IMAGES
of America

KANABEC COUNTY

On the Cover: These Kanabec County ladies were enjoying a refreshing dip in Lake Mora in 1907; pictured are, from left to right, Mrs. J.O. Werntz, Mrs. R.W. Pope, Mrs. J.C. Cravens, Mrs. John Grahek, and Mrs. C.E. Williams. (Courtesy Kanabec History Center.)

IMAGES
of America

KANABEC COUNTY

Amy Troolin and Earl J. Foster

ARCADIA
PUBLISHING

ISBN 978-0-7385-9056-1

Published by Arcadia Publishing
Charleston, South Carolina

Printed in the United States of America

Library of Congress Control Number: 2011944551

For all general information, please contact Arcadia Publishing:
Telephone 843-853-2070
Fax 843-853-0044
E-mail sales@arcadiapublishing.com
For customer service and orders:
Toll-Free 1-888-313-2665

Visit us on the Internet at www.arcadiapublishing.com

This book is dedicated to Ron Troolin (1951–2006).

Contents

ACKNOWLEDGMENTS

The photographs used in Images of America: *Kanabec County* are drawn from the collections of the Kanabec History Center in Mora, Minnesota. The authors send special thanks to codirectors Janet Franz and Sharon Vogt for all their help.

The authors would also like to thank the staff members at Proex Portraits in Coon Rapids, Minnesota—Melanie, Kris, Rose, Leslie, Lee, Rich, and John—for their efficient service.

Earl J. Foster would like to acknowledge his grandchildren, Peyton, Chloe, Earl III, Amelia, and Oliver, who love to look at his photographs and listen to him explain them.

Amy Troolin offers a special thank-you to T.J. Duchene for all his support, helpful suggestions, and solutions to a whole bevy of computer problems.

Finally, the authors would like to offer a special thanks and tribute to LaJune Troolin for her thorough research, editing, proofreading, organizational skills, excellent advice, and overall patience. We would not have been able to write this book without you!

INTRODUCTION

In photographs and stories, Images of America: *Kanabec County* offers a glimpse into the daily lives of the thousands of people who have made their homes in Kanabec County, Minnesota.

Long before people of European descent settled in East Central Minnesota, the Dakota and Objiwe resided in the region's ancient forests. They established camps and villages, hunted, gathered wild rice, and raised their families. In the 17th and 18th centuries, French explorers and fur traders arrived in the area. At least two groups of famous explorers traveled through the lands that would someday become Kanabec County. Adventurers Radisson and Groseilliers stopped near Knife Lake during the winter of 1659–1660 to trade with the Dakota, and in 1680, Father Hennepin passed through the territory during his exploratory journeys. By the mid-19th century, Native Americans had to contend with more than just the occasional visit from the "white man." Loggers and settlers had already begun to move into the region, and conflicts soon erupted between the newcomers and their Native American neighbors.

Lumbermen refused to be driven from the lucrative forests of East Central Minnesota. By the 1850s, logging was a popular and highly profitable activity. Logging company Hersey, Staples, and Bean had established its headquarters at Millet Rapids in Grass Lake Township. This company and several others were successful in their logging pursuits, harvesting millions of feet of white pine and clearing the forests to make way for homesteads and farms.

Kanabec County was officially established on March 13, 1858. Early residents created a local government and chose Brunswick as their first county seat. As the years passed, citizens worked hard to build successful farms and take full advantage of the land's resources. Farmers grew potatoes as their primary cash crop and cooperated to establish creameries and cheese factories. Other industrious entrepreneurs discovered a large outcropping of granite in the northern part of the county and organized a quarry.

Kanabec County's growth depended on attracting new settlers and shipping marketable goods to neighboring regions. Such activities required a solid transportation network. County residents navigated steamboats on local rivers, built roads and railroads, hitched up teams of horses to buggies and wagons, and eventually purchased the newfangled "horseless carriage."

Even though transportation gradually improved, most people in Kanabec County did not want to travel too far to access the goods and services they needed. They founded small towns like Brunswick, Grass Lake, Mora, Ogilvie, Grasston, Quamba, Warman, and Kroschel throughout the county as centers of trade. Citizens worked hard to improve their towns, building main streets and business districts, constructing cozy homes and grand Victorian houses, and establishing churches and schools.

For many years, Kanabec County's towns flourished, providing nearly everything their inhabitants required. In the days before supermarkets and huge discount retailers, small general and specialty stores lined downtown streets. Shoppers could check off everything on their lists in one visit to their town's business district. Most stores were packed full of fascinating and useful items. Everything from oysters to dolls to hair tonic to dresses was waiting for willing customers in local shops.

Kanabec County citizens worked hard, but they also knew how to have fun, even in the days before television, computers, and video games. The county's beautiful natural setting afforded a prime environment for outdoor activities like fishing, hunting, swimming, boating, and skiing. Sports like baseball, football, and basketball were popular pastimes as were plays and programs featuring local talent. Residents formed clubs and organizations for people of all ages and interests that offered countless opportunities for personal growth, socialization, and fun.

Images of America: *Kanabec County* explores each of these aspects of Kanabec County history with a special emphasis on the daily lives of the county's people, their work and play, their trials and joys.

One

A Meeting of Cultures

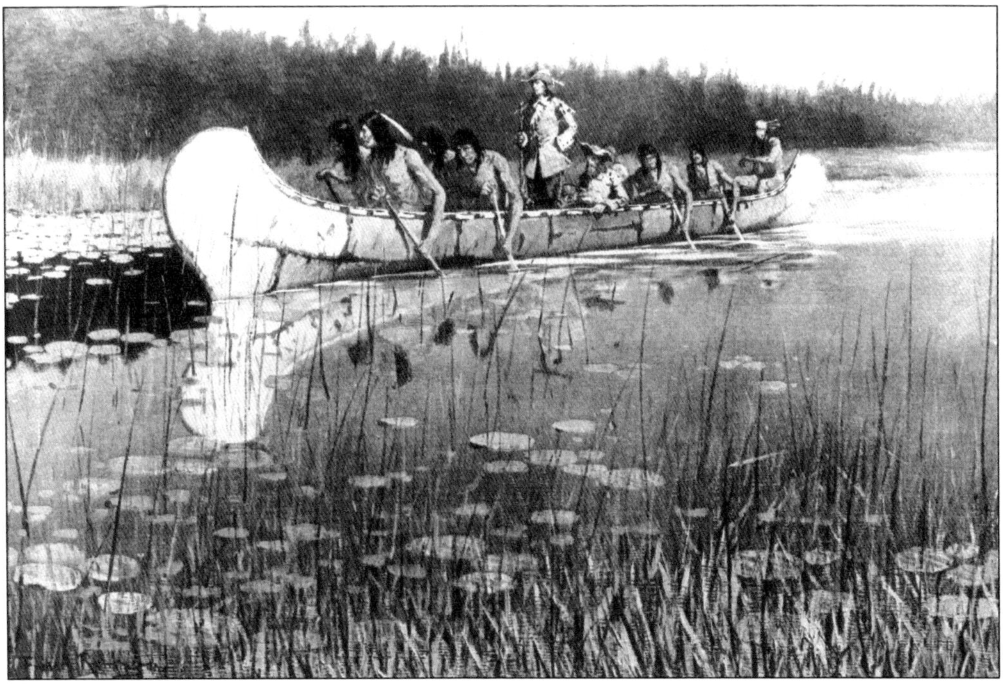

Native American people have lived on the land that is now Kanabec County for about 8,000 years. A group called the Mound Builders arrived first, followed later by the Dakota and Ojibwe. In 1660, a band of Dakota met French explorers Radisson and Groseilliers near the outlet of Knife Lake. The explorers presented the Dakota with a gift of metal knives, thereby giving the lake its name.

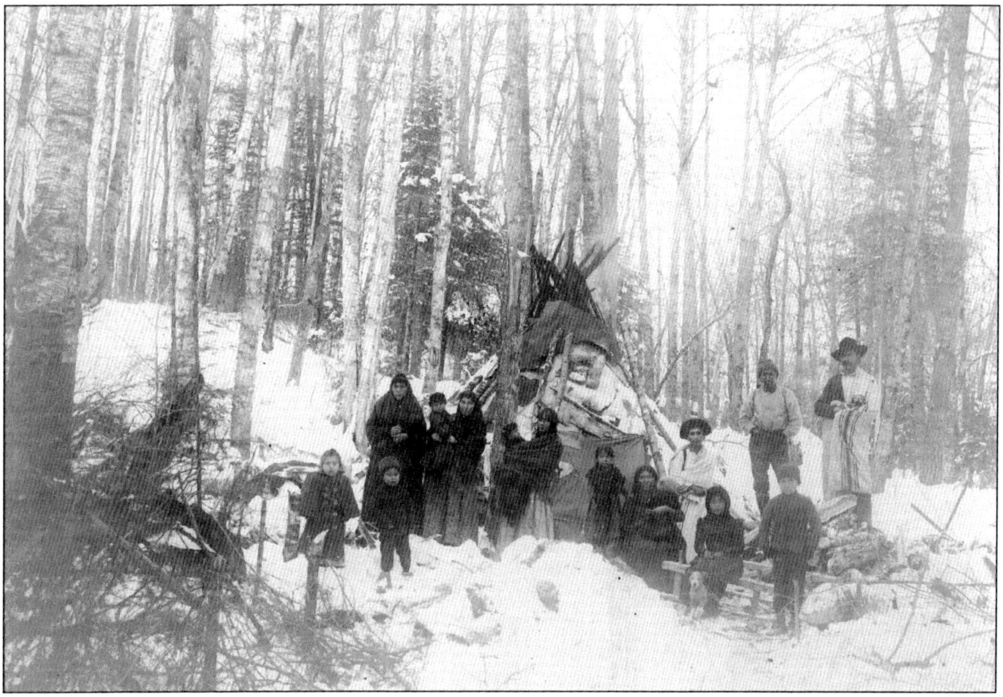

The Ojibwe people moved into the region beginning in the 1600s. After years of sporadic fighting with the Dakota over land, scarce food, and furs to trade with the Europeans, the two peoples forged a shaky peace. This Ojibwe family posed in front of their winter home near Ogilvie. Notice how they mixed Native American and European clothing.

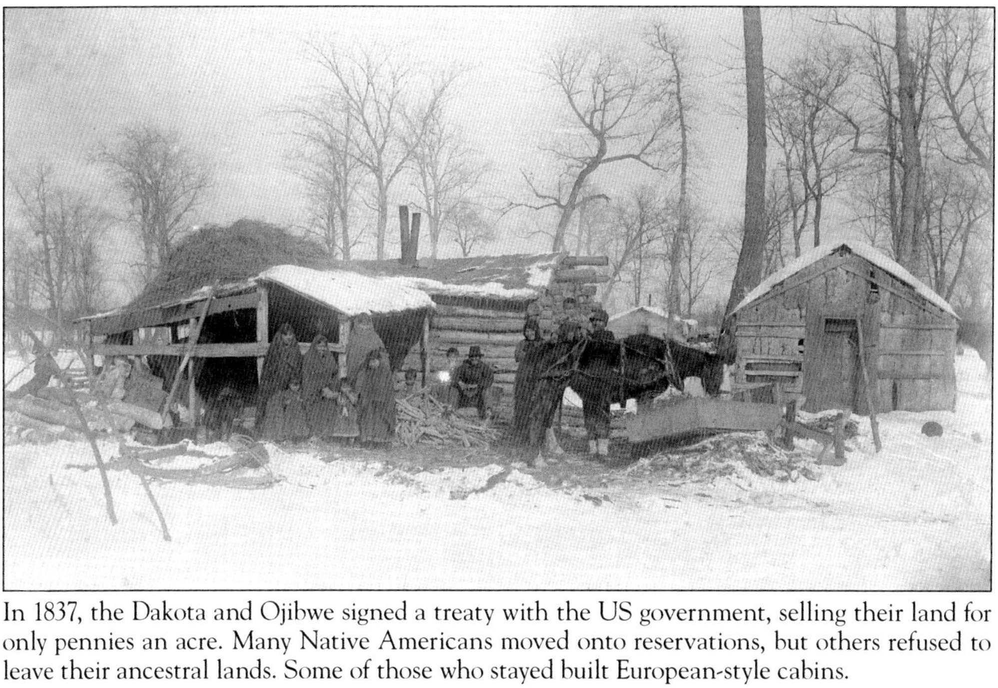

In 1837, the Dakota and Ojibwe signed a treaty with the US government, selling their land for only pennies an acre. Many Native Americans moved onto reservations, but others refused to leave their ancestral lands. Some of those who stayed built European-style cabins.

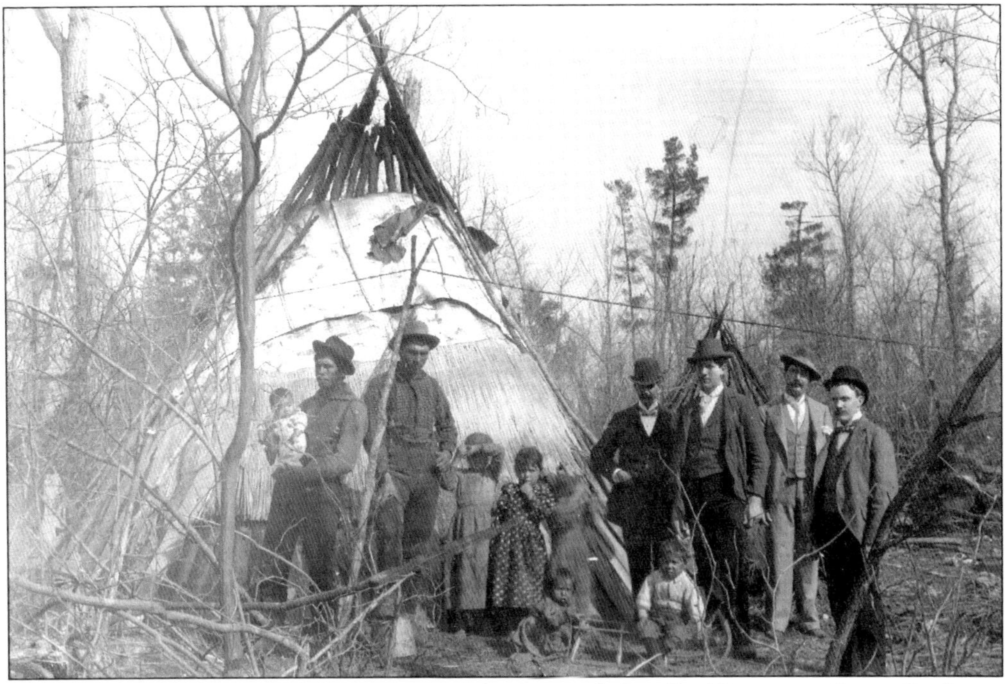

A group of Mora businessmen and community leaders, including Fred Pepperton, James Gordman, M.E. Rutherford, Henry Kern, Walter Andrist, and John P. Stenstrom, visited an Ojibwe family near Mora in 1898. This family chose to live in a traditional tepee as their ancestors had before them.

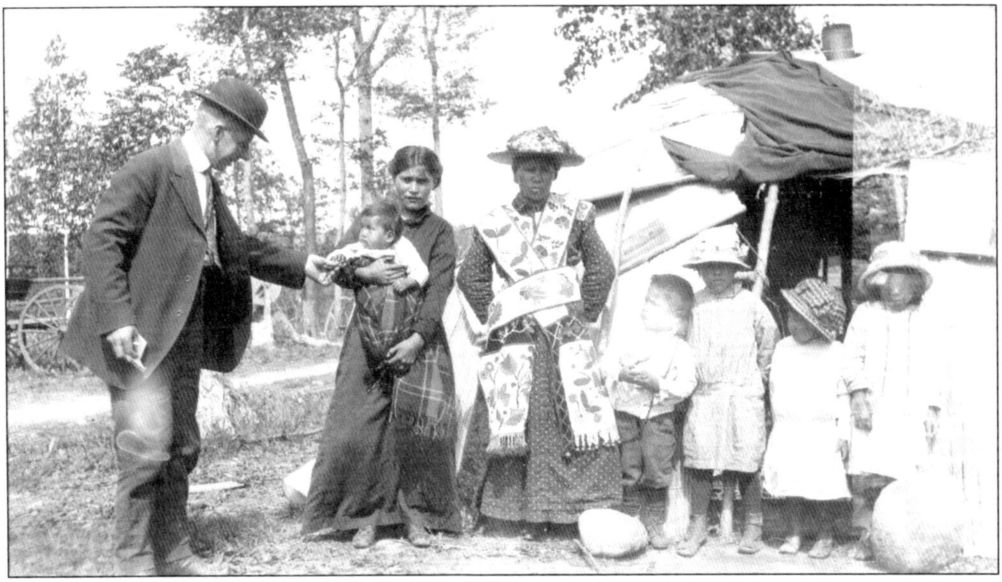

The family in this 1910s photograph also opted for a traditional home, a wigwam, even though they wore European-style clothing. Their ancestors had lived in villages throughout Kanabec County, including those at Fish Lake, Ann Lake, and Spring Brook Hill. A village at Knife Lake named Na-os-sing was an early trading post for Native Americans and Europeans.

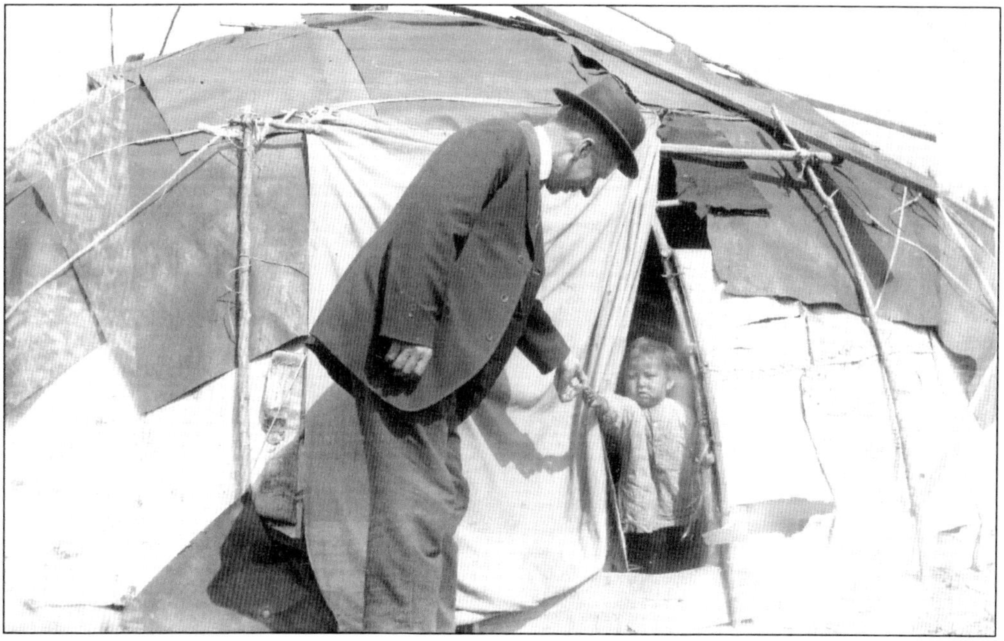

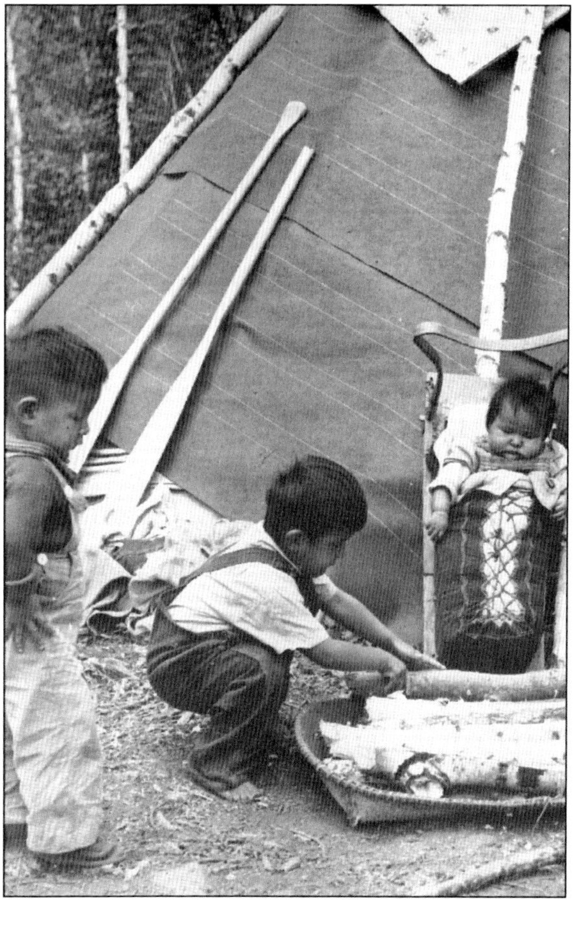

The child at the entrance of this wigwam looked a little hesitant to greet such a distinguished-looking stranger. The Ojibwe constructed their wigwams by bending saplings to create domed frameworks, which they covered with sheets of birch bark, woven cattail mats, or, in later years, canvas. Inside the wigwams, the Ojibwe built sleeping platforms and central, stone-ringed hearths.

The Ojibwe taught their children self-control and responsibility at a young age. Children fulfilled daily chores and learned necessary skills to help the community survive. When children misbehaved, their parents smeared charcoal on their faces as a humiliating sign to everyone that they had been bad. Ojibwe parents also made sure their youngsters had plenty of playtime to enjoy stuffed animals, dolls, and games like hide-and-seek and lacrosse.

Ojibwe mothers carried their infants in cradleboards or *dikinaaganan*. Mothers firmly secured their babies to the wooden boards with blankets. Then they could carry their children on their backs or prop the boards against trees while they completed their daily tasks. The wooden bow at the top of each cradleboard prevented the baby's head from hitting the ground if the board should tip or fall.

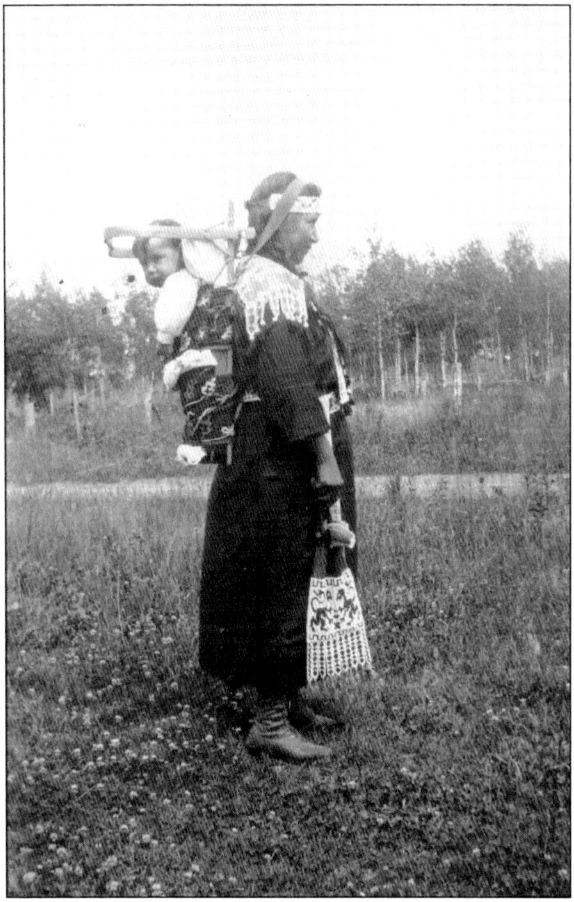

Native American life changed with the seasons. Both the Dakota and Ojibwe moved their camps according to their food sources. At the first springtime thaw, they set up sugar camps to collect maple sap and boil it down into syrup and sugar. This was a labor-intensive process. Native American women collected and prepared 30 to 40 gallons of sap to make one gallon of syrup.

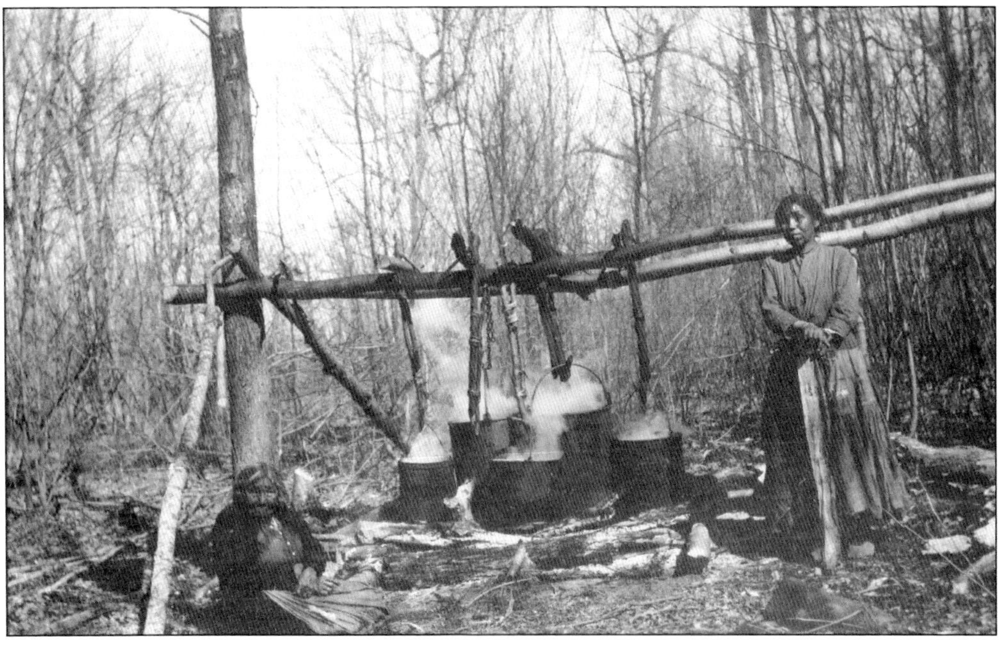

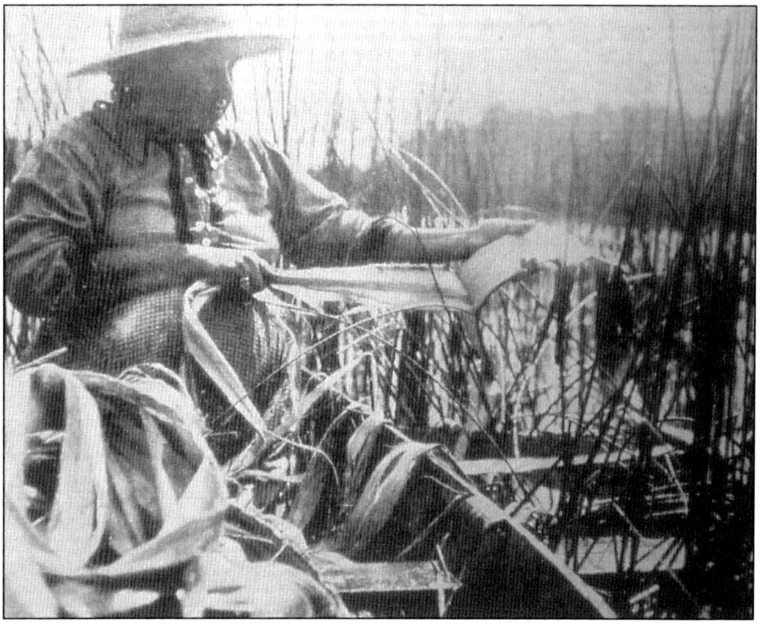

After the corn harvest, Native Americans gathered the wild rice that grew in the shallow waters of lakes and ponds. First, they tied the rice stalks into bundles and allowed them to dry for a few days.

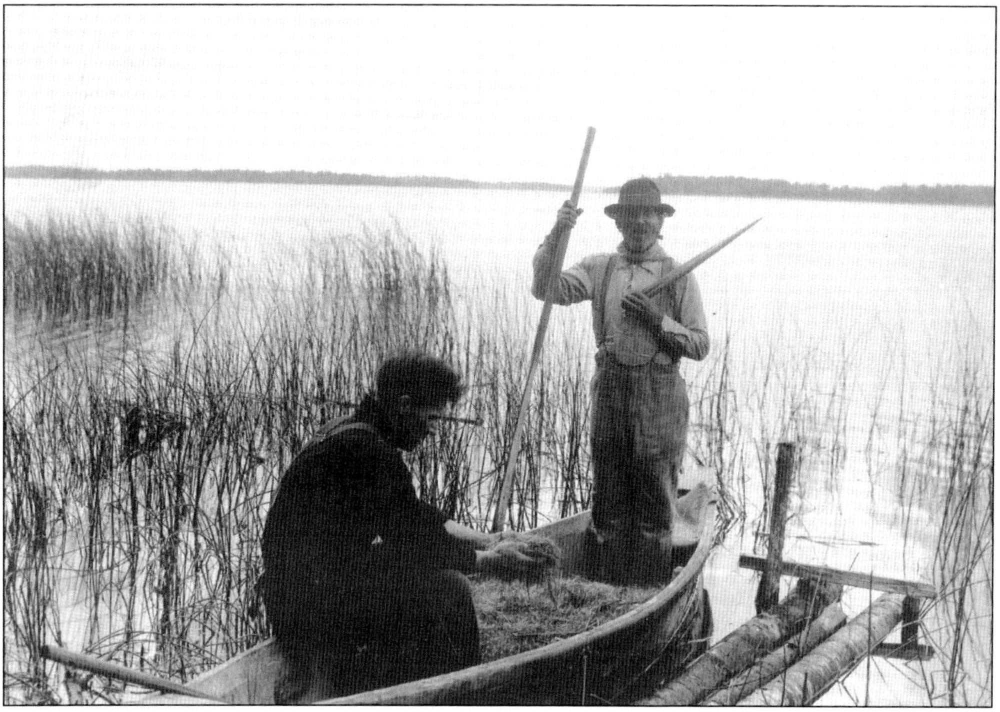

The next phase of the rice harvest required team effort. One person pushed a canoe through the rice paddy using a long pole to avoid damaging the plants. Another person pulled the bundled stalks over the edge of the canoe and used wooden ricing sticks to knock the rice kernels into the bottom of the canoe.

Wild rice was a primary food source for Native Americans, but it also had spiritual and communal aspects. Wild rice was viewed as a gift from the Creator, and harvest time provided an opportunity for social interaction. When the first rice arrived on shore, the women prepared and cooked a small amount. The chief blessed the cooked rice, and the assembly presented it as a ritual offering to the spirits.

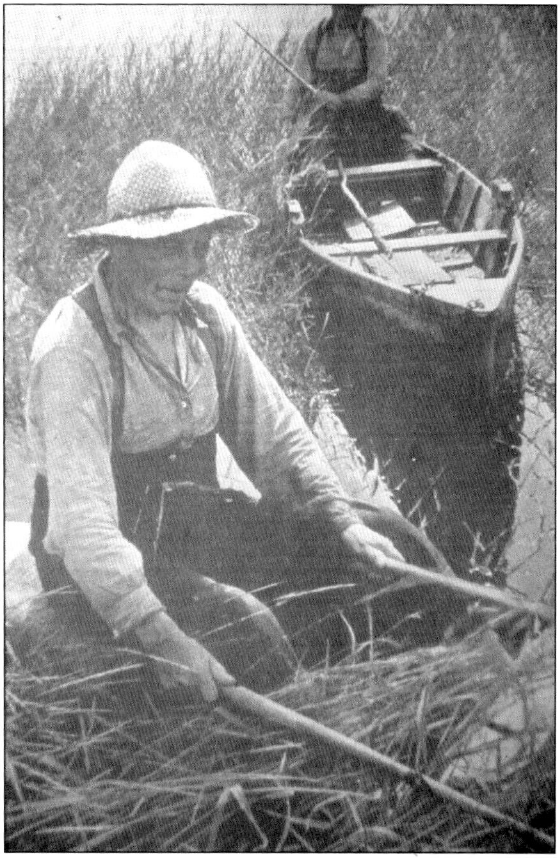

After the rice was harvested, it was brought to shore, laid out on mats to dry, and then parched. Boys wearing special moccasins "danced" on the rice to grind off the husks. Finally, the rice was winnowed so that the chaff blew away in the wind, leaving only the rice kernels, which were now ready for storage.

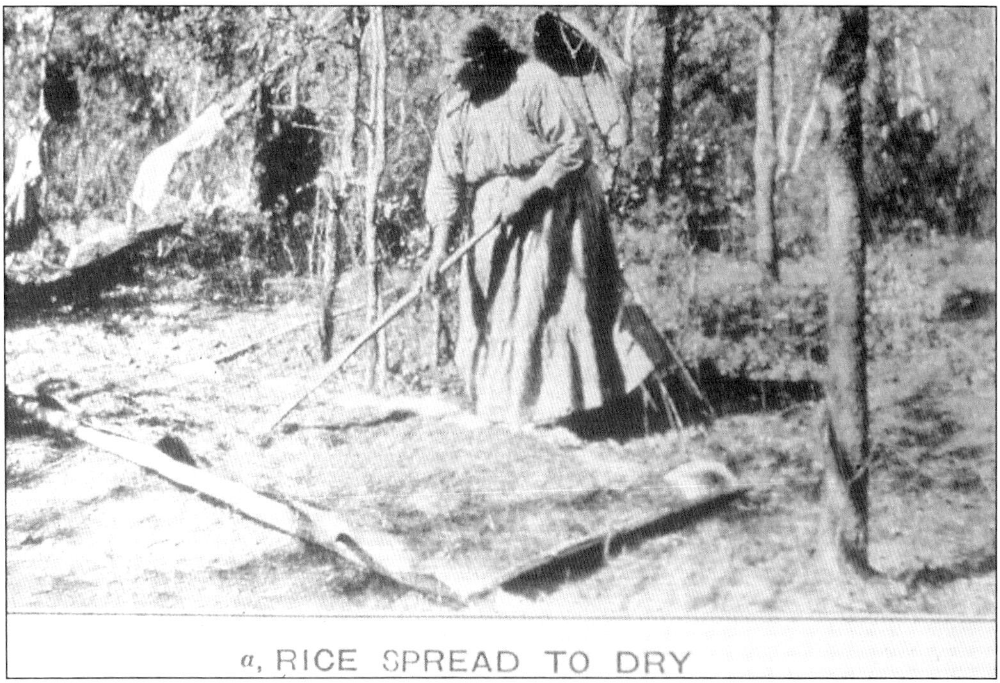

a, RICE SPREAD TO DRY

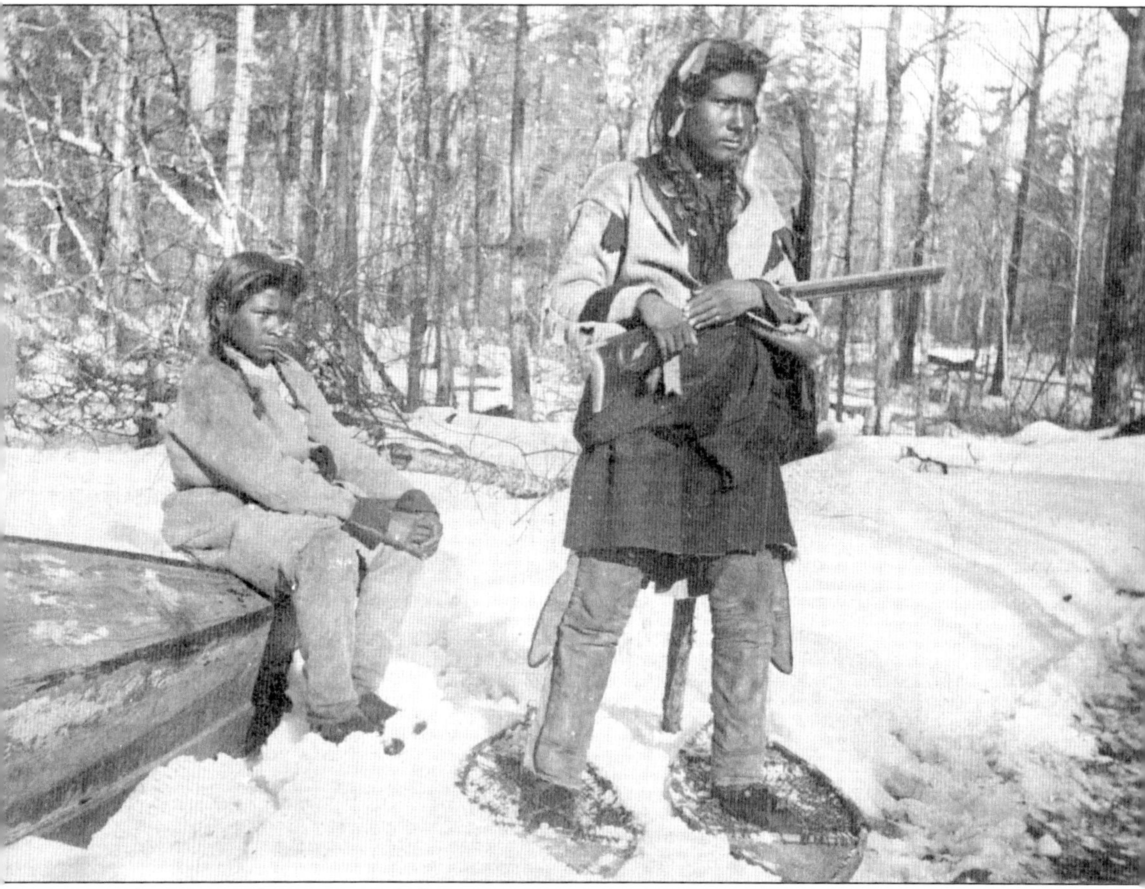

When the rice harvest ended, the Native Americans began to prepare for the autumn hunt, which often lasted until January. The whole community worked hard during the hunt. While the men and boys did the hunting, the women and girls prepared, cooked, and preserved the meat. In this 1870 photograph, an Ojibwe brave was setting out on a deer hunting expedition. During the winter, Native Americans spent their time ice fishing, tanning hides, making clothing, telling stories, and discussing community issues in the village council. Winter was also filled with dangers like blizzards, bitter cold, and food shortages. The community huddled close together as an extended family to survive until spring when the year's work began again.

After the Dakota and Ojibwe signed the 1837 treaty that deeded their lands to the US government, loggers moved in to harvest valuable trees. As they finished their work and moved on, settlers of European descent followed and established homesteads and towns. Settlement meant financial gain for railroads and land companies, who published pamphlets like this one to attract residents.

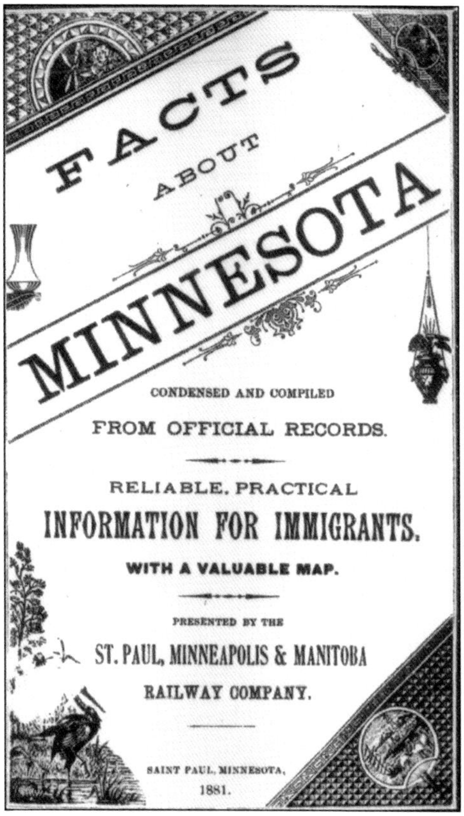

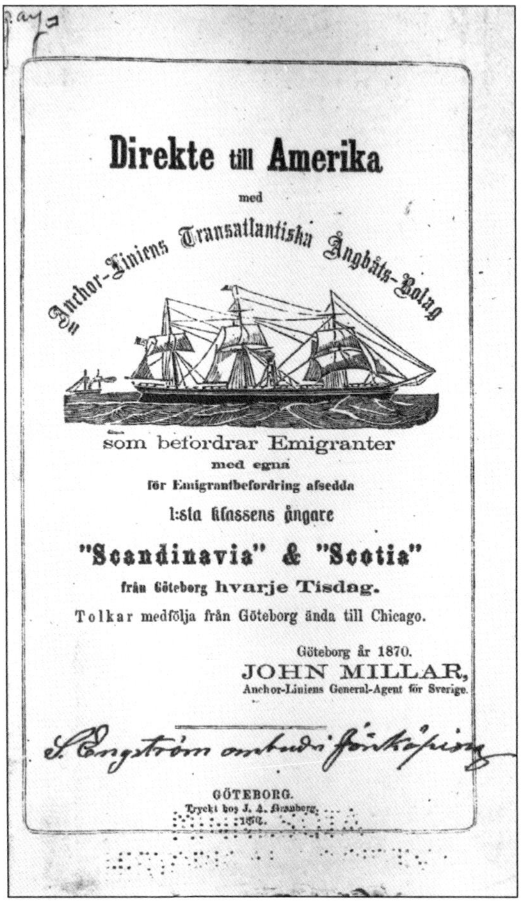

Many of Kanabec County's early settlers were Swedish immigrants, who homesteaded in Brunswick and Grass Lake Townships beginning in 1871. Some of them had received booklets like this one that exalted the climate and fruitful farmland of the Midwestern United States but neglected to mention the hazards of immigration and homesteading in the wilderness. Nevertheless, Swedish settlement spread rapidly through the southern part of the county in the 1870s.

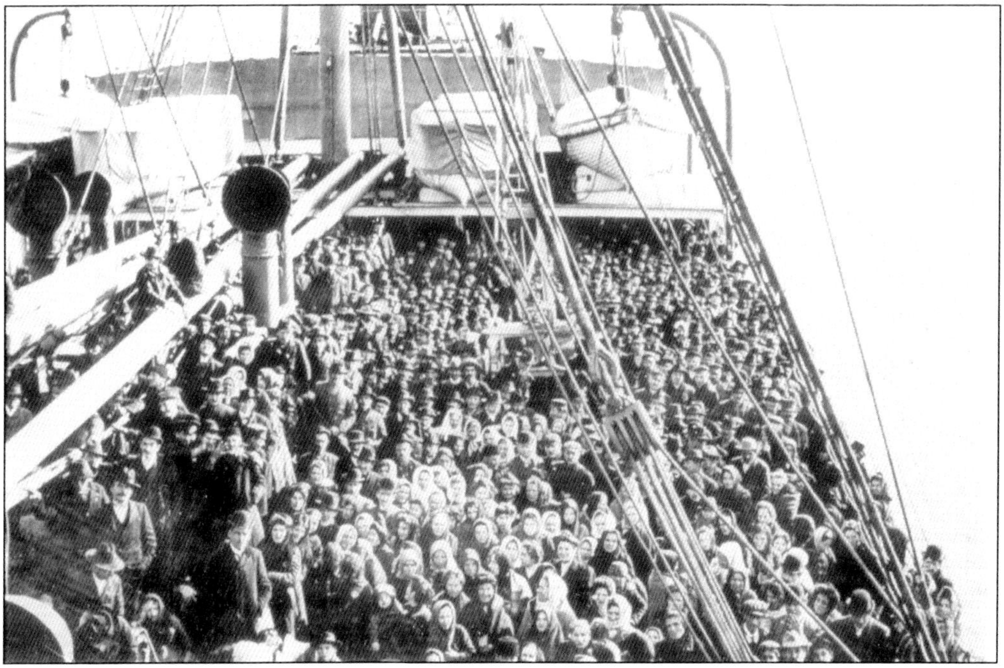

As settlement in Kanabec County expanded and towns sprang up along railroad lines, county leaders turned their attention to recruiting new residents who would establish more businesses, farm more land, and help the area's economy grow. In March 1891, the Kanabec County Immigration Society was founded with the purpose of attracting European immigrants like these, who landed at Ellis Island in 1906.

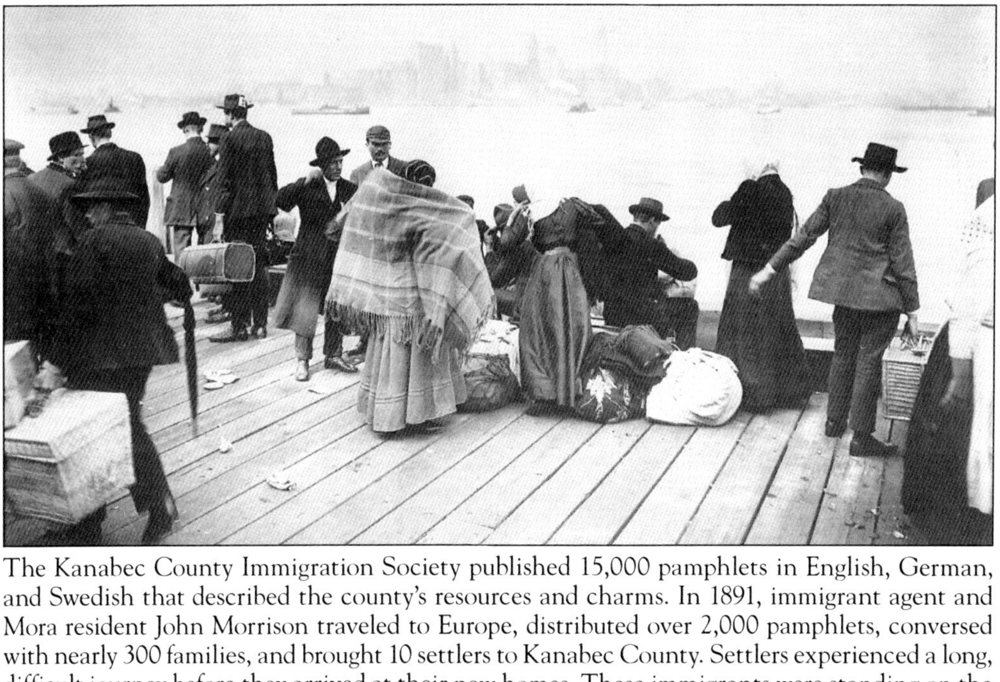

The Kanabec County Immigration Society published 15,000 pamphlets in English, German, and Swedish that described the county's resources and charms. In 1891, immigrant agent and Mora resident John Morrison traveled to Europe, distributed over 2,000 pamphlets, conversed with nearly 300 families, and brought 10 settlers to Kanabec County. Settlers experienced a long, difficult journey before they arrived at their new homes. These immigrants were standing on the dock at Ellis Island in 1912.

Two

Clearing the Land

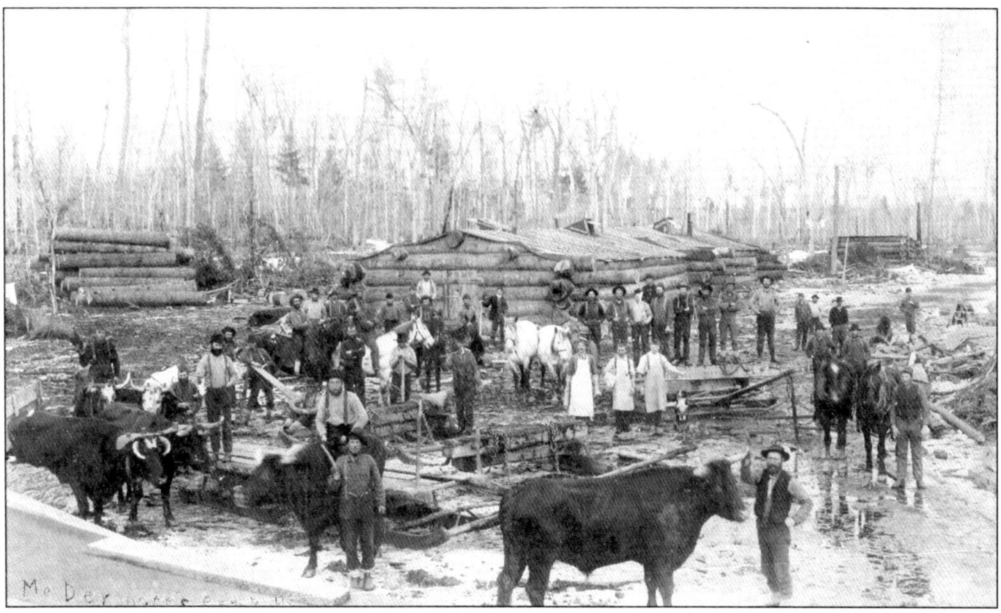

Following the 1837 treaty with the Native Americans, logging began in earnest in East Central Minnesota. By the winter of 1846–1847, lumberjacks were harvesting the majestic pines near Kanabec County's Fish Lake. Lumbermen like Samuel Hersey, Isaac Staples, and Jacob and Charles Bean purchased timberlands from the government for $1.25 per acre and established logging camps like this one along the Snake River and its tributaries.

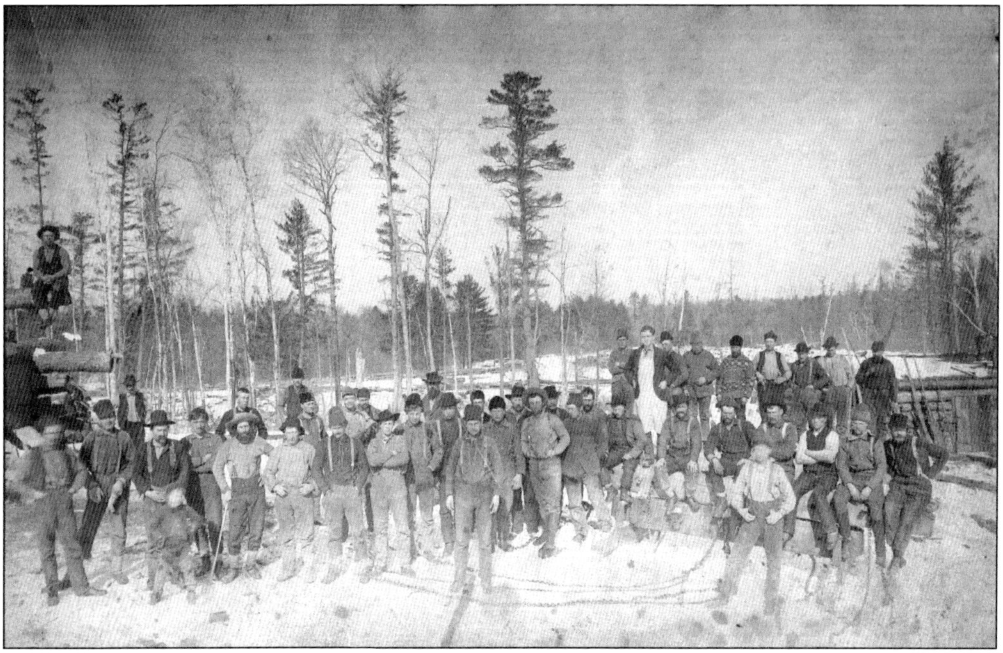

Each logging camp housed 50 to 100 men, who arrived at camp in the fall and stayed until the spring log drive. Lumberjacks worked six days a week from sunrise to sunset for a wage of between $18 and $30 per month, depending on each one's job and experience. They usually received their wages in a lump sum at the end of the season.

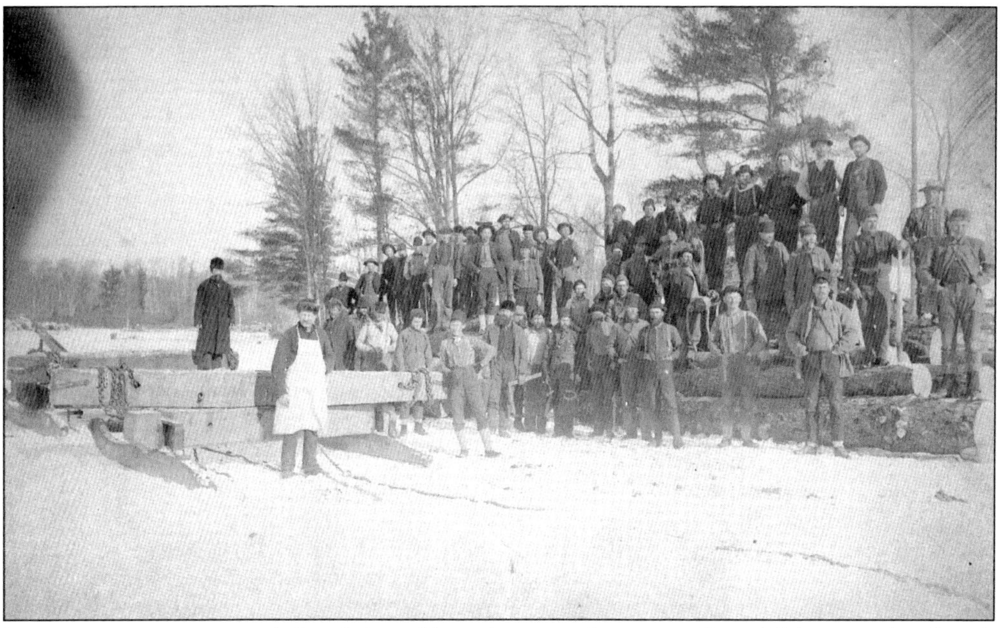

Logging camps were crowded and dirty. Typical camp cabins were 40 by 25 feet, insulated with moss and clay, and heated by stoves burning green birch logs. At least two tiers of bunks lined the walls. Sometimes each man had a bed to himself; sometimes he had to share. Lumberjacks were plagued by pests like lice and boiled their clothes each week to try to maintain some level of cleanliness.

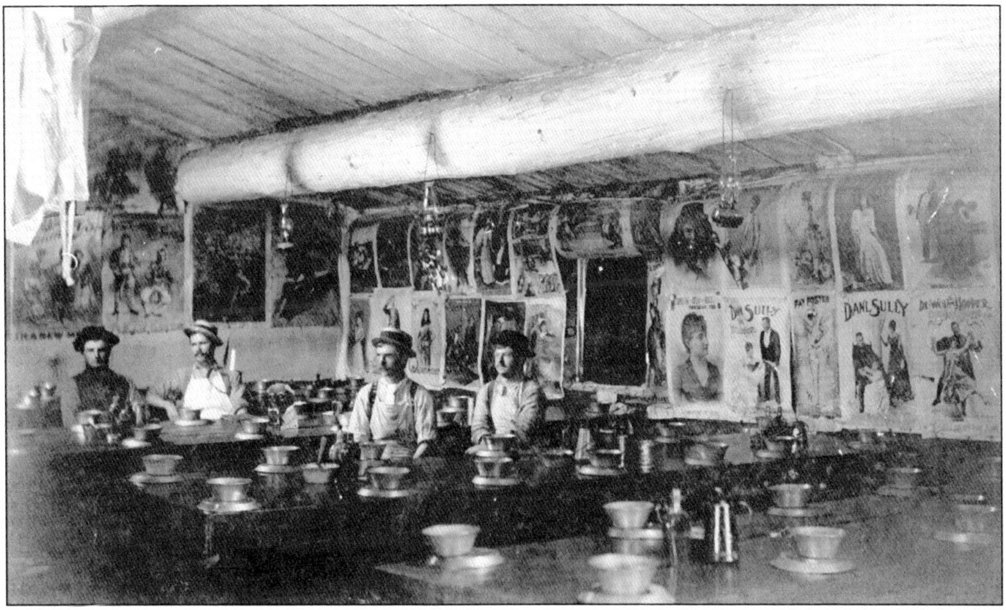

Food was very important in lumber camps, and cooks earned just as much or more than lumberjacks. Loggers ate well, consuming three large meals per day of pork and beans, salted mackerel, flapjacks, fried potatoes, codfish, biscuits, rice pudding, molasses, gingerbread, dried apple pie, cookies, tea, and coffee. Meals lasted 15 to 20 minutes. No talking was allowed, but the clanking of tin plates and cups created plenty of noise.

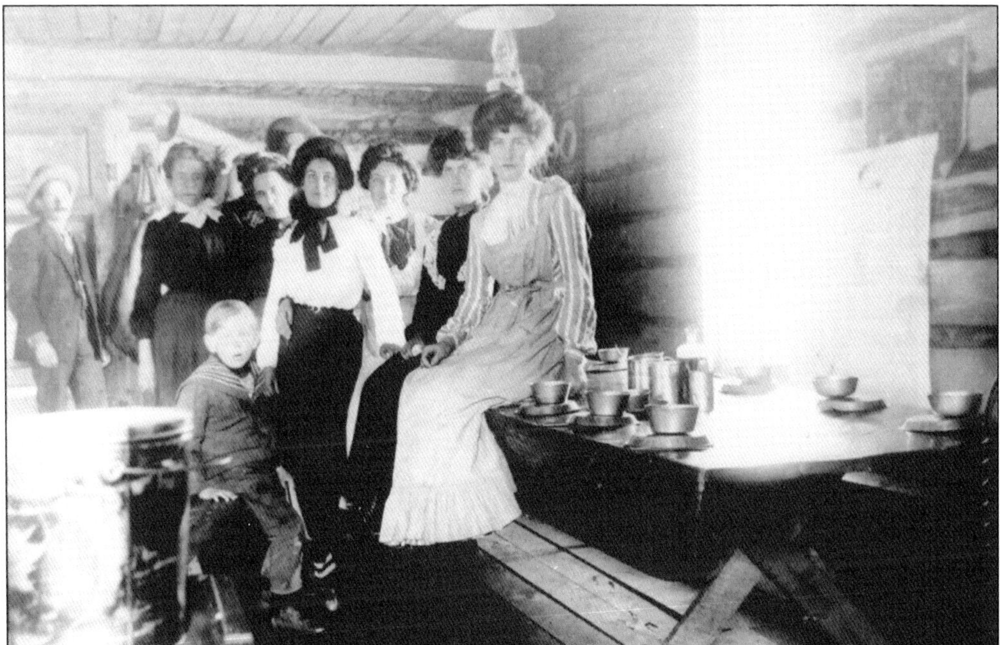

Sundays were rest days for lumbermen. They played cards, made music, told stories, washed clothes, and visited with friends and relatives, who might travel several miles just to spend an afternoon with their loved ones. Lumberjacks would also hold Sunday prayer services, especially if a "sky pilot," or traveling preacher, happened to be in camp.

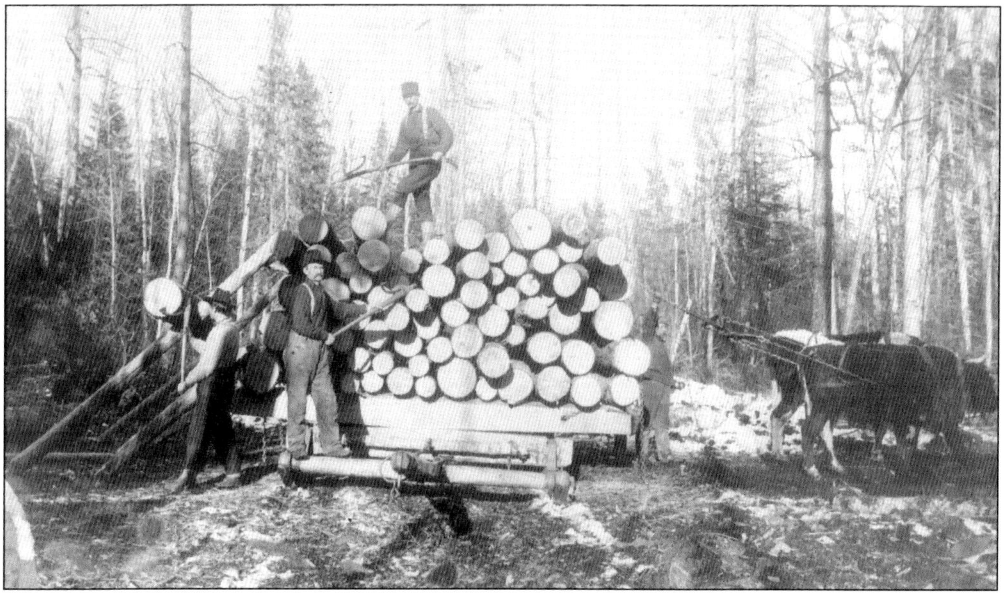

Lumbering was strenuous work. Timber cruisers began the process by surveying the stands of pines. Undercutters notched trees to be cut. Sawyers cut the trees. Then lumberjacks using oxen skidded newly cut logs out to roads or trails cut by the swampers. A teamster and two loaders stacked the logs onto sleds.

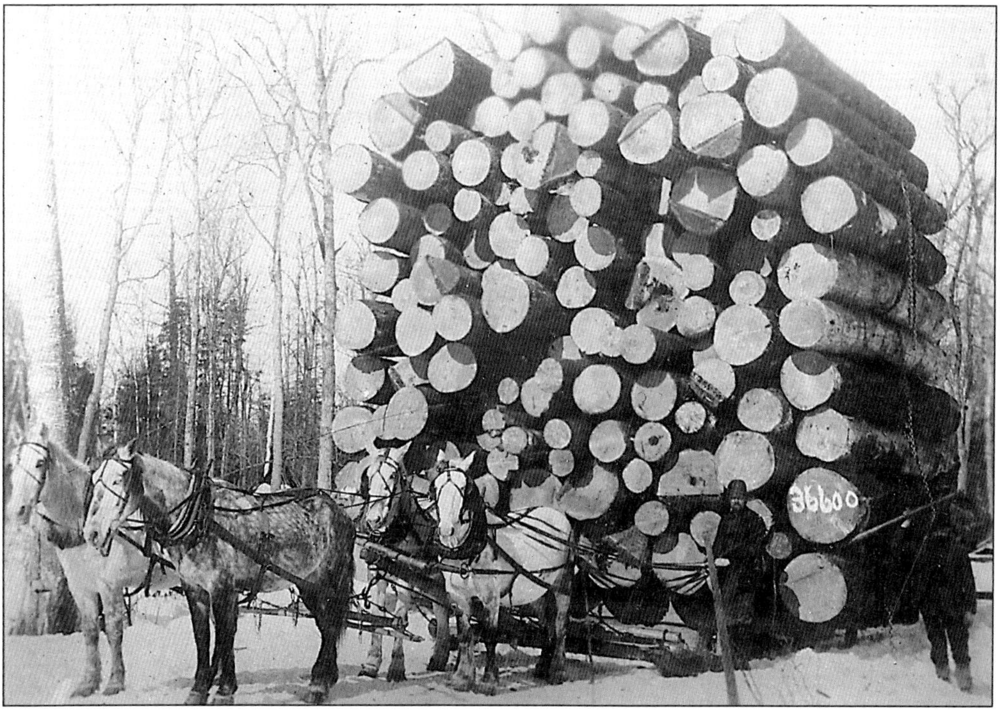

Lumberjacks liked to see how many logs they could stack on a sled. The largest stacks contained up to 40,000 board feet in eight or more tiers. Usually, these loads were too large for horses or oxen to actually pull. They were merely "show loads" that displayed the loggers' prowess and the sheer volume of timber available in the pineries of Minnesota.

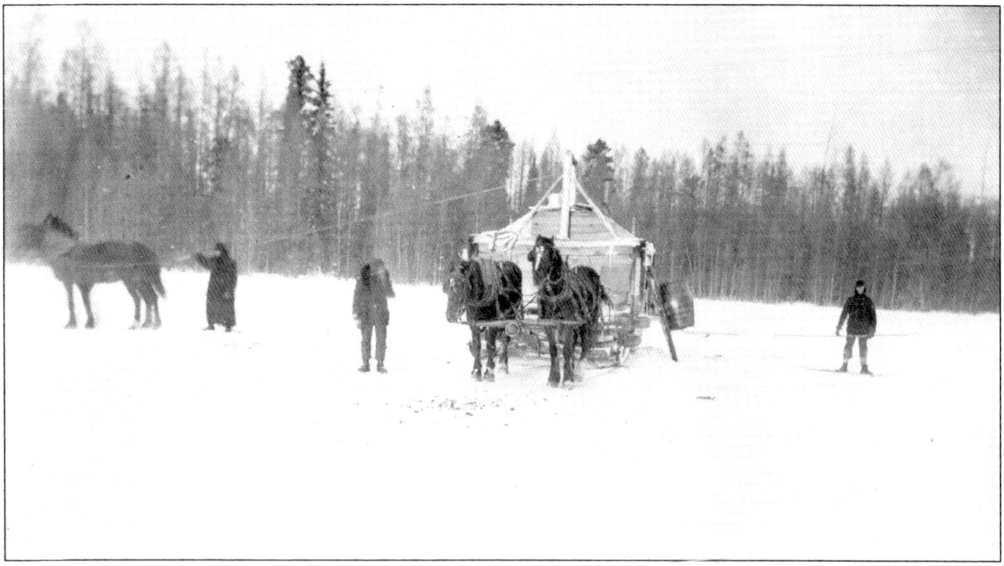

Lumberjacks called "road monkeys" hauled water from nearby lakes to ice logging roads and help sleds glide more smoothly. In this picture, road monkeys were using horses to pull barrels of water out of a frozen lake. They dumped the water into a specially designed wagon that had a wood-burning stove and smoke stack to keep the water from freezing.

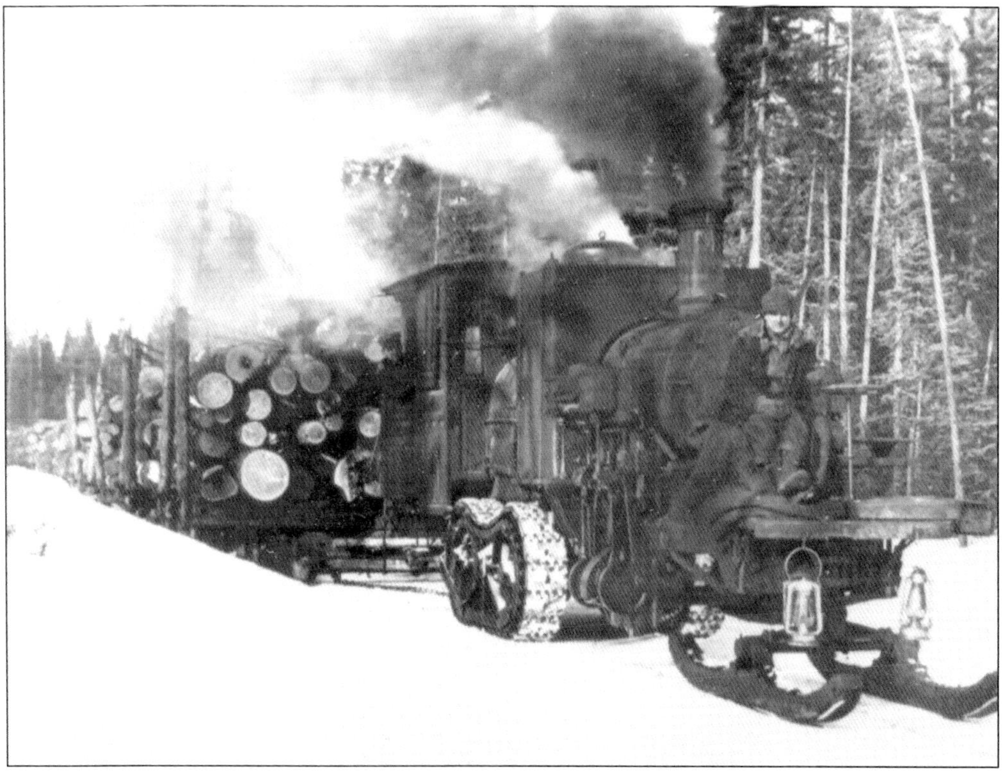

As technology advanced, some logging companies tried a new method of hauling logs out of the woods and off to the sawmill. Steam trains like this one could haul more logs for longer distances than horses or oxen.

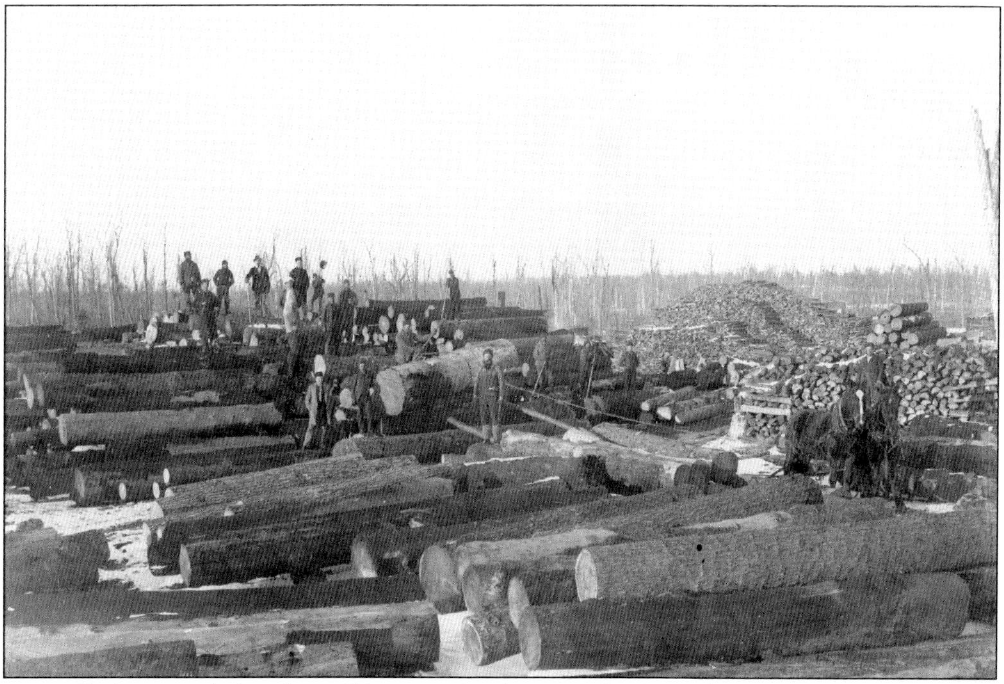

Normally, logs traveled to the mill by water. Each winter, lumberjacks stacked thousands of logs beside the nearest lake or stream to await the spring thaw. Log piles often extended onto the ice, fell through, froze together, and had to be blasted apart with dynamite when springtime arrived.

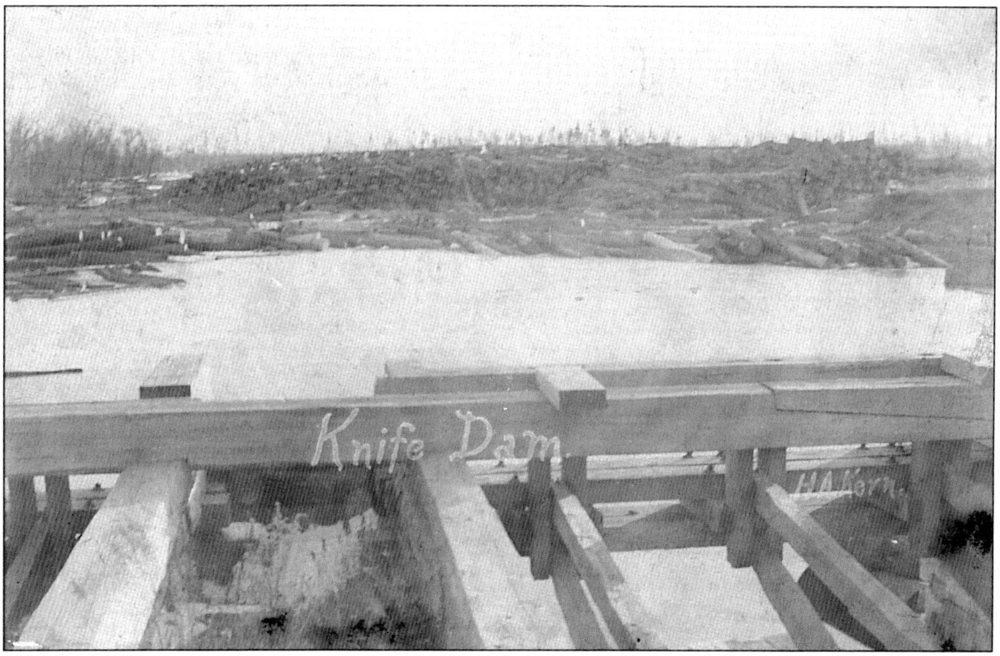

As the spring thaw began, 20 to 30 loggers set out from camp to prepare for the annual log drive. They checked the waterways, making sure they were free from obstructions, and inspected dams, like this one on Knife Lake, that were designed to regulate the flow of logs downstream.

Before the logs set off to the mill, each one was branded with a unique symbol so mill workers could identify its owner. Ideally, logs floated smoothly downstream, like those pictured here.

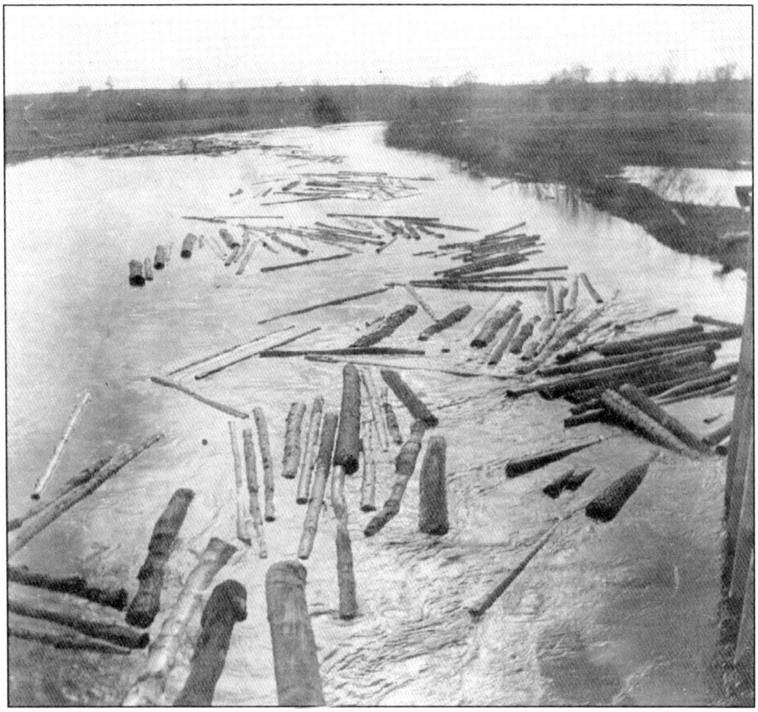

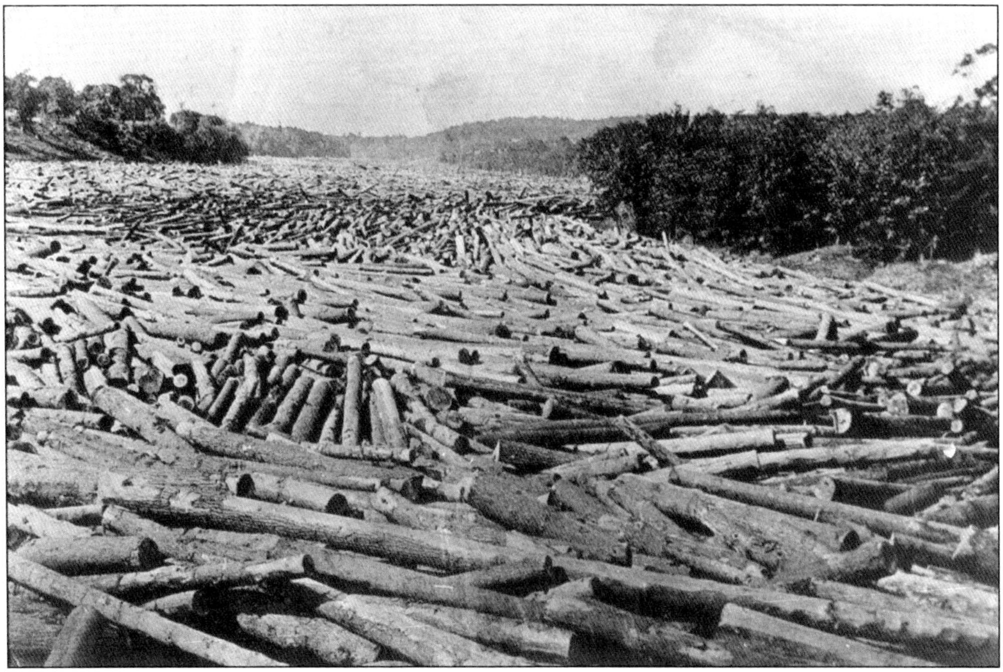

Occasionally, however, log jams occurred. Then it was the job of the 40-to-50-man crew of "river hogs" to find the key logs causing the trouble, release them using dynamite and long, pointed poles called peaveys, and set the whole mass flowing freely again. Many men lost their lives performing this dangerous work.

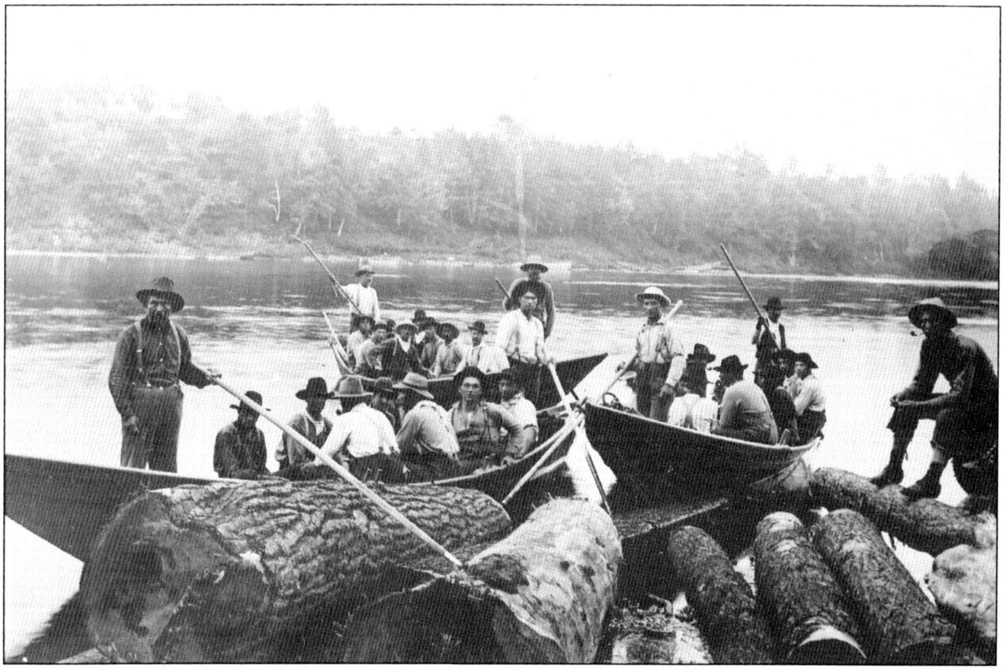

River hogs typically worked from two hours before sunrise until it was too dark to see. They even worked on Sundays if the river was flowing and logs were moving. River hogs earned $2.50 to $3.50 per day, which was a much higher wage than that of the average lumberman or laborer.

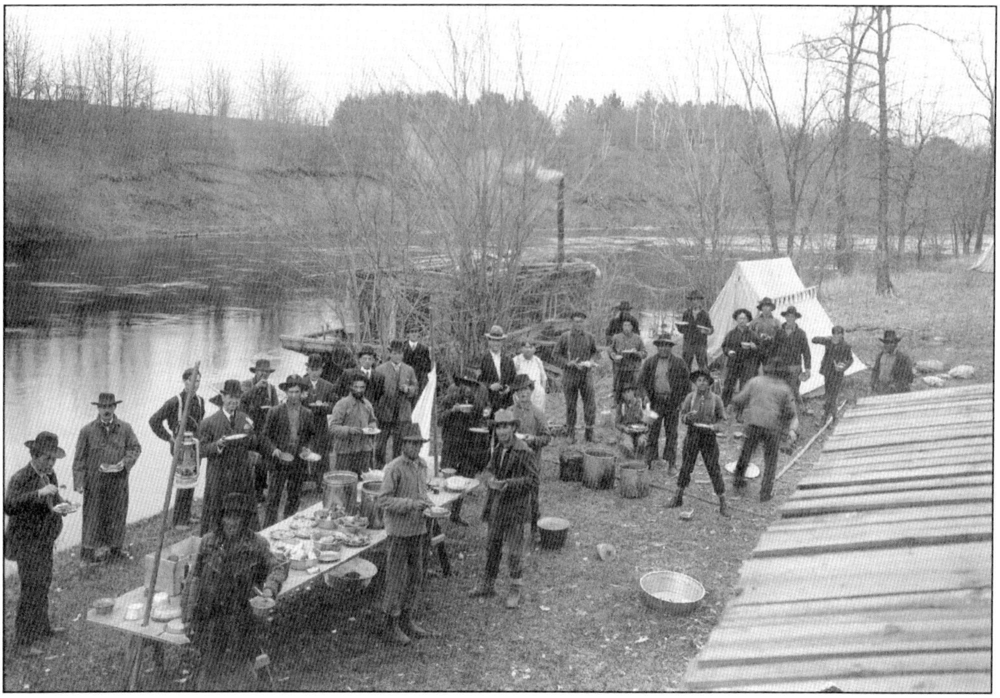

River hogs ate four hot, hearty meals every day. Cooks followed the log drives downstream on covered boats called wanagans, which hauled food and other supplies and offered limited sleeping space. These men were enjoying a well-earned repast along the shore of the Snake River.

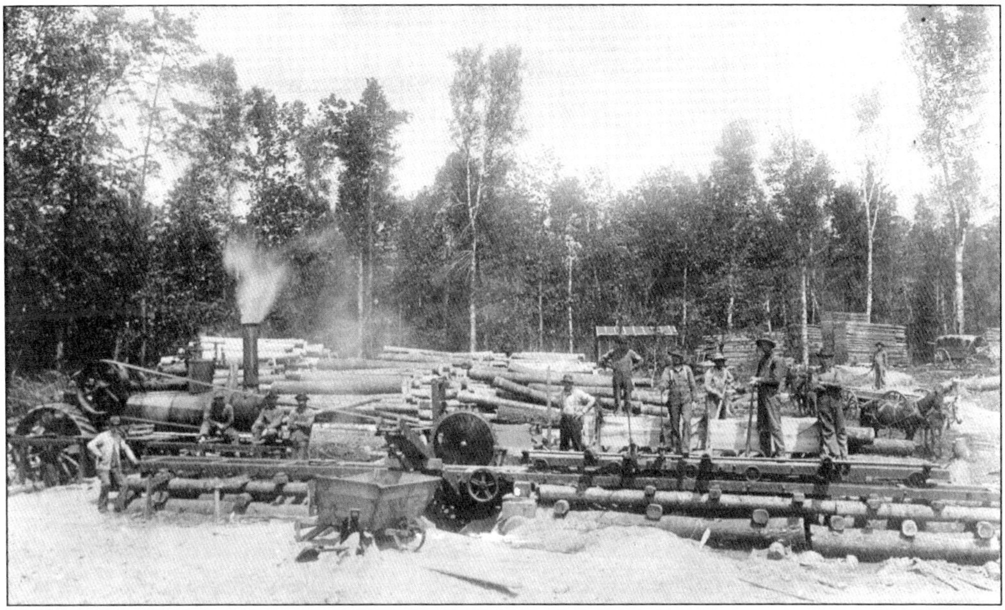

Howard Aldrich owned a sawmill in Mora, but he also operated this portable, steam-powered sawmill near Warman in 1900. Such mills were especially useful for sawing lumber to build logging camps and villages.

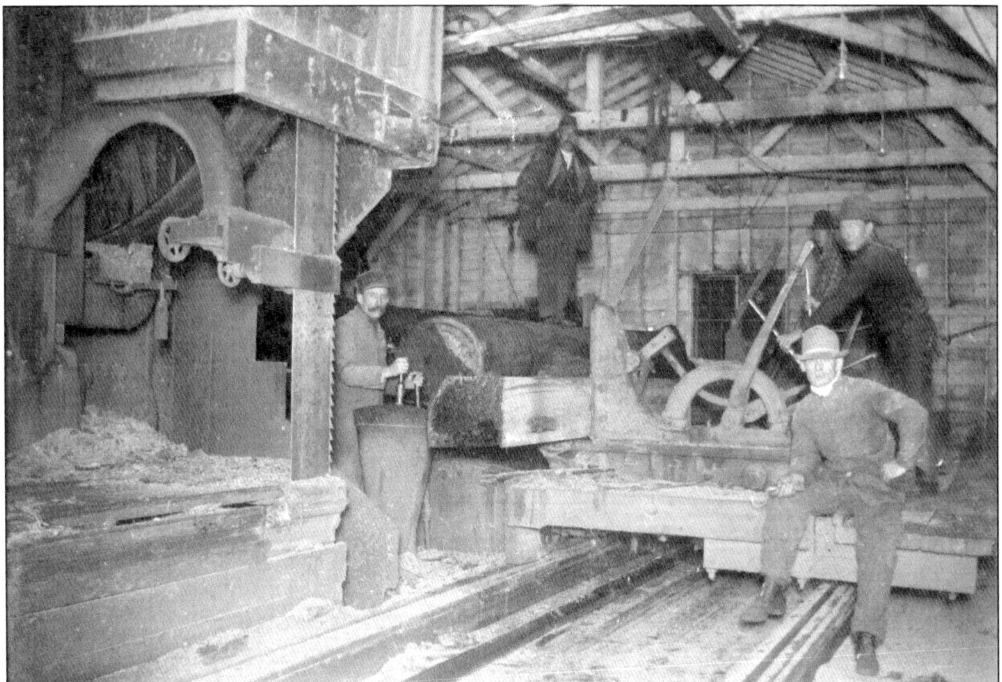

Permanent sawmills like this one processed logs into lumber and shingles. When a load of logs arrived, mill workers removed their bark, used circular saws and large band saws to cut the logs into boards, and edged the boards to produce flat edges. Milling was dangerous work. Millers often lost fingers or even limbs when they accidently got in the way of the saws.

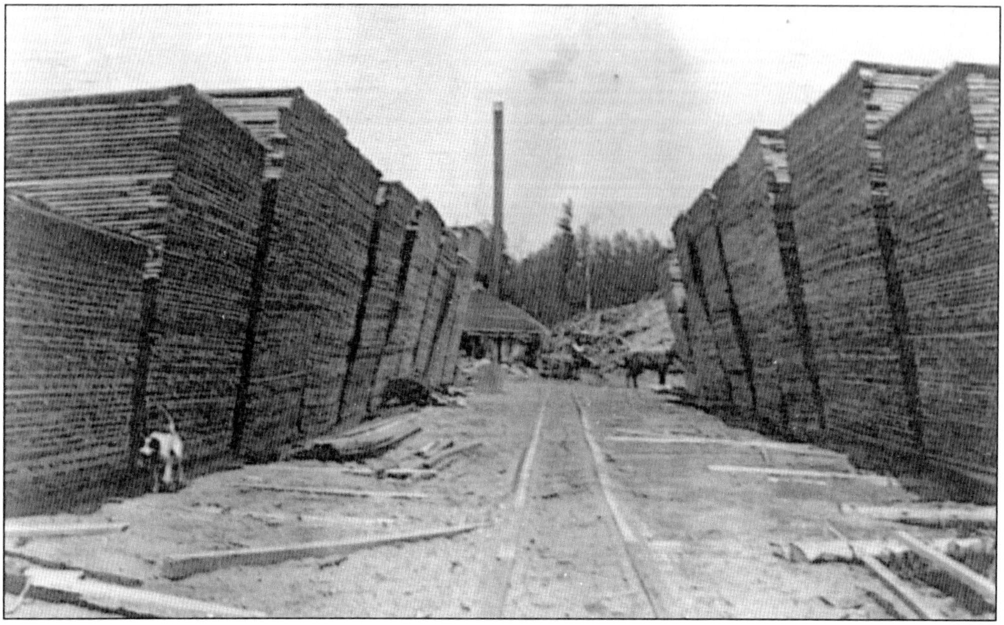

After milling, lumber was stacked in yards to dry. Drying made boards stronger and prevented decay, warping, and splitting. Mora's Williams Lumber Company, shown here, was founded by C.E. Williams in 1894. The company could handle up to 85 train carloads of lumber in a year. Fire destroyed the lumberyard in 1909, but the lucrative business was rebuilt in only two weeks.

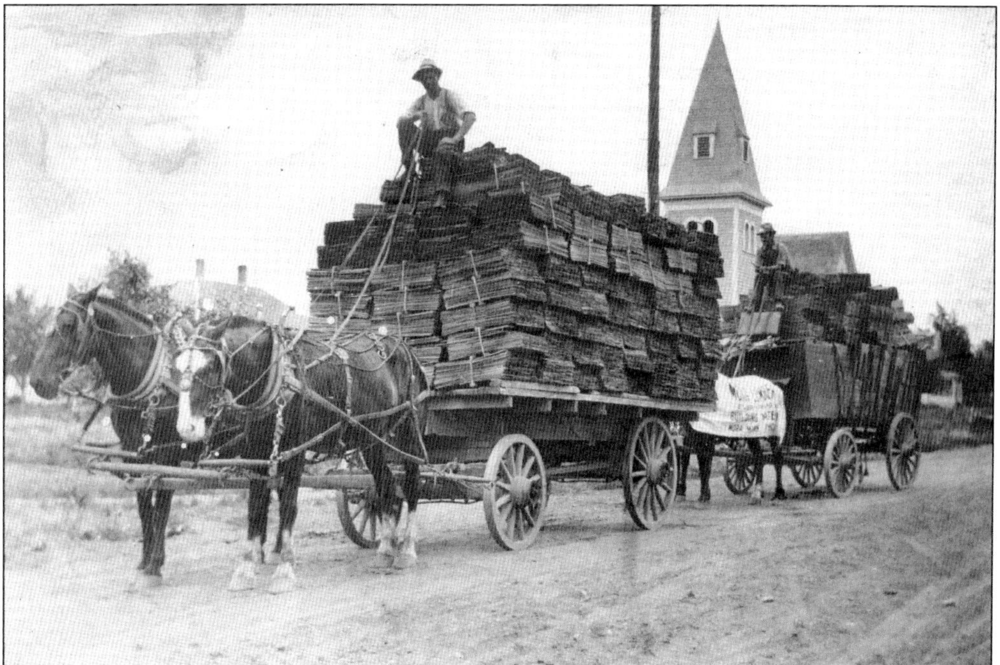

Lumber was plentiful in Kanabec County's early days. Plain boards cost only $5 to $10 per thousand feet, shingles 35¢ per bundle, and nails $1.35 per keg. A settler could build a new house for $300 to $400 plus labor. In this photograph, the Mora Lumber Company was showing off its abundant supplies in the village's annual parade.

Three

Building a County

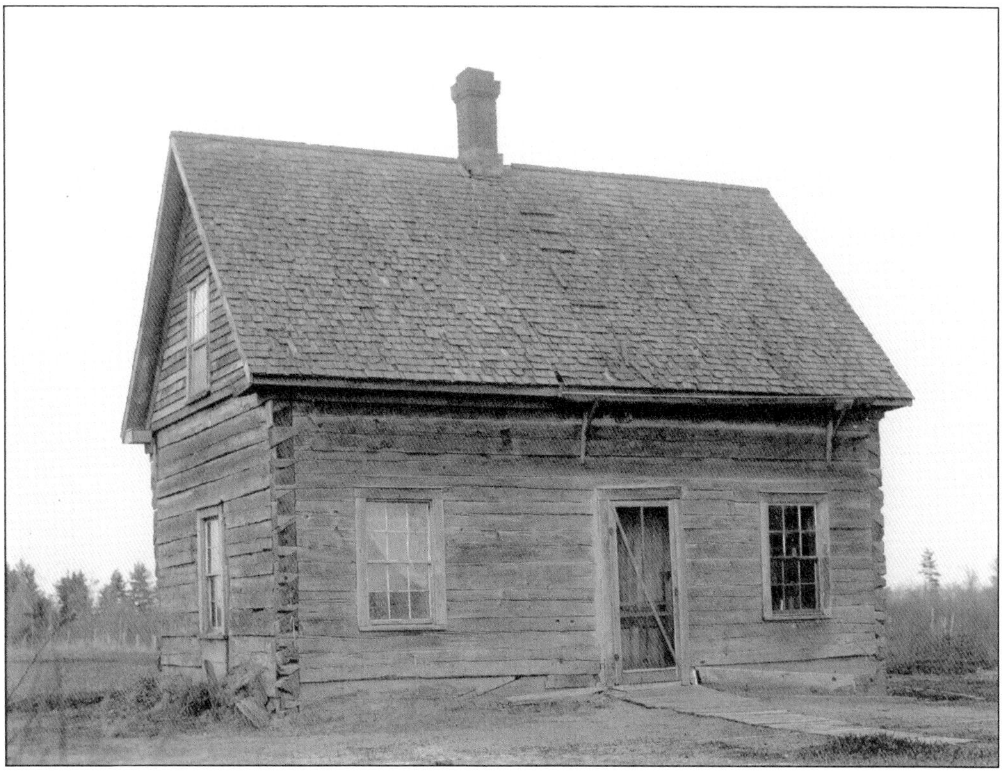

The Minnesota legislature established Kanabec County as an independent governmental entity on March 13, 1858, and chose the logging village of Brunswick as the county seat. Governor Sibley appointed Benjamin L. Gifford, George L. Staples, and Daniel Gordon as members of the county board. Kanabec County's first courthouse, shown here, was a 16-by-30-foot, two-room log cabin built in 1876.

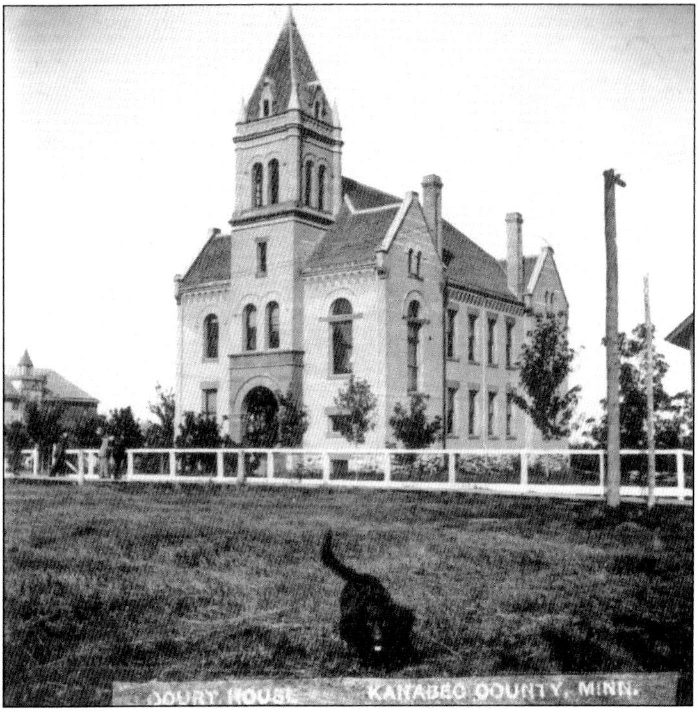

The village of Mora was founded early in 1882 alongside the newly constructed Minneapolis & St. Cloud Railroad. The town prospered, attracting so many settlers and businesses in its first year that Kanabec County citizens voted 166-2 to move the county seat to Mora. A $4,000 courthouse, built in 1883, was destroyed by fire in March 1894. The new courthouse, pictured here, was completed that fall.

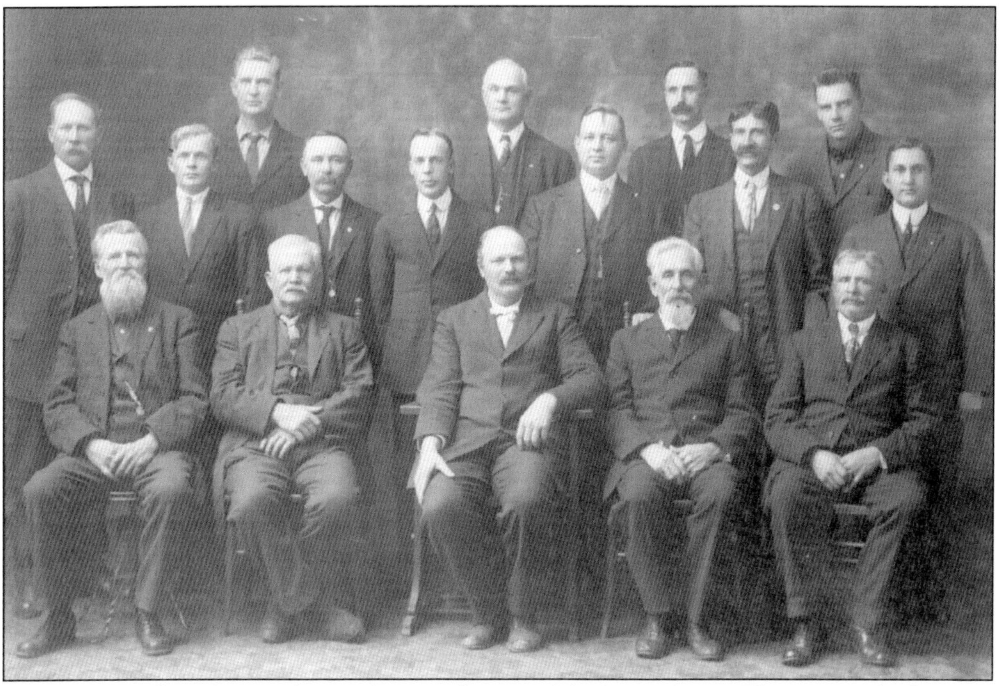

By 1910, Kanabec County boasted a population of 6,461 residents. The county had grown immensely since 1860 when it was home to only 30 people. County government had expanded, too, from a three-member board to the distinguished-looking county board that posed for this photograph in 1913. These civic-minded men were dedicated to fostering the continued growth and success of their county.

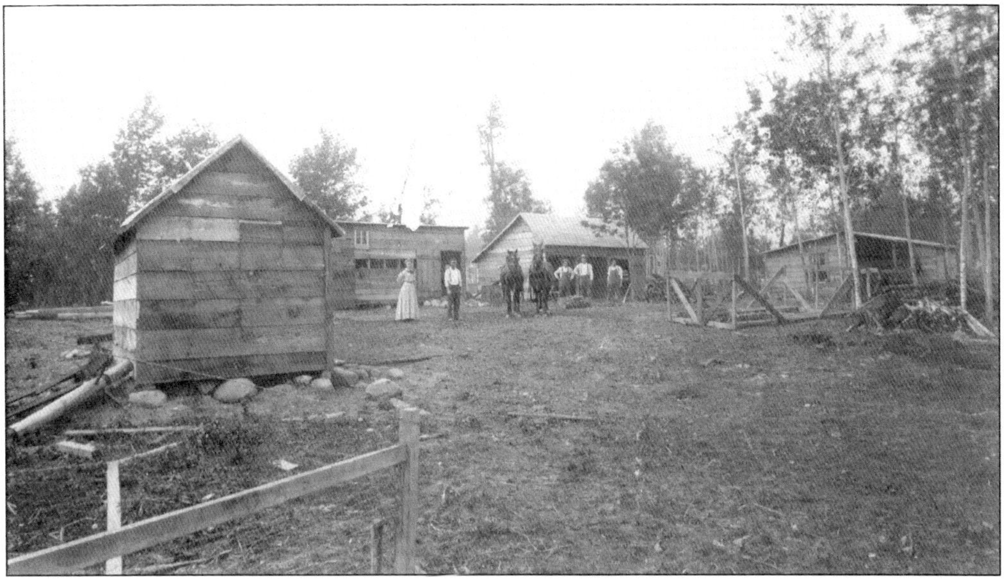

Loggers established the first farms in Kanabec County to grow food for themselves and their animals. After the lumber companies finished clearing the land, settlers moved in, took up permanent residence in the county, and built small farmsteads like this one. By 1880, sixty-five farms, valued at an estimated $35,755, dotted the county's landscape, covering 8,680 acres.

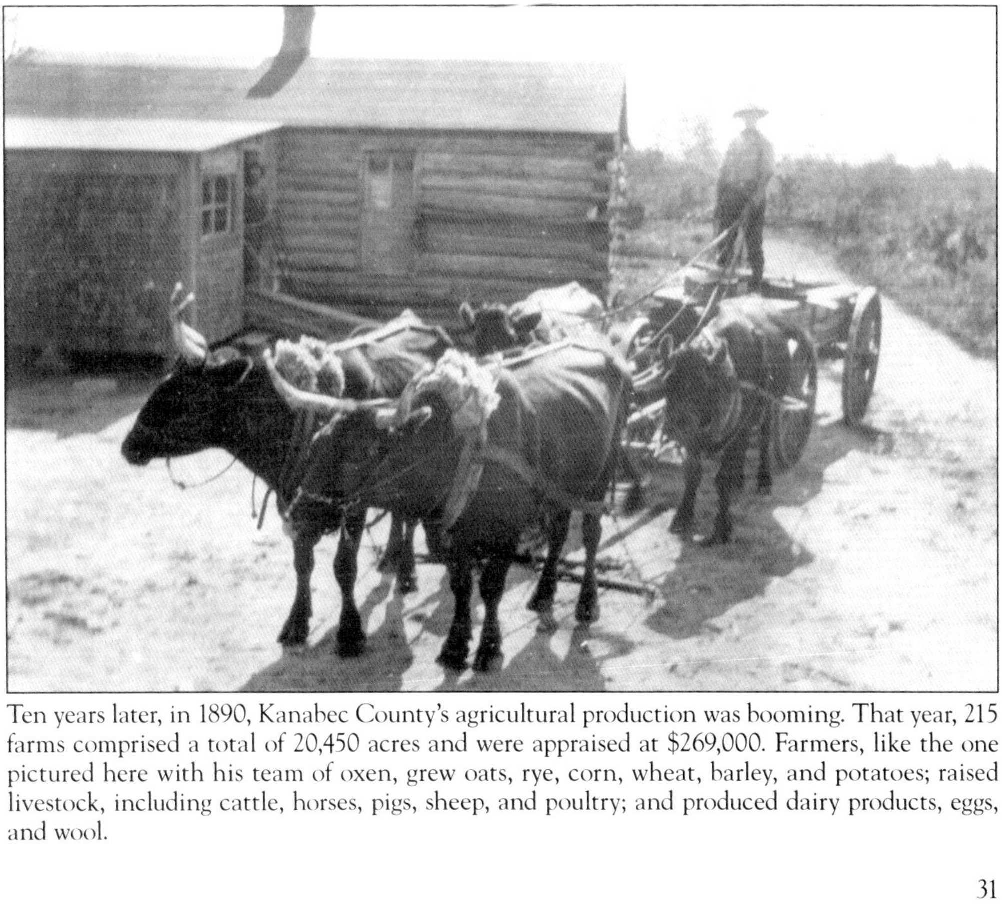

Ten years later, in 1890, Kanabec County's agricultural production was booming. That year, 215 farms comprised a total of 20,450 acres and were appraised at $269,000. Farmers, like the one pictured here with his team of oxen, grew oats, rye, corn, wheat, barley, and potatoes; raised livestock, including cattle, horses, pigs, sheep, and poultry; and produced dairy products, eggs, and wool.

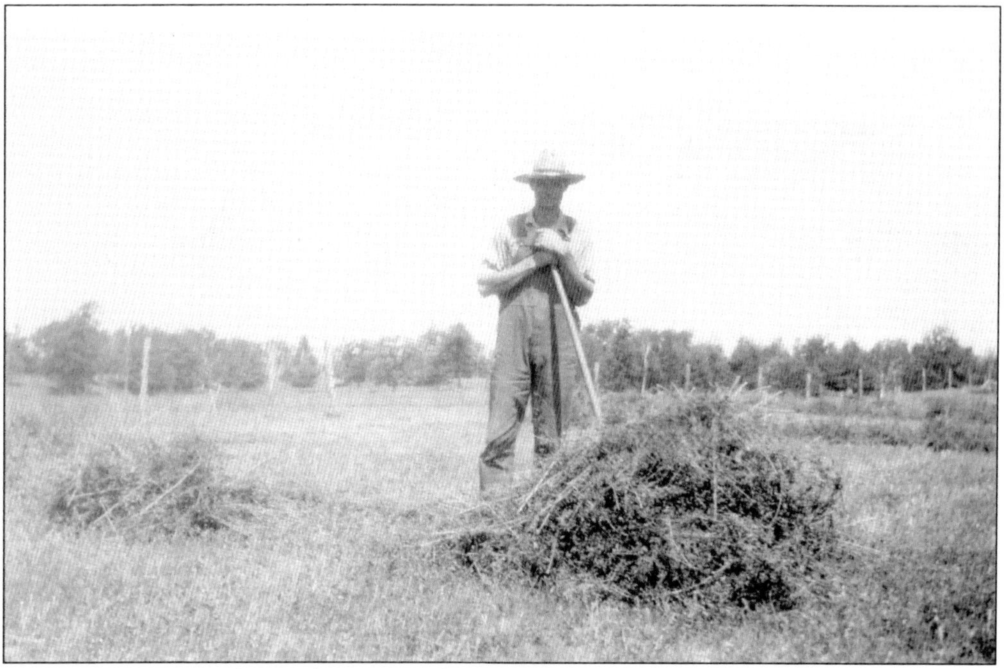

Life was not easy on early Kanabec County farms. Farming was a 24-hours-a-day, seven-days-a-week job, and farmers and their families did most of their chores by hand, without the conveniences of modern machinery. This man was hand-stacking hay with only a pitchfork.

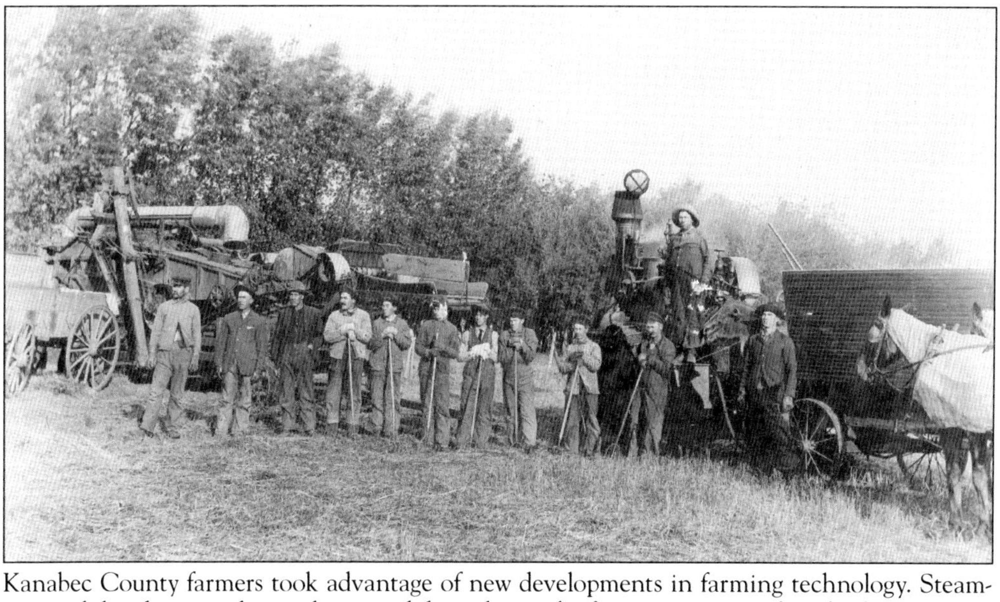

Kanabec County farmers took advantage of new developments in farming technology. Steam-powered threshing machines eliminated the tedious job of separating grain from husks and stalks by hand. Threshing crews traveled from farm to farm during the threshing season, and neighbors worked together to support the crews. The men and boys helped in the fields, and the women and girls cooked massive meals for the whole neighborhood.

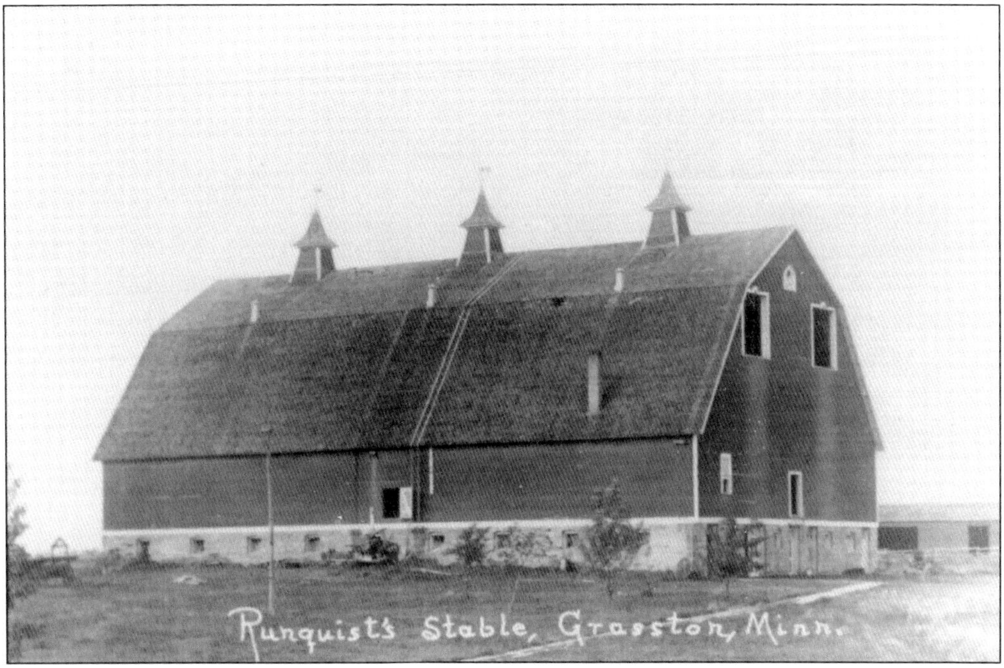

For nearly 60 years, Kanabec County could boast of being home to the largest barn in Minnesota. Built by John Runquist of Grasston in 1907 for $22,000, the massive structure was 125 feet long, 75 feet wide, and 79 feet high. The barn featured an eight-foot-high sandstone foundation, an interior silo and granary, and space for up to 100 cows. The barn burned in 1963.

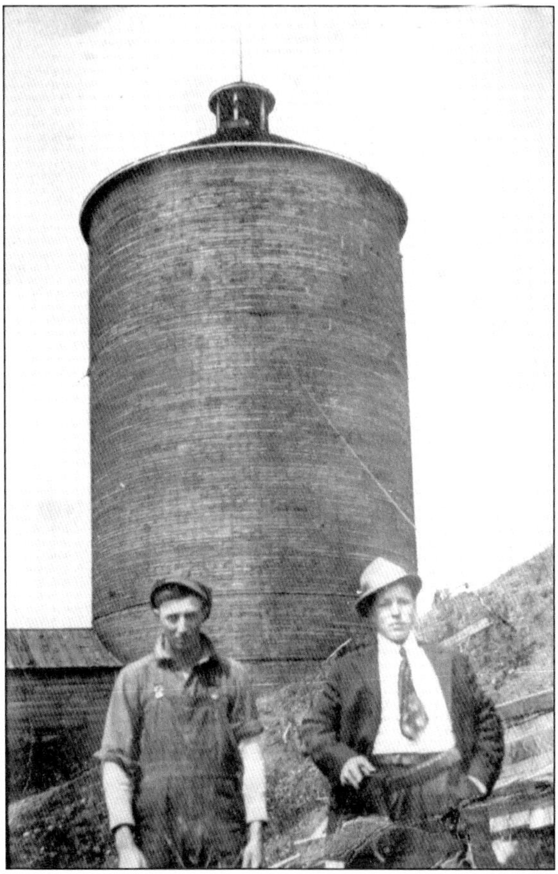

The Bronson farm two miles west of Mora was the county's largest farm for several decades. Founded as a logging farm in the early 1880s by lumberman Isaac Staples, the Bronson farm served as a local headquarters, post office, warehouse facility, and summer stables for the logging company. When this picture was taken in 1916, the Bronson farm was a commercial operation owned by Hiram Elliot of Duluth.

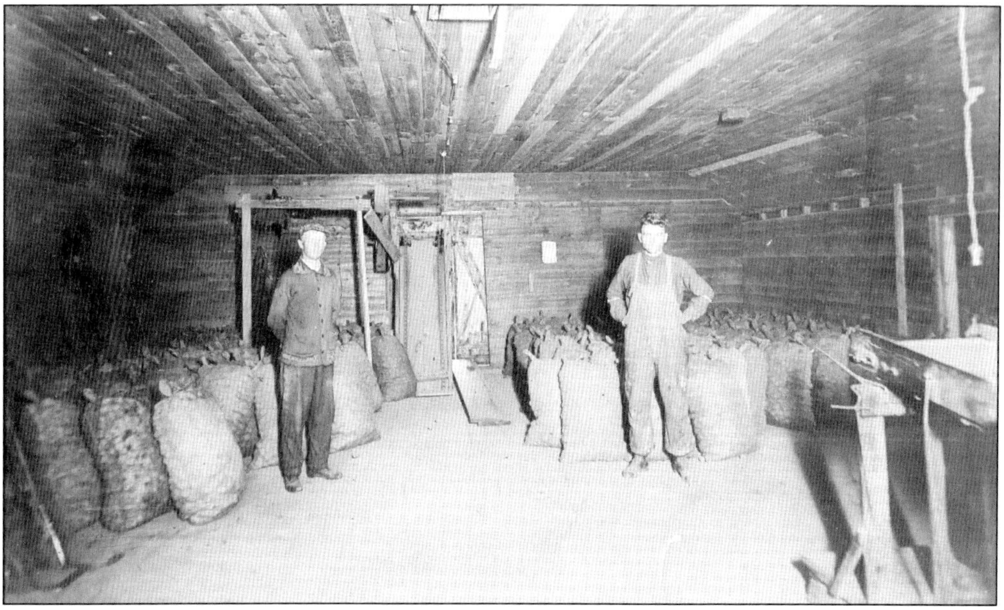

In the early 1900s, potatoes were Kanabec County's primary cash crop. Farmers planted 40-acre potato patches that produced 200 to 250 bushels per acre. Faced with a surplus of potatoes, businessmen began building warehouses to store the spuds and prepare them for shipping. Ed Schultz's facility in Mora, shown here, could hold 22 carloads of potatoes (600 bushels per car). That is 13,200 bushels of potatoes!

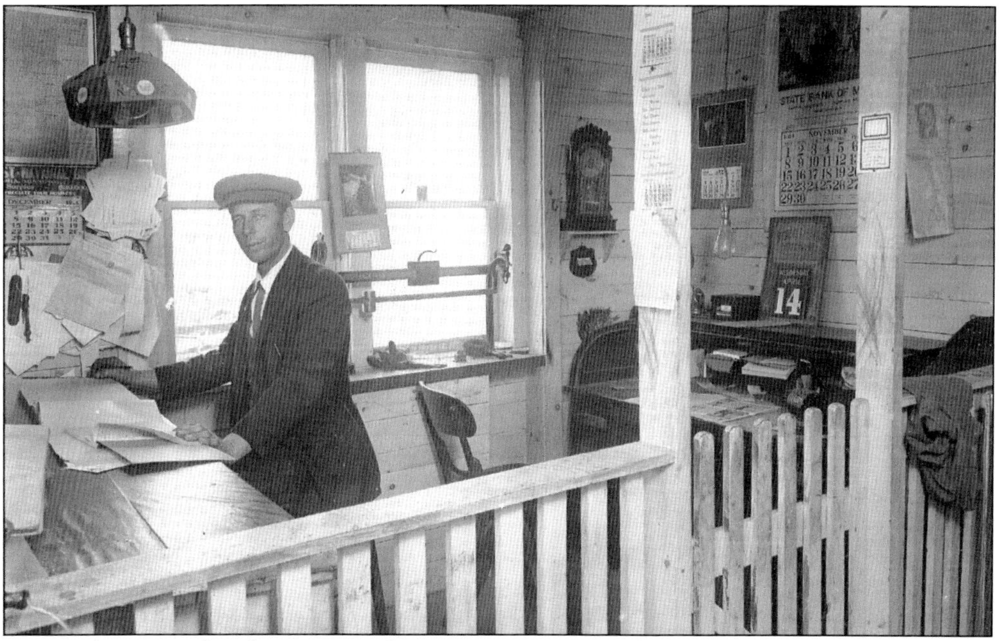

During the years of peak potato production, Mora supported nine potato warehouses. Ogilvie had five. Often, all 14 were full. Farmers sometimes waited up to three hours to weigh and sell their spuds and deposit them at a warehouse. Potato prices varied from 65¢ to $4.50 per bushel between 1910 and 1930. In this 1914–1915 photograph, John Check was looking over the records at the McFarland potato warehouse in Mora.

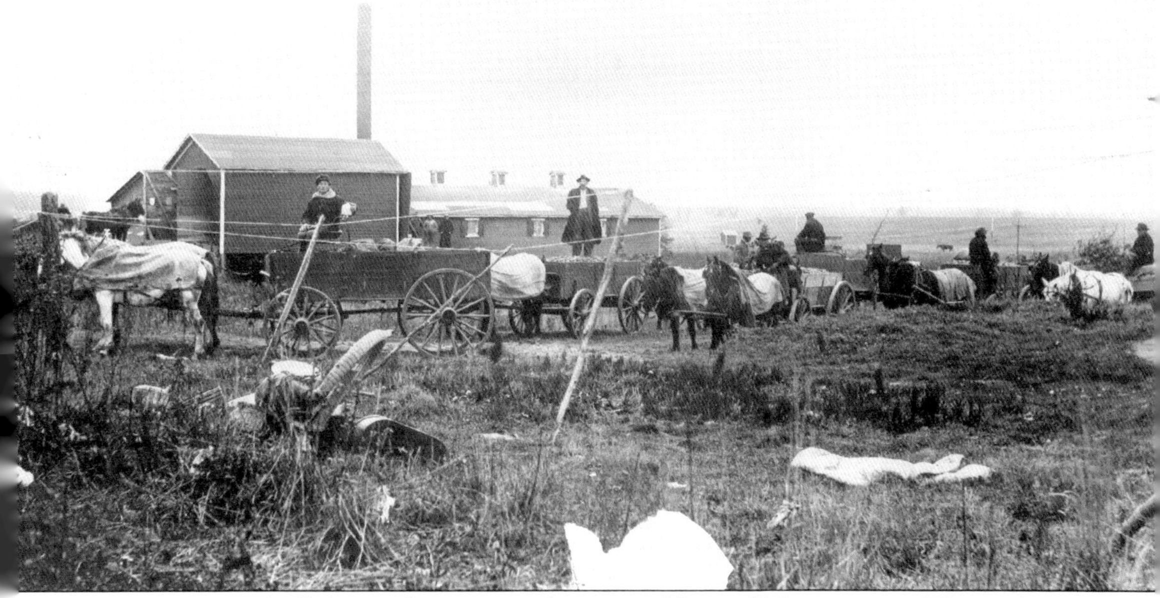

Sometimes, even with all the warehouse space, farmers could not sell their potatoes. The surplus was too large, or the potatoes did not meet buyers' standards. To avoid wasting potatoes, several Grasston businessmen, including John Runquist, S.O. Person, John O. Serline, P.M. Peterson, D.O. Anderson, Karl Anderson, and Jonas Birch, decided to form the Grasston Starch Manufacturing Company in 1904. The factory began buying potatoes and turning them into starch in 1905. Unfortunately, the company was not particularly successful. Financial difficulties occasioned heavy borrowing and debt, and the factory was destroyed by fire in the 1920s. In the 1930s, a potato blight and low prices ended Kanabec County's potato years. Farmers turned to the dairy business. The warehouses fell into disrepair and were gradually torn down. The last one, Ed Schultz's warehouse, was demolished in 1954.

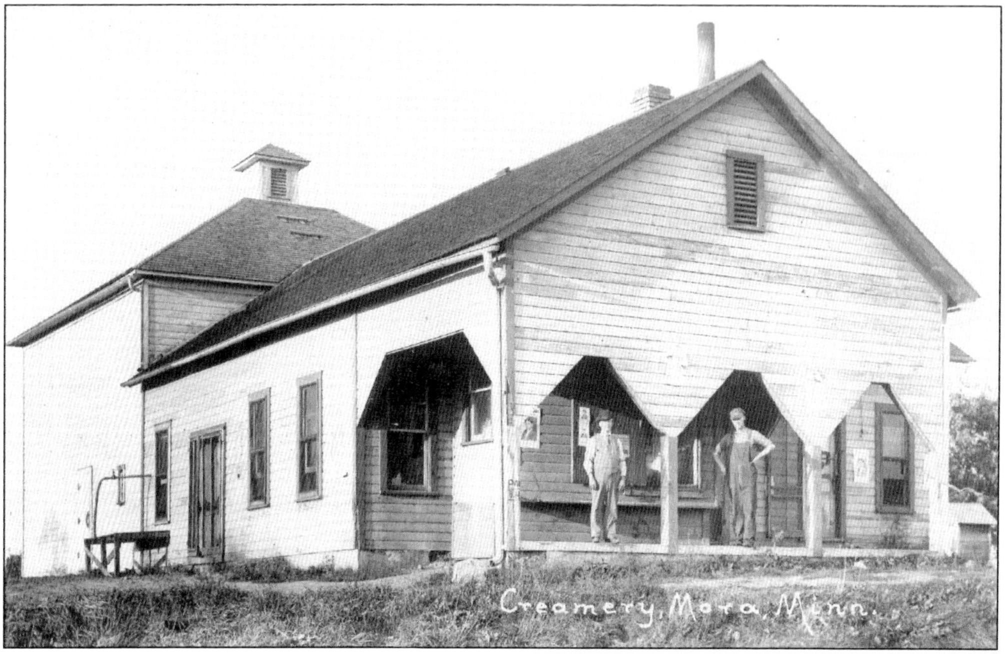

Farmers and businessmen organized Mora's first cooperative creamery in 1895 in hopes of earning larger profits for their surplus butter and cream. They built a small creamery on a local farm, only to watch the building burn the following year. In 1899, the organization tried again, constructing the creamery shown here. This building was destroyed by fire in 1901.

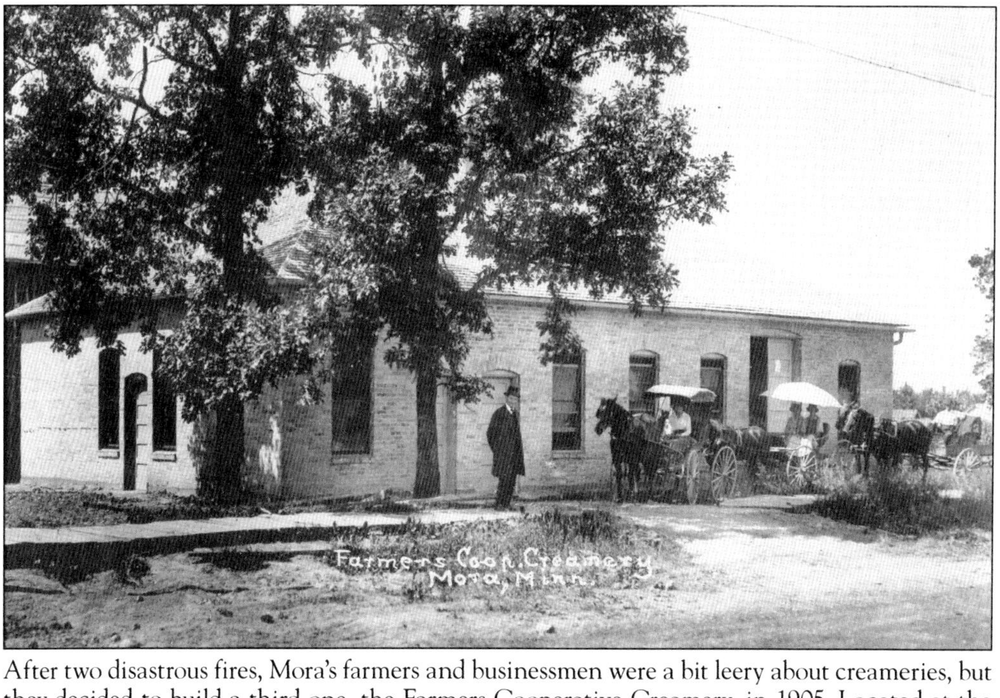

After two disastrous fires, Mora's farmers and businessmen were a bit leery about creameries, but they decided to build a third one, the Farmers Cooperative Creamery, in 1905. Located at the corner of Maple Avenue and Grove Street, this creamery lasted longer than the others, but it, too, burned in 1915.

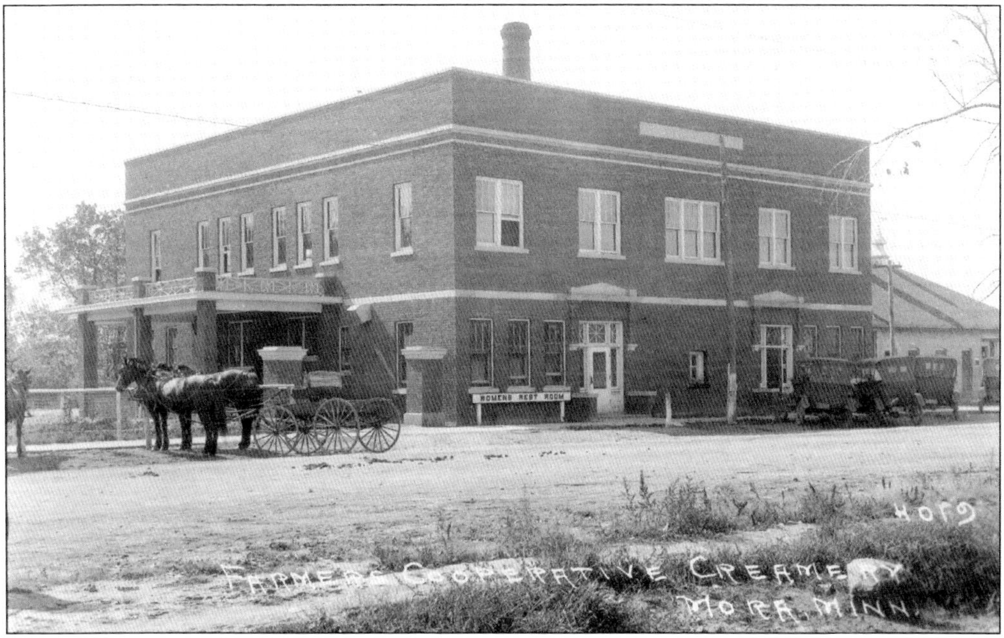

Farmers had become accustomed to the convenience of a cooperative creamery, but they wanted one that would not go up in flames every few years. In 1916, the Farmers Cooperative Creamery organization constructed a new, fire-resistant brick creamery that would stand the test of time. For 80 years, this creamery building provided services to farmers, jobs for workers, entertainment in the "creamery hall," and even educational facilities for local schools.

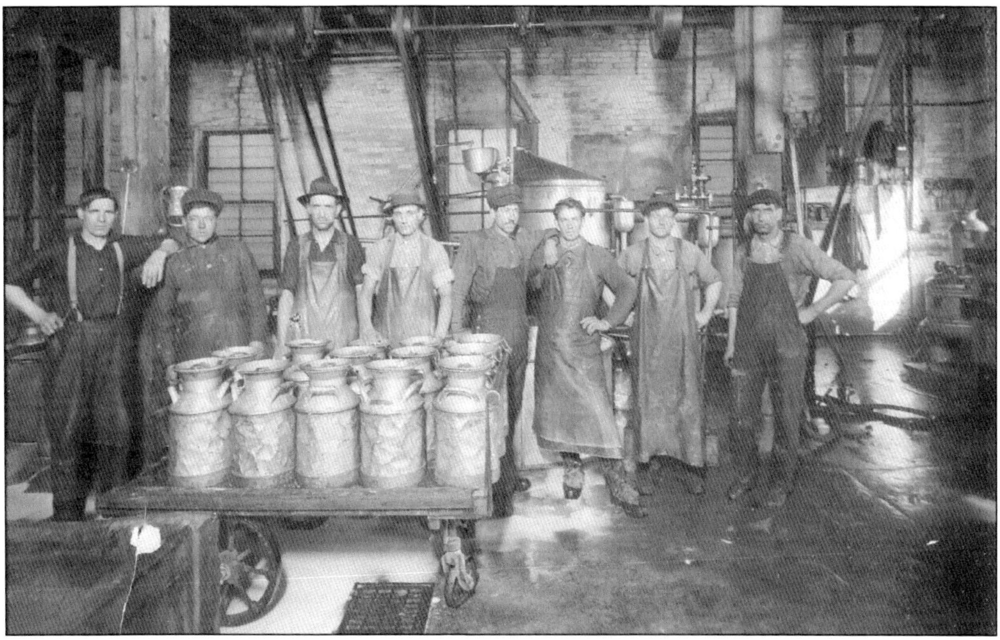

Mora's Farmers Cooperative Creamery did brisk business beginning in the 1920s. During its "banner years" of 1928 and 1929, the creamery produced over 900,000 pounds of butter per year. These early creamery employees took a short break from their work to pose for their photograph. Notice the dented milk cans, which had clearly been well used.

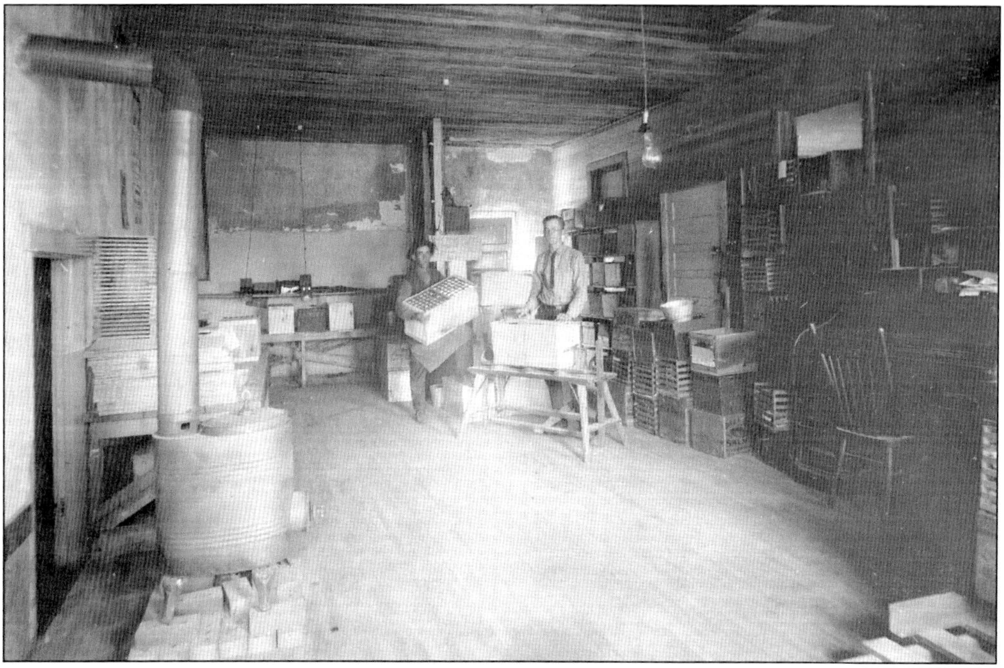

By the 1930s, the creamery business had expanded to include an egg plant and poultry building. Many area farmers had been raising poultry and selling their eggs to local stores. Often, however, the eggs were inedible because they were not candled or accurately graded. The creamery's new additions helped raise the quality of local eggs and provided opportunities for farmers to purchase higher-grade feeds and properly dress their poultry.

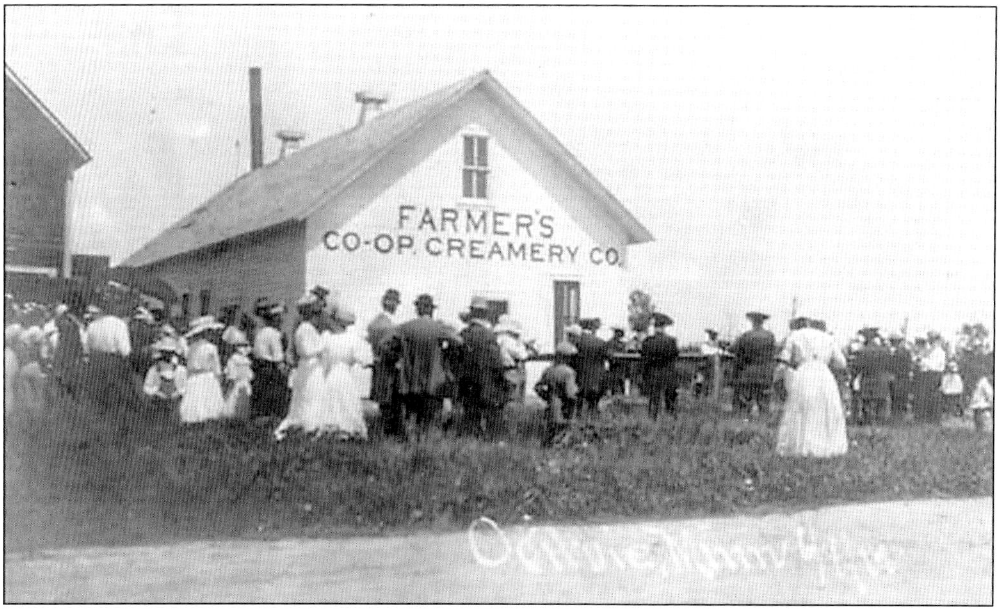

The Ogilvie Farmers Cooperative Creamery was incorporated on March 15, 1911, with a net worth of $6,000 in 240 shares of stock. Butter production was the creamery's primary activity, with 274,849 pounds sold for a total of $118,396.47 in 1923 and 934,569 pounds for $542,532.21 in 1956. Ogilvie's creamery also produced cheese in the 1940s and 1950s.

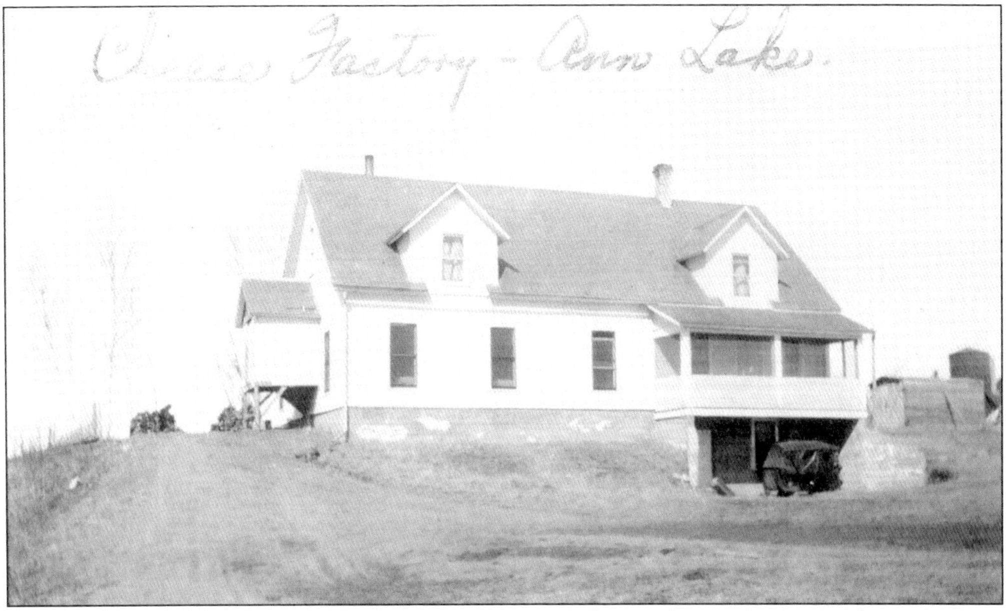

Hoping to take advantage of Kanabec County's growing dairy industry, the Ann Lake community decided to build a cheese factory in January 1917. C.A. Nelson constructed the Ann Lake Cheese Factory later that year on land donated by Carl Brettingen. By August, the factory was paying 54¢ per pound for butterfat. The price rose to 94¢ per pound in 1919.

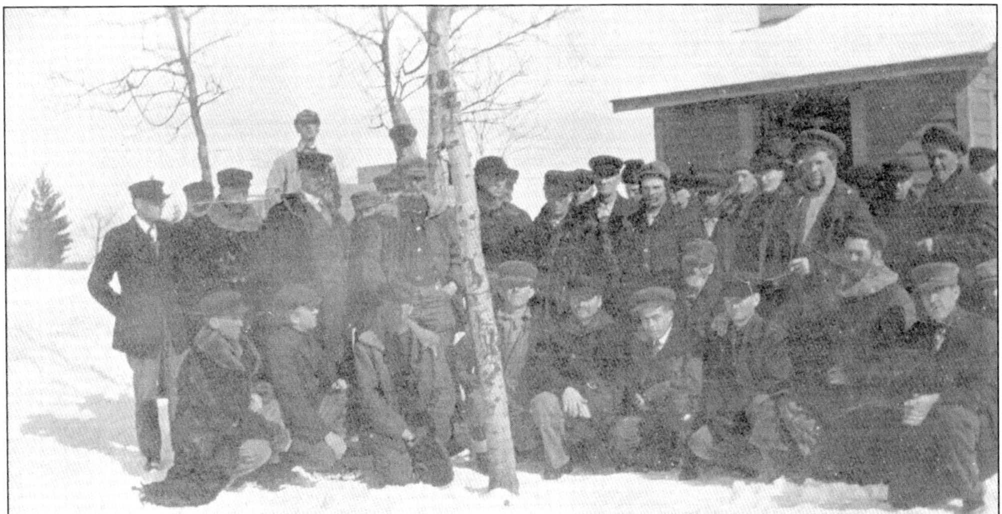

The organizers of the Ann Lake Cheese Factory gathered for a group photograph in 1917. William Achterkirch served as the organization's president, Guy Hart as vice president, R.J. McCartney as secretary, Carl Brettingen as treasurer, and G.F. Vanetten, C.O. Hill, and A.M. Bergren as directors. The cheese factory closed in 1924 due to a lack of funds to buy milk and pay for normal operations.

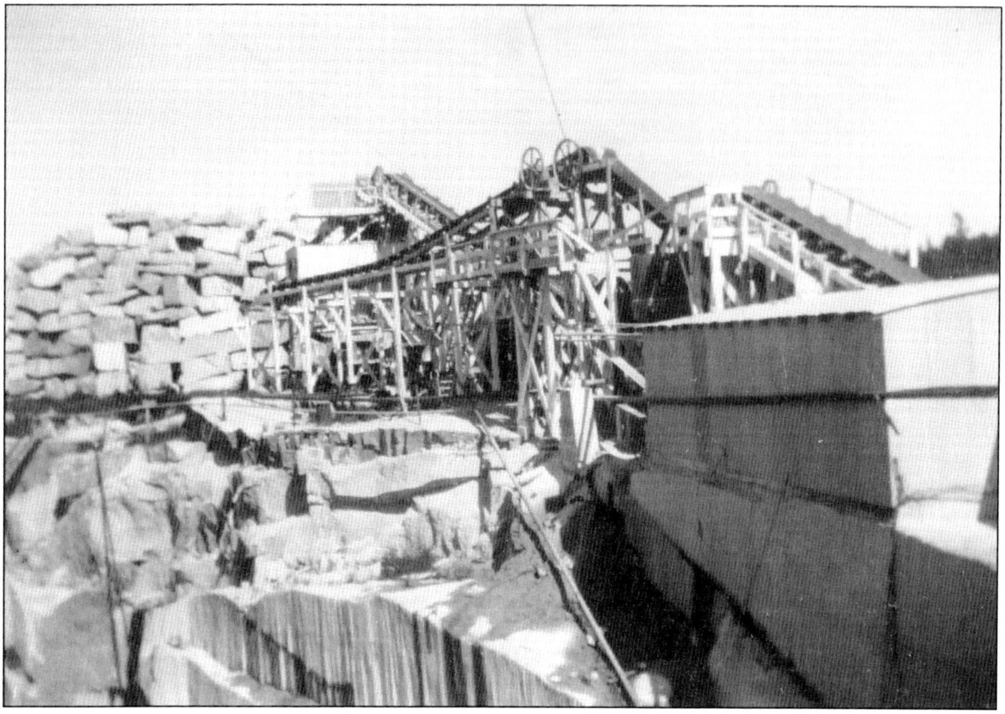

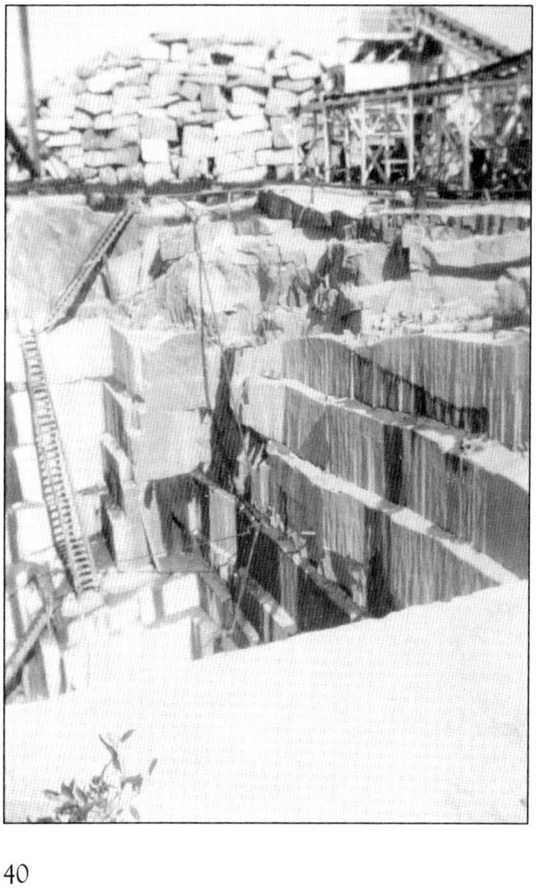

Although Kanabec County's economy was built primarily on logging and agriculture, a few ambitious entrepreneurs decided to tap into another of the county's resources: granite. In 1907, Samuel Warman established the Warman Creek Granite Company and constructed a quarry 16 miles north of Mora to extract the distinctive, high-quality, gray stone. Warman and his wife, Sarah, platted the town that bears their name shortly after founding the quarry.

The Pike-Horning Granite Company was also interested in harvesting "Warman granite" and built its own quarry in July 1907. N.C. Pike platted his own village just east of Warman and named it North Mora. The two competing communities eventually merged under the name Warman. Quarrying in the area ended in the mid-1950s.

Four

A County in Motion

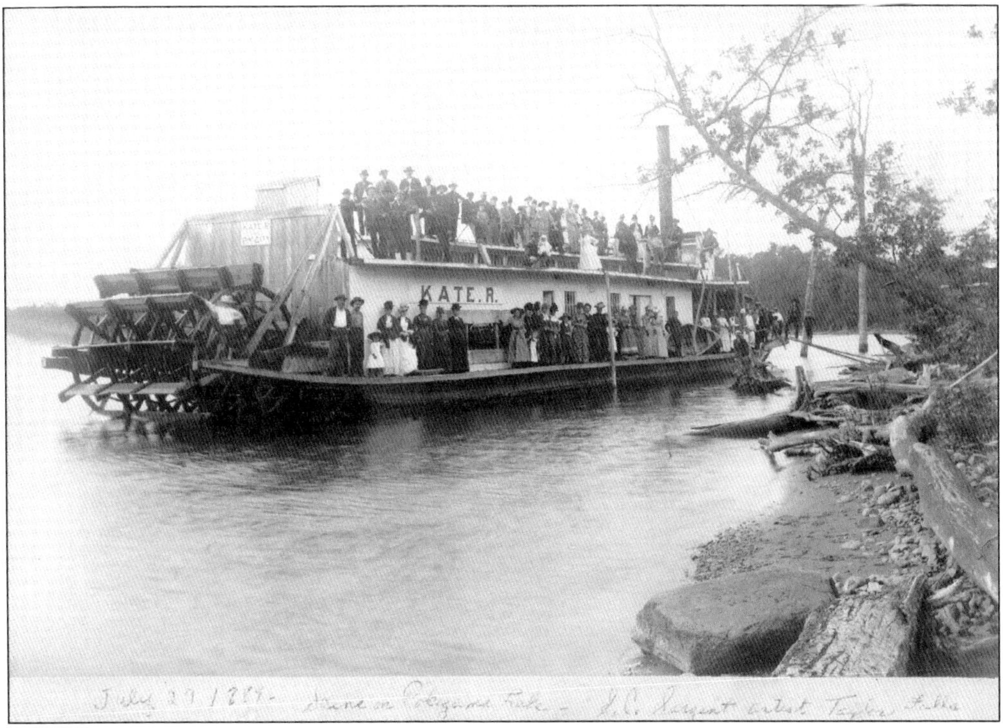

Kanabec County has always been a county in motion. During the logging era, log dams raised water levels in the county's rivers and streams so logs could float easily down to the southern sawmills. These higher water levels allowed for steamboat transportation along the Snake River and Rice Creek as far north as Brunswick. Capt. E.L. Seavey piloted the steamer *Kate R.*, shown here in 1889.

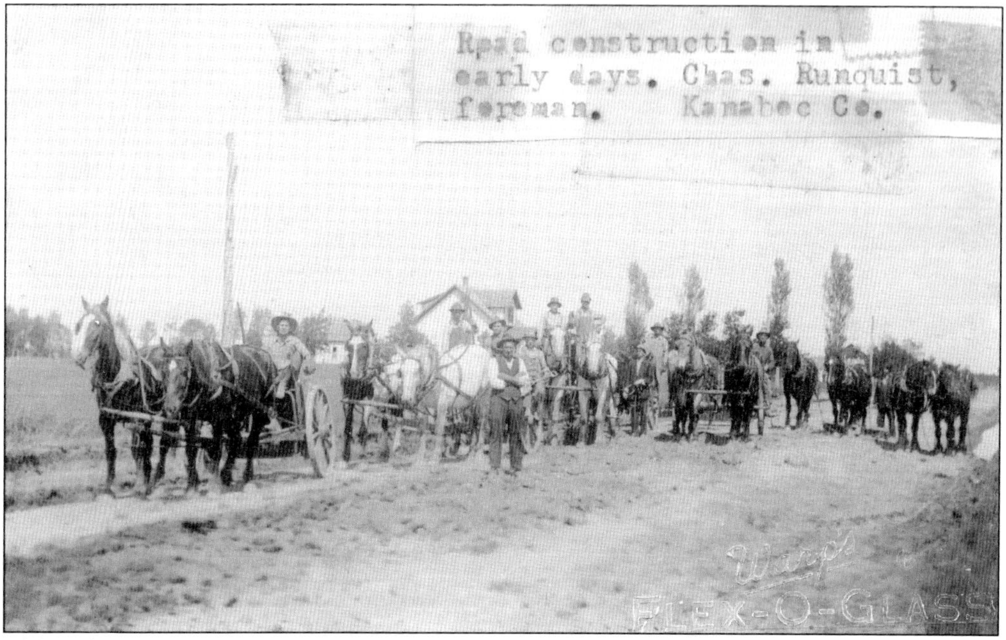

Although Native Americans created the first trails in Kanabec County, loggers built the first tote roads by 1851. These were constructed on frozen ground for the winter logging season but were muddy, rutted, and useless the rest of the year. In 1859, the county board established a county road system to improve roads and build bridges. Charles Runquist was the foreman of this group of road workers.

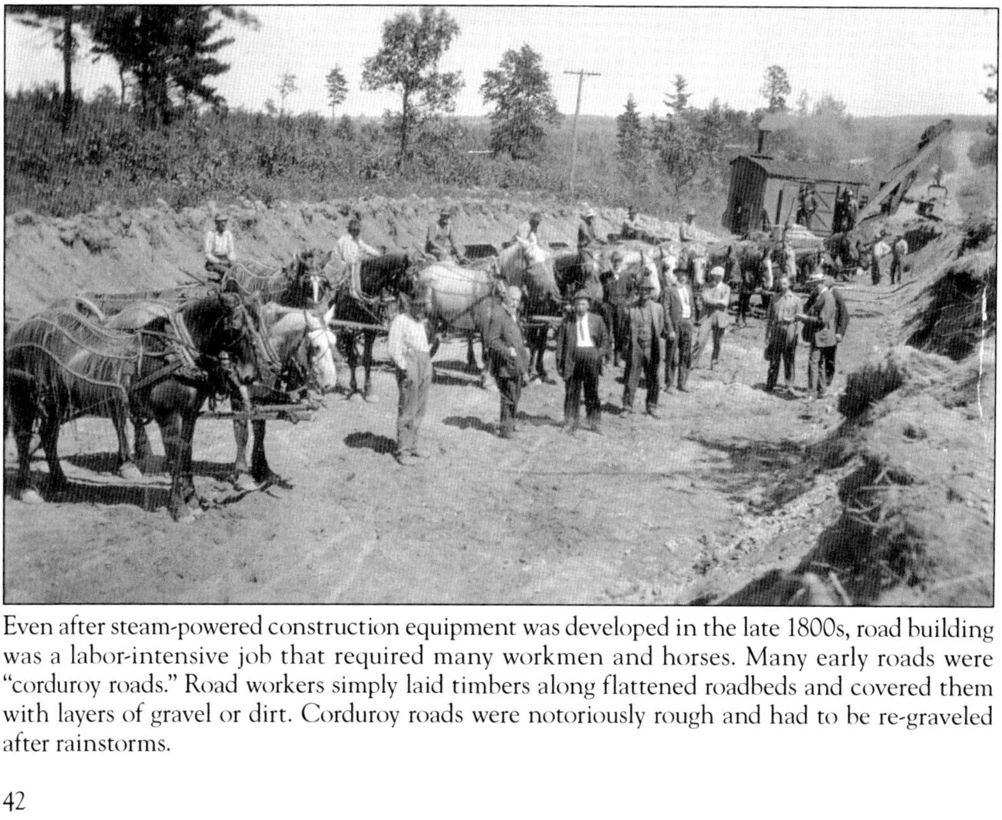

Even after steam-powered construction equipment was developed in the late 1800s, road building was a labor-intensive job that required many workmen and horses. Many early roads were "corduroy roads." Road workers simply laid timbers along flattened roadbeds and covered them with layers of gravel or dirt. Corduroy roads were notoriously rough and had to be re-graveled after rainstorms.

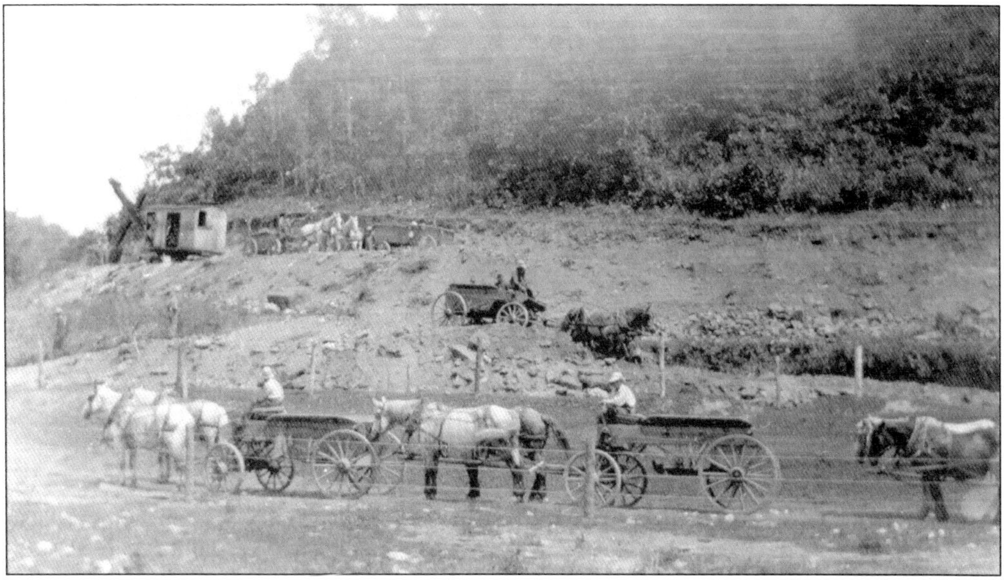

Kanabec County's first bridge was built across the Snake River at Brunswick in 1874. It required 1,300 feet of fill and cost $5,000, an enormous amount in those days. Five years later, a second bridge was constructed over the Snake River, this time at Grass Lake. This bridge was too low to allow for steamboat traffic, so it was rebuilt in 1884 for a total cost of $8,000.

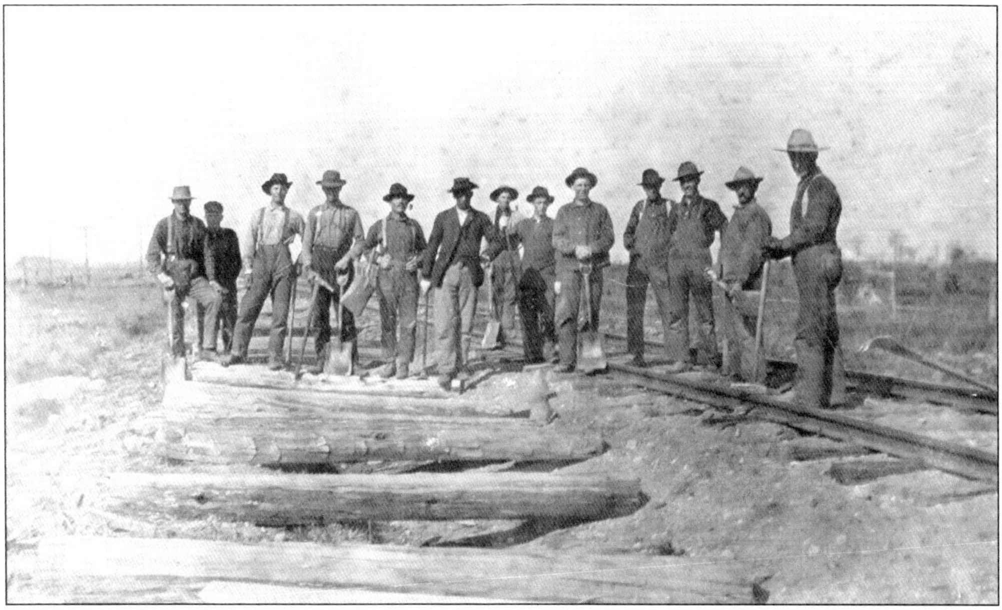

The Minneapolis & St. Cloud Railroad laid Kanabec County's first railroad line in 1882. The town of Mora was founded as a station stop along the new line. In 1898–1899, the Eastern Minnesota Railway ran its road through the southern part of the county and built a depot in the newly established village of Grasston. These early railroad workers took a quick break from their work to pose for their photograph.

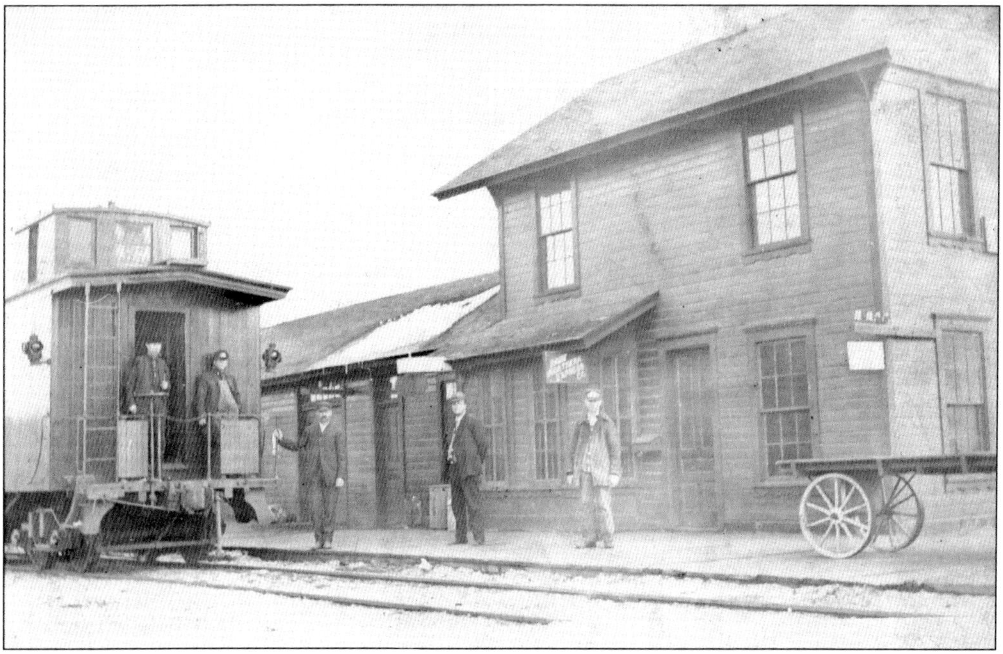

Railroads provided Kanabec County with an economic boost as they carried settlers into the area and transported goods like potatoes, wood, and cream to distant markets. The village depot was a bustling hub of activity. Mora's first depot was built in 1882 and located downtown on the north side of the tracks. The depot shown here was constructed around the turn of the century just east of the village.

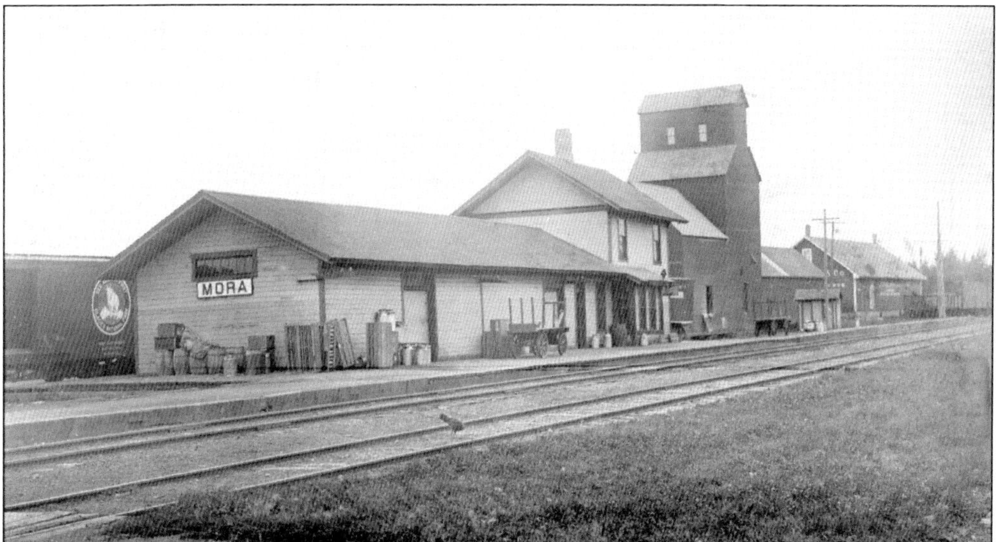

In the early 1900s, Mora's Great Northern Railway yard was a busy complex with a depot, a feed elevator, and several warehouses. Village residents often walked out to the depot to meet passenger and mail trains, and local hotels sent livery rigs to pick up customers. The complex was always expanding and improving. In 1902, for instance, a 50-foot addition to the depot provided large, comfortable waiting rooms for travelers.

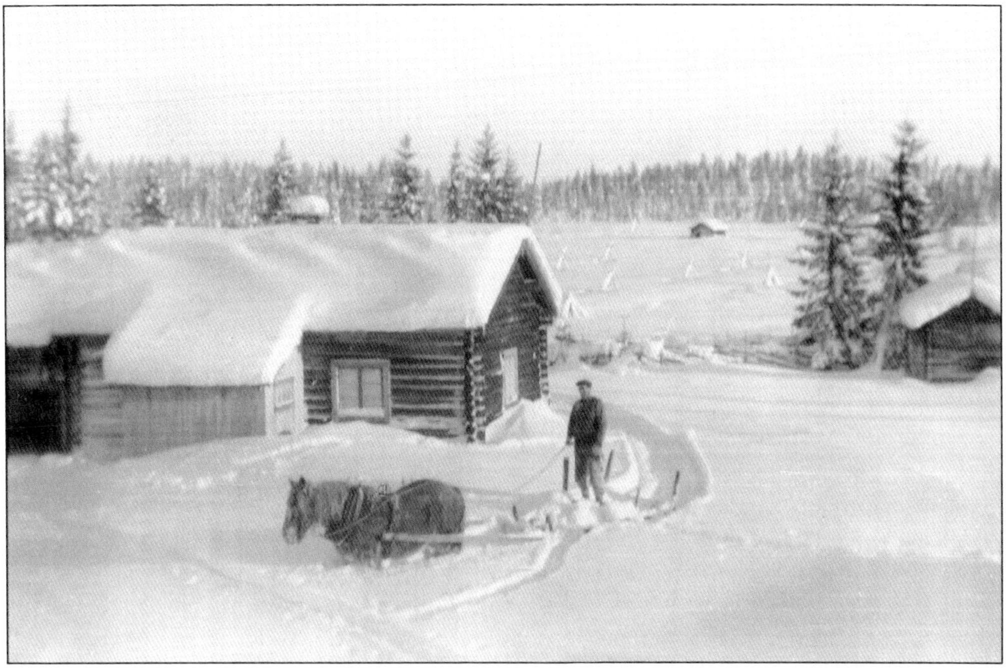

Even after the railroad arrived in Kanabec County, travel remained slow and difficult. Although most families owned horses or oxen to pull their wagons, buggies, or sleds, they did not wander too far from home, especially in the winter. Since horse-and-buggy travel averaged four to eight miles per hour even in the best conditions, long journeys were few and far between.

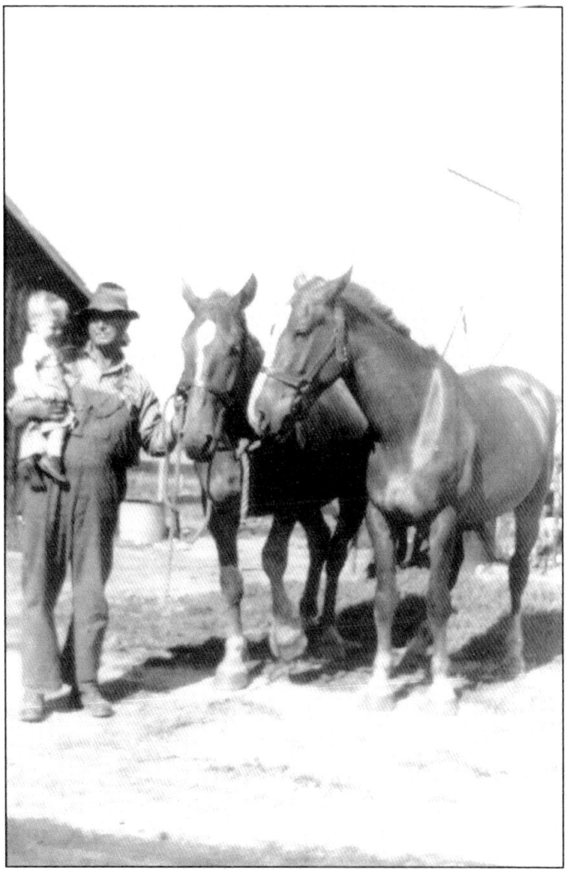

Horses were more than just transportation or working animals on many Kanabec County farms. They were members of the family that were treated with respect. In this 1946 photograph, Kanabec County farmer Curtis Points was introducing his grandson, author Earl "Jim" Foster, to the family's equine members.

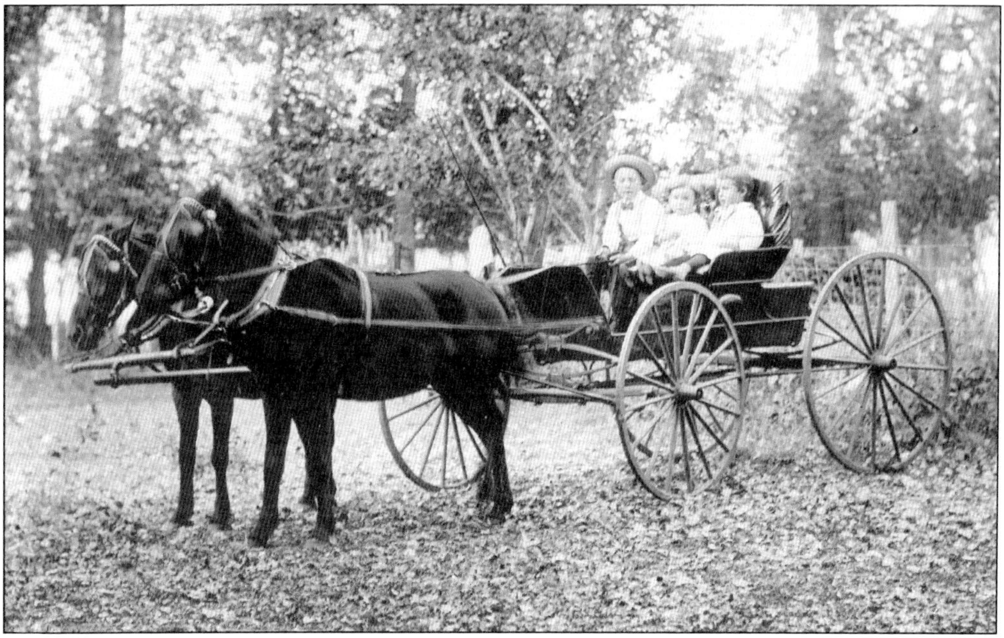

These three siblings from the Fetchenheir family were ready for a short jaunt in their family's buggy. Boys learned to handle horses at a young age.

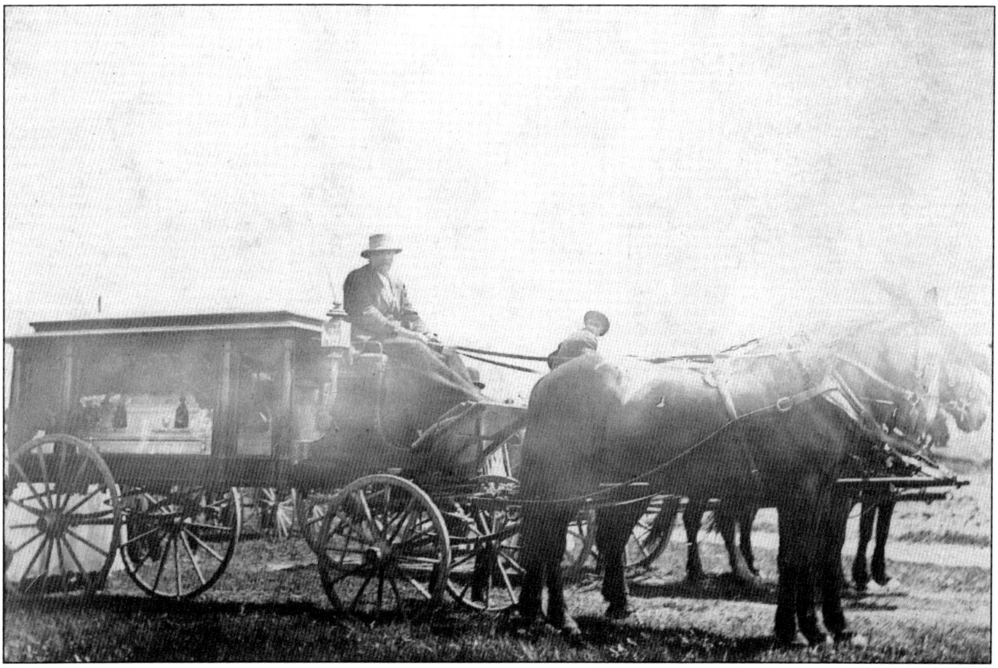

This horse-drawn hearse was probably owned by the local undertaker. Early funeral homes were typically located in furniture stores, and proprietors made or ordered caskets as part of their standard line of merchandise.

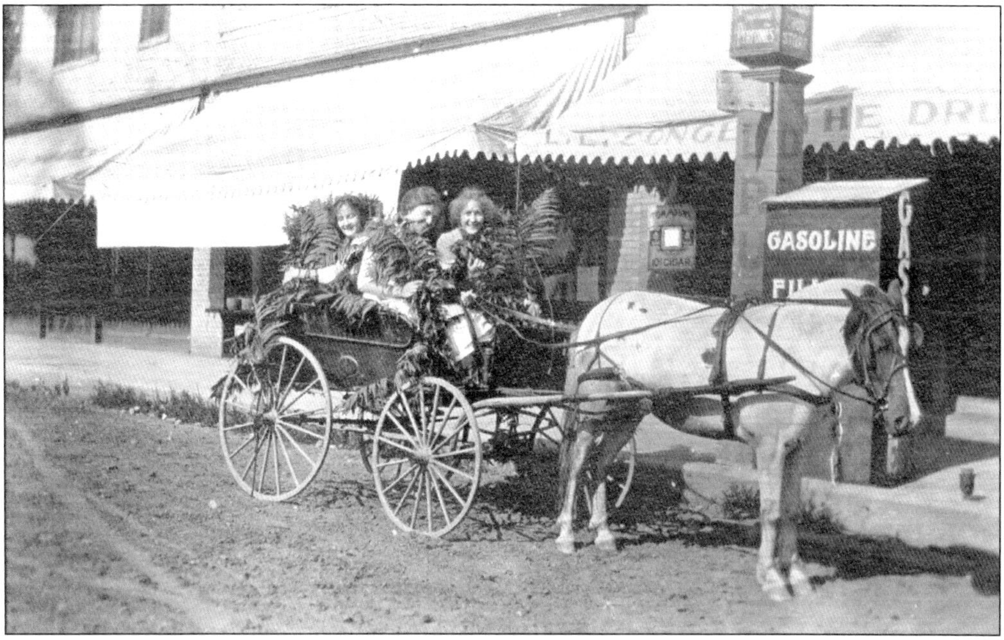

In the first two decades of the 20th century, transportation in Kanabec County was changing. Many families still owned horses and buggies, but the "horseless carriage" was becoming more popular and widespread. This 1913 photograph visually reveals the transportation transition. Notice that the horse was standing next to a gasoline pump outside L.E. Conger's Drug Store in Mora.

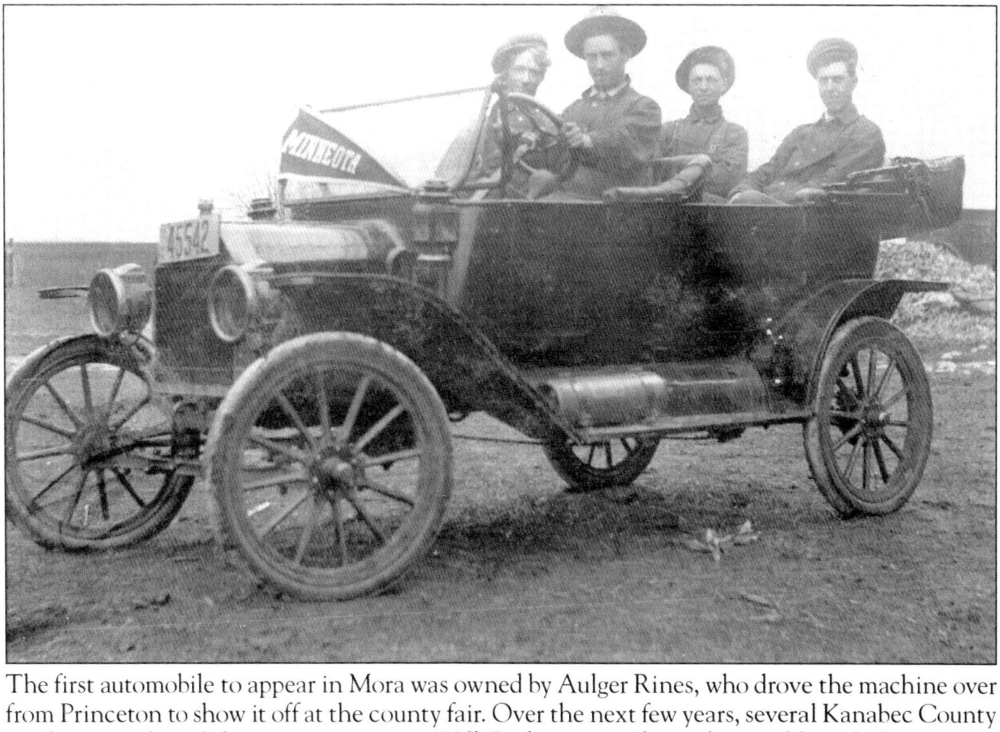

The first automobile to appear in Mora was owned by Aulger Rines, who drove the machine over from Princeton to show it off at the county fair. Over the next few years, several Kanabec County residents purchased their own motorcars. Will Gorham owned one that could reach the amazing speed of 20 miles per hour, and Oscar Nyquist's auto could get two or three miles per gallon.

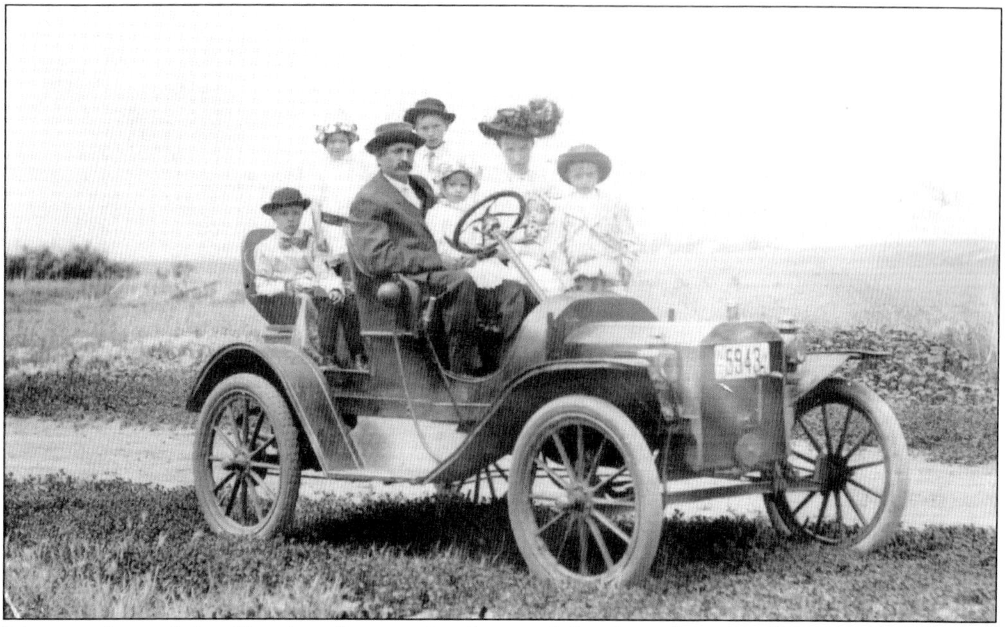

The members of this Kanabec County family posed for their photograph in their shiny, new automobile. Most county residents simply could not afford early motorcars. When the Ford Model T was released in 1908, it cost $850, which is equivalent to over $20,000 in today's money. Other 1908 cars cost between $2,000 and $3,000. The Model T's price dropped to $550 in 1913, $440 in 1915, and $290 by the 1920s.

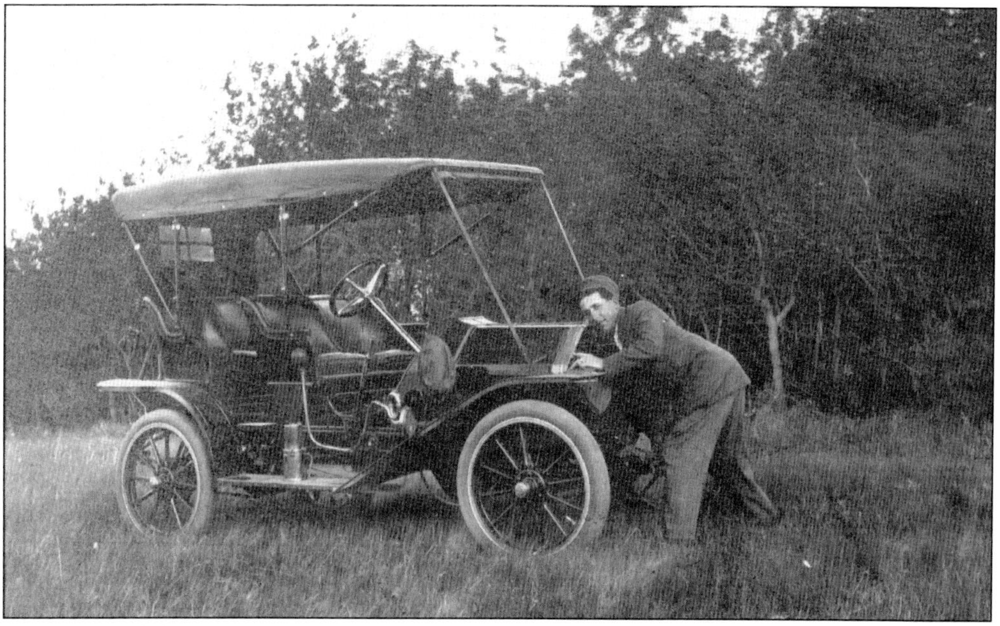

Early automobiles came with a whole assortment of troubles. According to one old-timer, they were "quite an education" and took "considerable tinkering" to remain in "reasonable running condition." Drivers quickly learned to be prepared for breakdowns, flat tires, and overheated motors by carrying tool kits complete with various wrenches, screwdrivers, pliers, a jack, a pump, and a tire patching kit. This early car was stalled near Quamba.

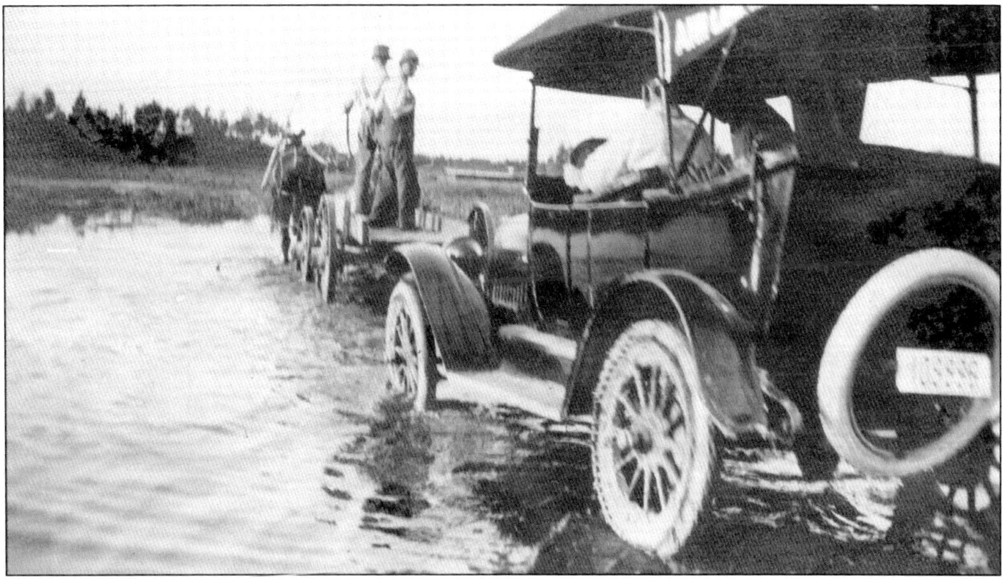

Not everyone appreciated motorcars. These "demons of the road," as some called them, created traffic problems, scared horses, and elicited anger and profanity from horse drivers who struggled to control their animals as they plunged in terror at the noisy machines. Ironically, the automobile driver in this picture needed some equine help to remove his car from Ann Lake.

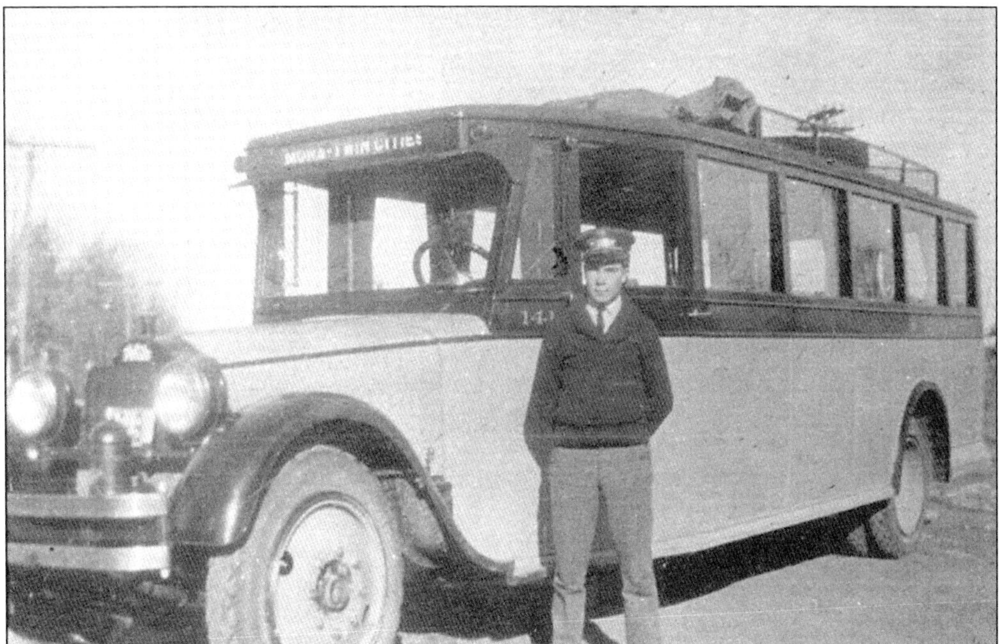

Because early motorcars were expensive and undependable, many Kanabec County residents relied on public transportation for long journeys. By the 1920s and 1930s, bus travel was becoming more common and more convenient as roads improved. This bus covered the route between Mora and the Twin Cities of St. Paul and Minneapolis.

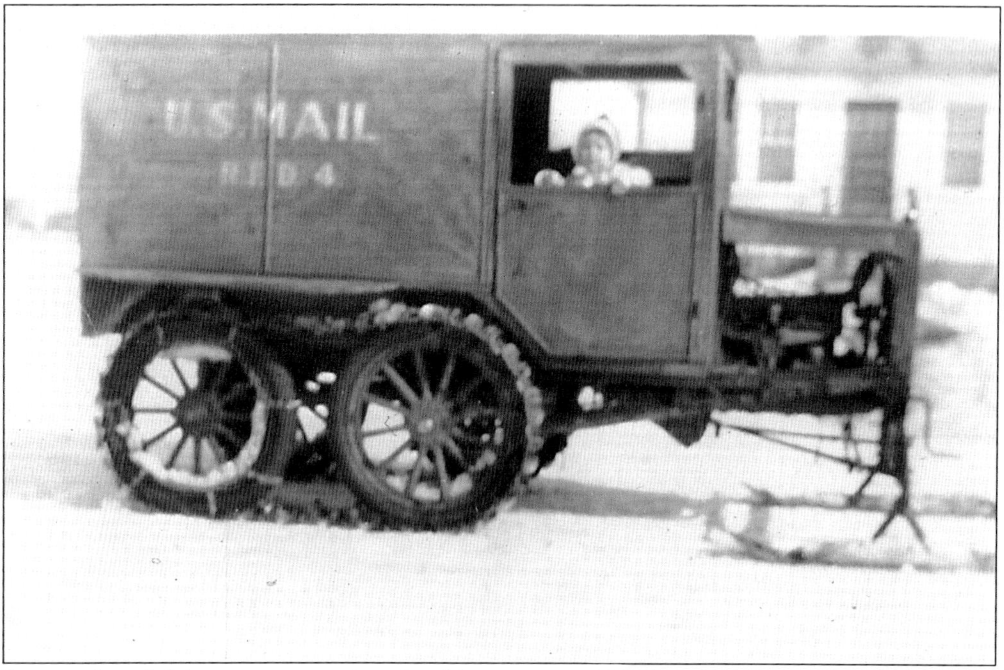

Free rural mail delivery was introduced in Minnesota in 1897. By 1904, it was an official part of the US Postal Service. Delivering mail on Kanabec County's snow-packed winter roads was not an easy task, but vehicles like this one used on Route 4 helped postmen complete their duties.

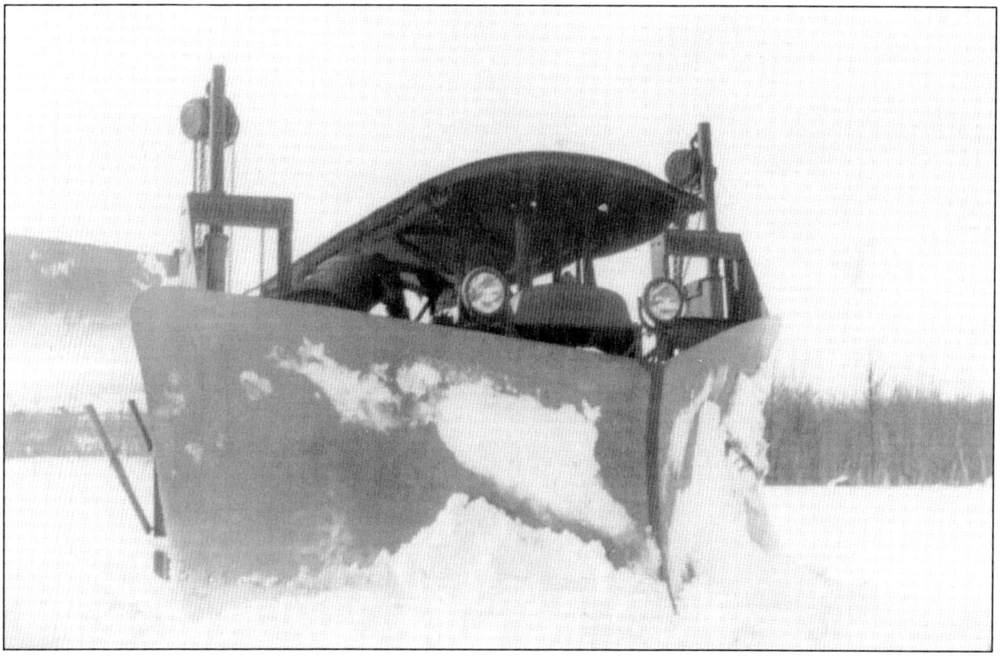

As the years passed and cars became the most common mode of transportation in Kanabec County, keeping the roads open during the harsh winter months was essential. Snowplows like this one made valiant efforts, but many rural residents were still snowed in for days after a major snowstorm.

Five

MAIN STREET, KANABEC COUNTY

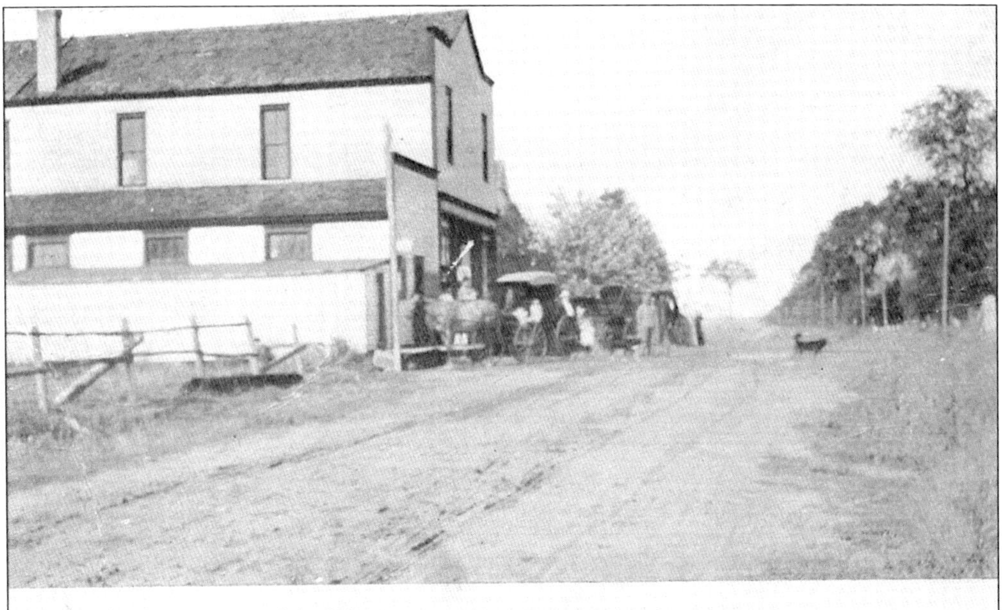

In 1856, lumbermen George and Isaac Staples platted Brunswick, Kanabec County's first town, on the site of their lumber camp at Millet Rapids on the Snake River. In 1864, the camp and town moved about a mile upstream. Brunswick moved again in 1882, this time to the site of S.E. Tallman's mill on the Groundhouse River. The Skoglund store, established by Andrew Skoglund in 1889, was Brunswick's primary general store.

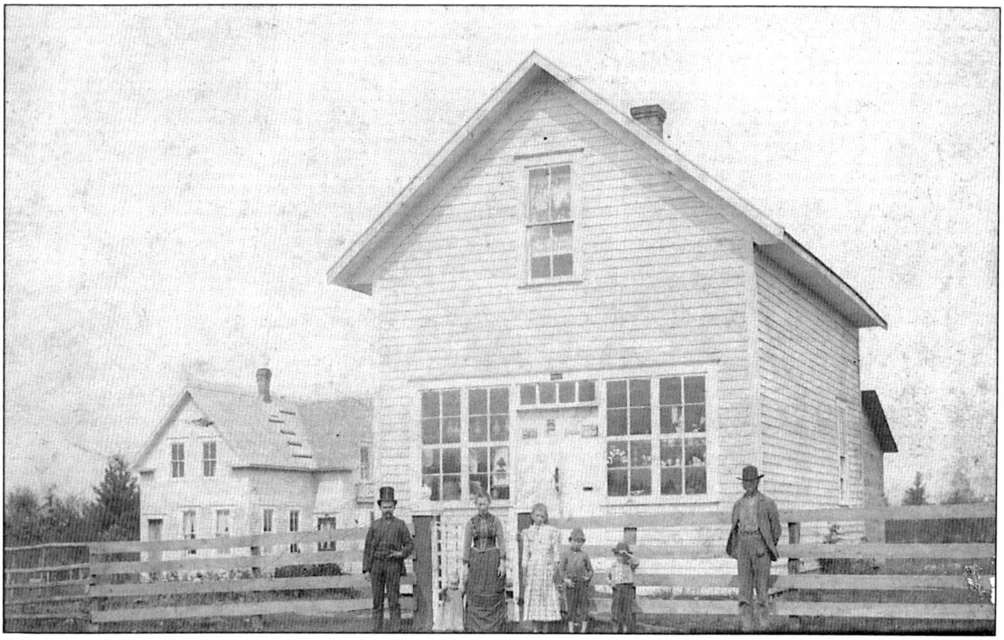

Settlement in the Grass Lake area of southeastern Kanabec County began in 1872. Swedish immigrants built farms and homes, and L.E. Dennewith founded a general store, shown here about 1894. Dennewith's original last name was Peterson, but since there were so many Peterson families in the area, Dennewith took the suggestion of a German neighbor and changed his name in order to stand out amongst the crowd.

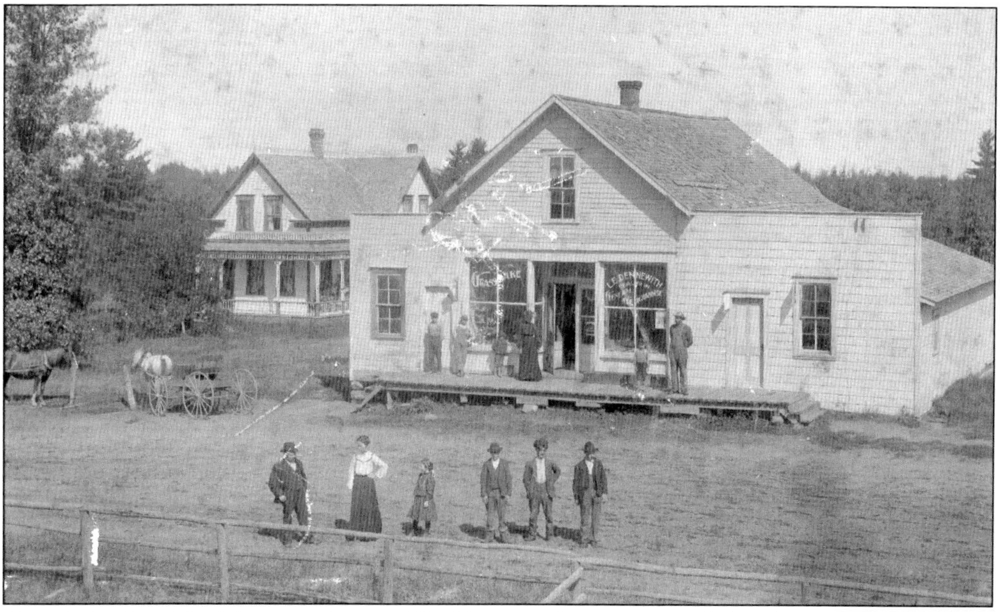

Grass Lake flourished for several years. The Dennewith store expanded and was joined by a post office, two churches, a school, a blacksmith shop, a sorghum mill, a dance hall, a sawmill, and a "halfway house" for travelers. In 1899, the Great Northern Railway bypassed Grass Lake and ran its new line just to the east through the neighboring community of Grasston. Grass Lake rapidly declined.

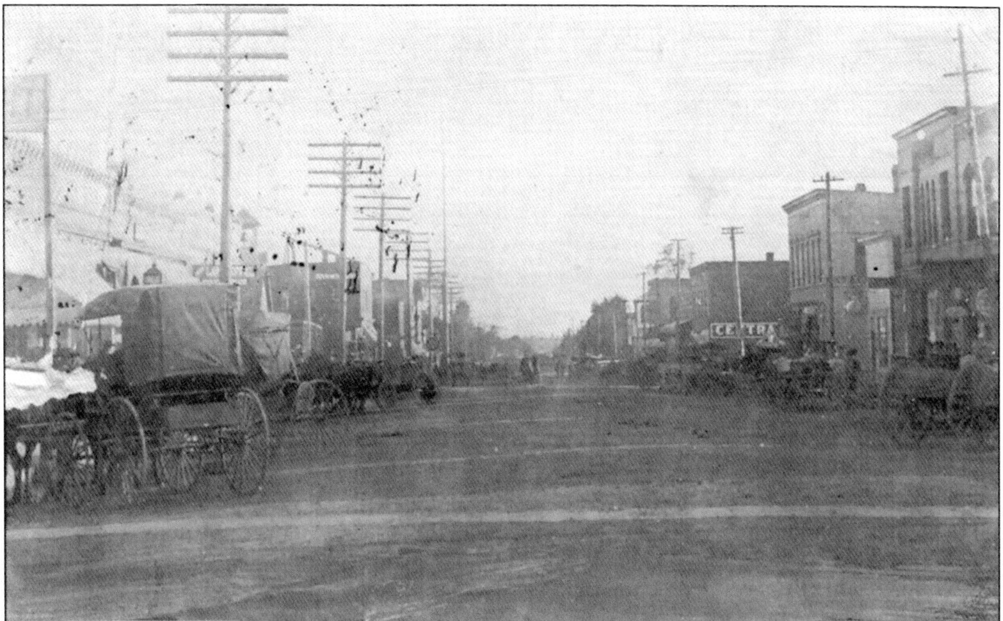

UNION STREET, LOOKING SOUTH, MORA, MINN.

When Myron Kent filed the first plat of Mora in May 1882, the village consisted of nine blocks, three streets, and two avenues with a railroad line running through the center. Settler Israel Israelson suggested the village's name in honor of his hometown of Mora, Sweden. As the town grew, the business district developed on Union Street just west of the original plat. This photograph was taken in 1911.

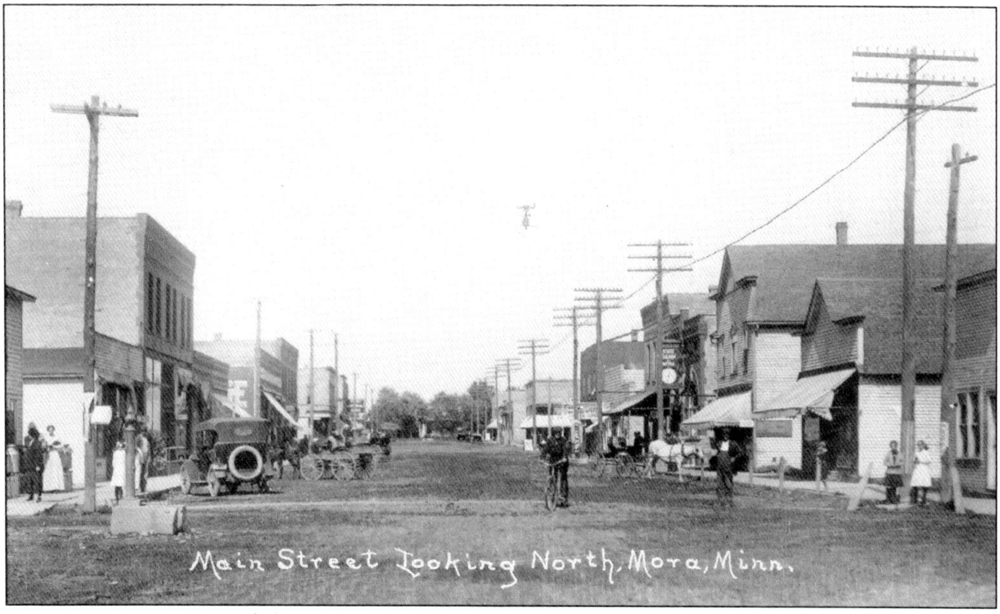

Myron Kent constructed the first building in Mora. He sold the little log structure to A.J. Conger, who completed it and opened a hotel on July 4, 1882. By 1888, Mora was home to two hotels, five stores, a lumberyard, three saloons, a courthouse and jail, a school, and many homes. By the early 1900s, when this photograph of Union Street was taken, the town was flourishing.

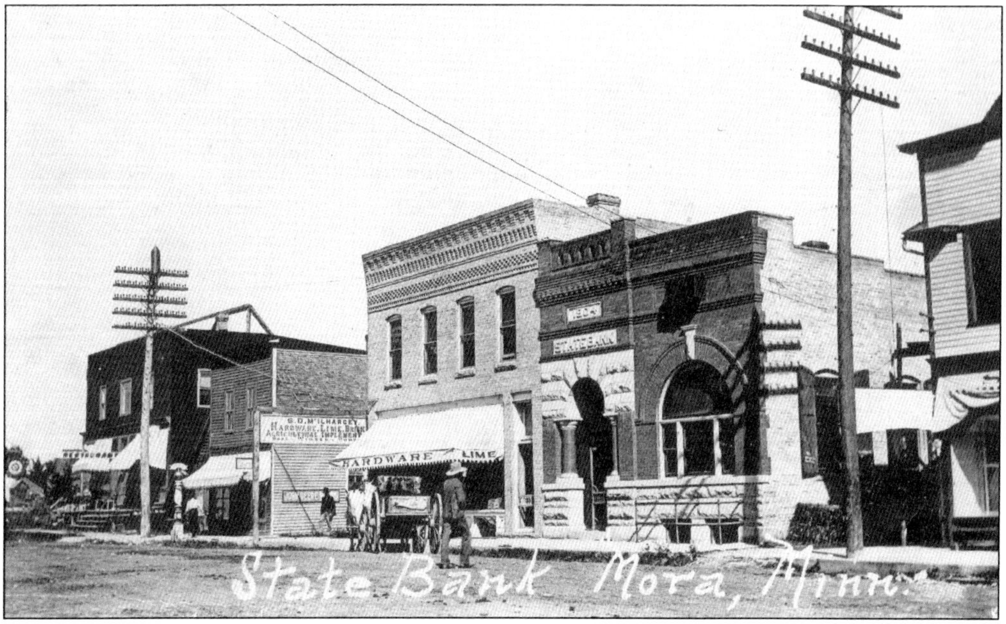

A thriving town like Mora needed a bank, so local businessmen organized the Kanabec County Bank on July 1, 1894. Nine years later, on July 8, 1903, the State Bank of Mora, shown here, opened for business. Early banks often printed their own paper money, which was good for trade in local establishments like the Grahek Hardware Store next door.

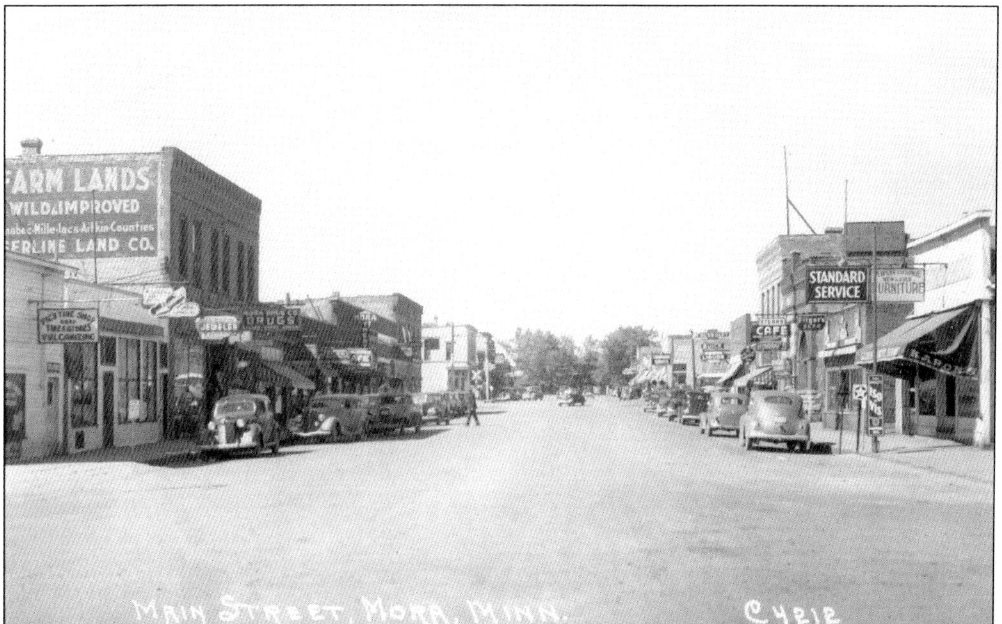

By 1930, Mora boasted a population of 1,014 residents. Businesses lining Union Street included City Meat Market, Globe Meat Market, Mora Drug Company, L.E. Conger's Drug Store, Fairway Market, Red & White Store, Economy Shoe Store, Cohen's Clothing, Peterson Bros. General Store, Ole Sundstrom's Harness Shop, Andrew Erickson's Furniture Store, Mora Motor Company, Tinker Auto Company, Gillepsie Auto Company, Charles Serline's land office, and several cafés.

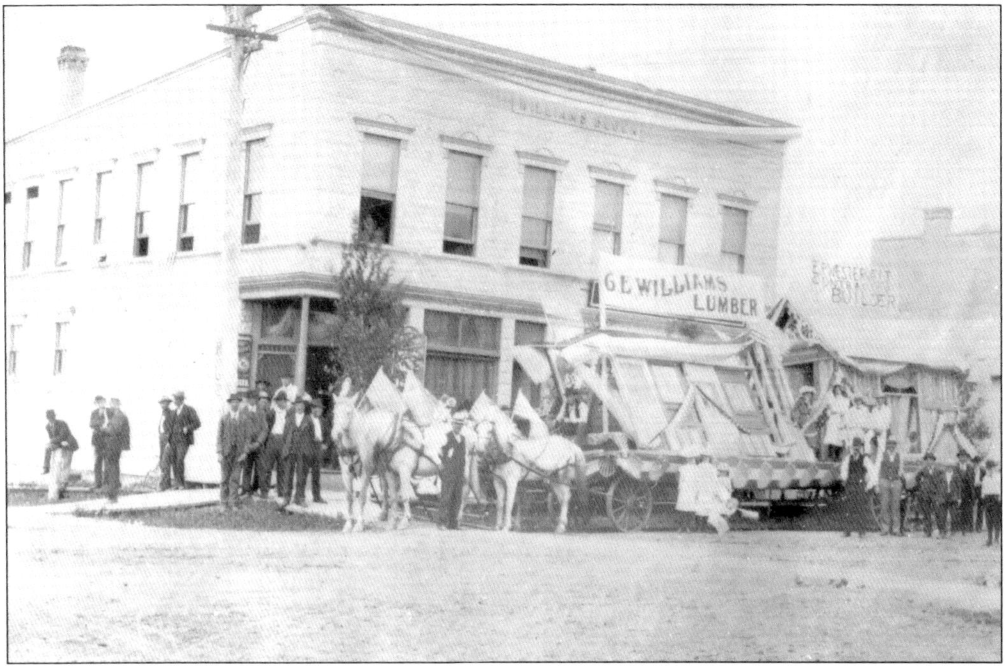

When C.E. Williams built his two-story brick "Williams block" at the northwest corner of Union Street and Railroad Avenue in 1898, his fellow citizens thought he was foolish to construct such a large building in a small town. Williams's investment paid off. The block's two store spaces and its upstairs offices, meeting rooms, and apartments have been almost continuously occupied for over 110 years.

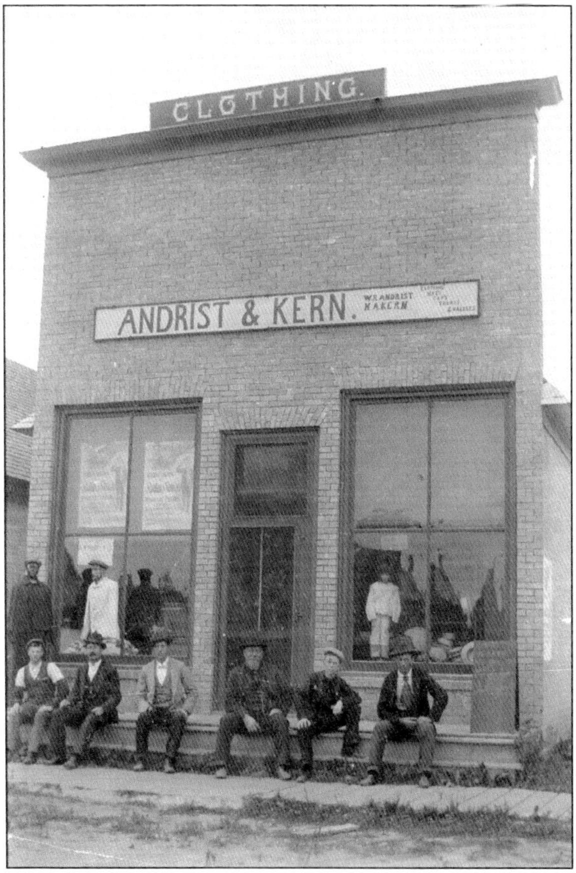

Andrist & Kern was one of Mora's earliest clothing stores. Businessmen Hilding Borgeson, Walter Andrist, Henry Kern, George Kern, and Hilding Eckman took a seat on the store's front step to pose for this 1898 photograph. Notice the hand-painted sign and the posters and displays in the front windows.

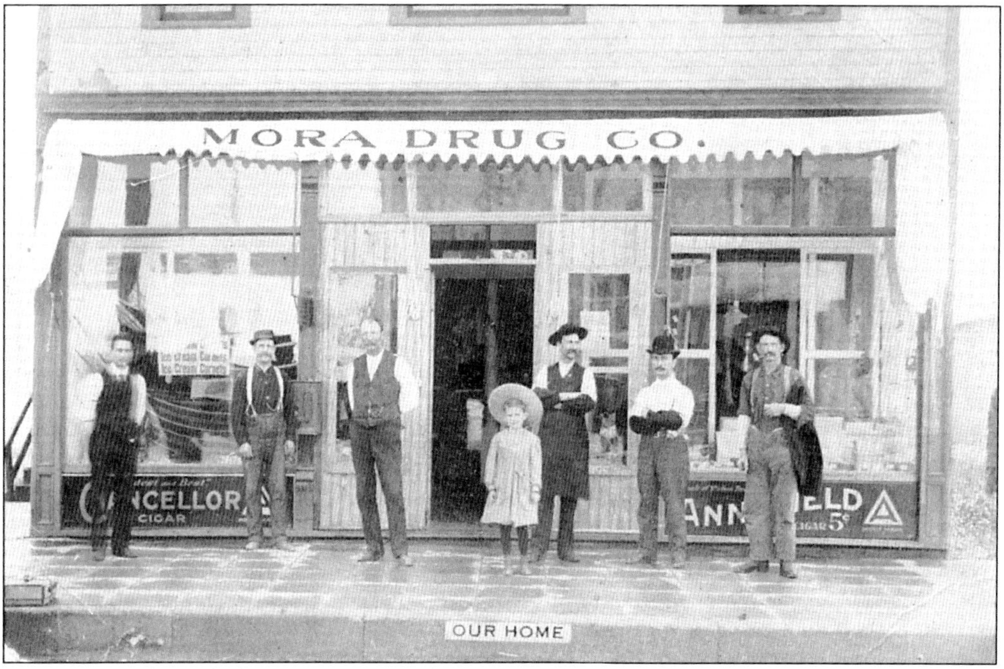

Willis Fairbanks and pharmacist J.G.C. Johnson founded the Mora Drug Company in the spring of 1904. Like most drugstores of the era, the establishment offered a wide variety of medicines and tonics as well as personal care items, postcards and stationery, and the ever-popular soda fountain. Owner Willis Fairbanks posed next to his daughter Ruth in this 1914 photograph.

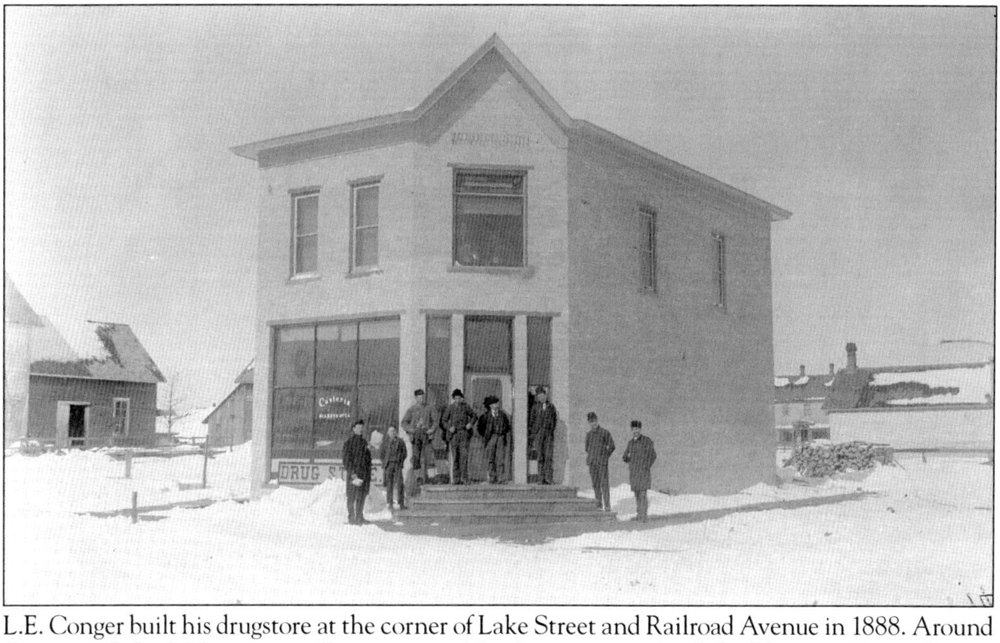

L.E. Conger built his drugstore at the corner of Lake Street and Railroad Avenue in 1888. Around the turn of the 20th century, Conger moved his business to a brick building on Union Street. During his 48 years in business, Conger was active in the Mora community as a school board member, village recorder, and county coroner. He sold his store to Virgil Hall in 1936.

D.R. Eaton's general store was one of Mora's favorite businesses around the turn of the 20th century. In May 1901, it was destroyed by a fire that ignited near a defective chimney flue. Dozens of teams of horses hauled water to fight the blaze while nearby residents ran in and out of the store, carrying much of the merchandise to safety. Eaton still estimated his loss at $10,000.

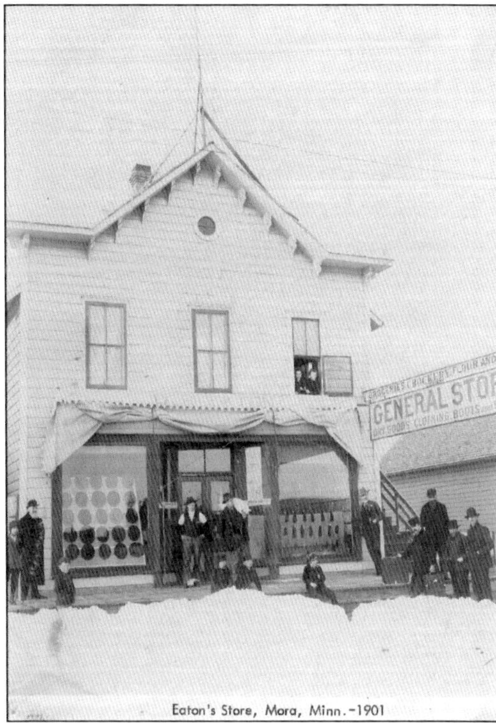

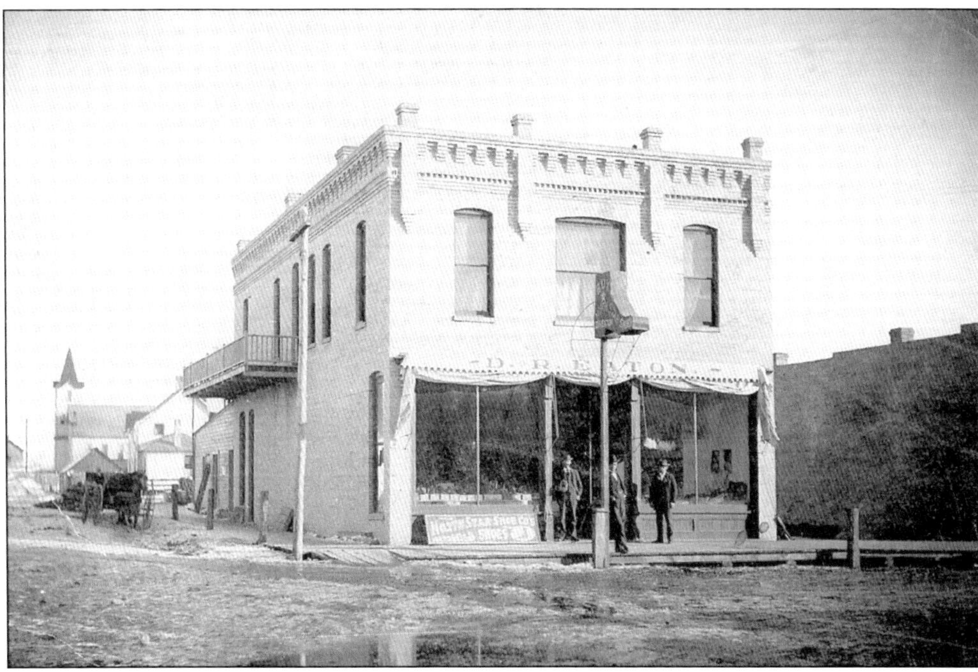

Eaton began rebuilding immediately and, by September, opened his new brick, two-story store on the corner of Union Street and Maple Avenue. A souvenir booklet raved about the business, calling it "the finest and largest store" in the county and "one of the cleanest and best kept stores in the state." Eaton carried everything from groceries to fabric but chose to focus specially on selling shoes.

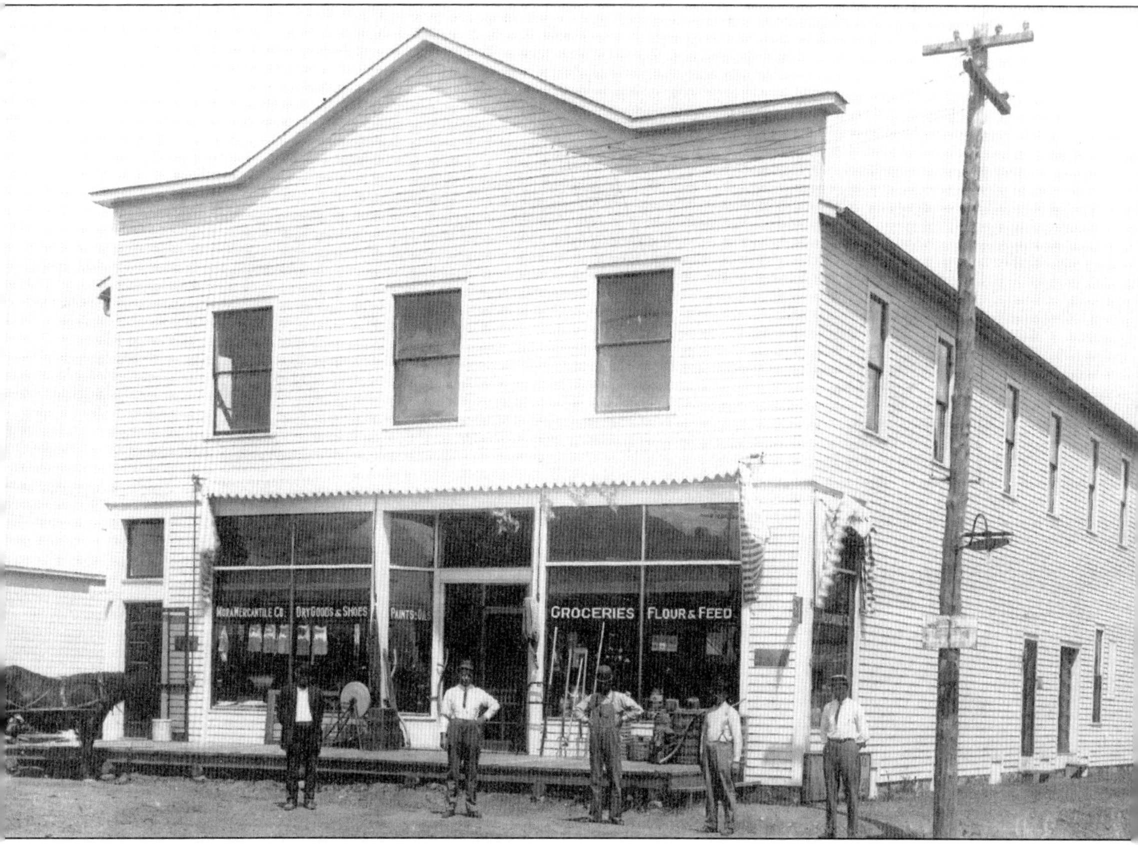

Peter Zetterberg immigrated to America from Sweden in 1893 and found work near Mora as a lumberjack. He started a second job as a salesman for Champion farm machinery and established his own firm, Zetterberg & Co., before 1903. In 1912, he paid $550 for a parcel of land on the east side of Mora and built his own store and warehouse. Zetterberg's store carried a huge assortment of general merchandise, groceries, hay and feed, hardware, and farm machinery. The building's second story housed a dance hall that was the site of several decades' worth of good music and festive parties. Peter's sons, Marcus and Linnea, joined the family business in 1926 and 1928, respectively. Zetterberg's remained a fixture in Mora until it closed in 1986.

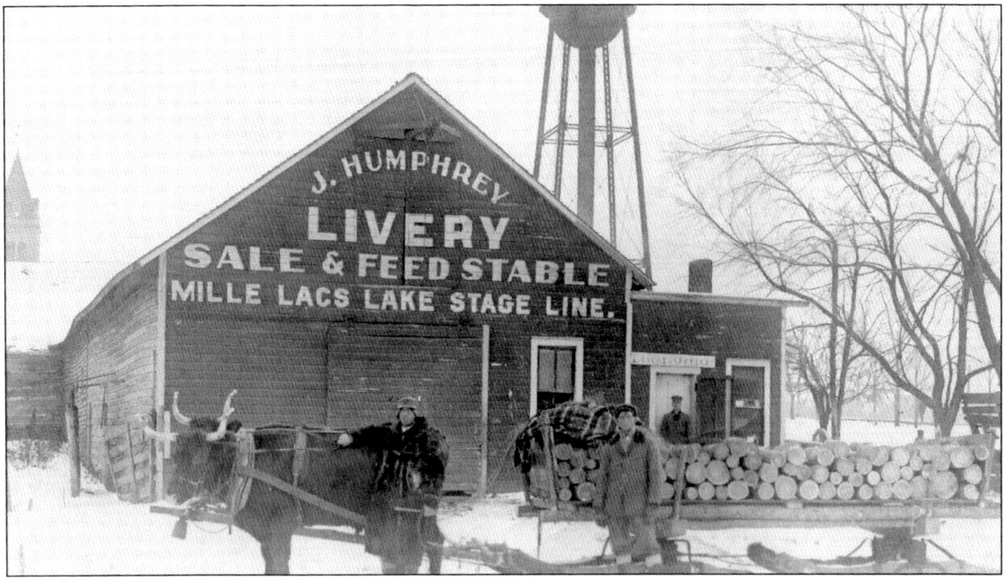

Mora's J. Humphrey Livery offered horses, teams, and wagons for hire; boarded privately owned horses; and sold hay and feed. Beginning in 1899, the Humphrey Livery operated a stage line between Mora and Lawrence (Wahkon) in Mille Lacs County that transported passengers, mail, freight, and supplies. The stage line offered daily service each way and provided a "halfway house" in Hillman Township where travelers and drivers could rest on their journey.

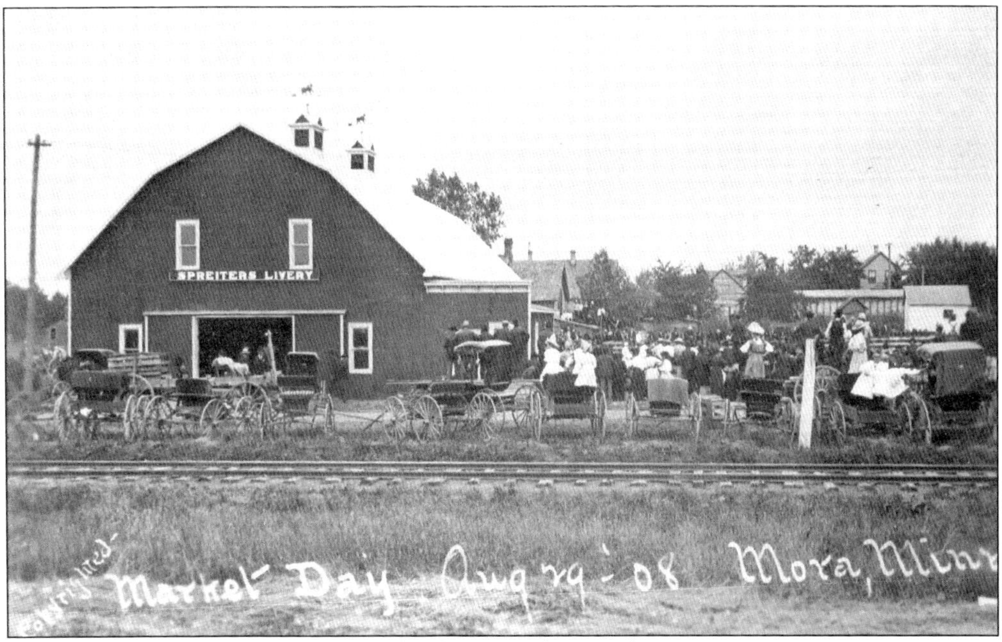

Hundreds of people gathered in Mora for the town's first Market Day on August 29, 1908. Visitors were treated to a free lunch, special sales at the local stores, prominent speakers, music from the Boys' Band, an auction, and a horse sale. Market Day was so successful that village leaders decided to repeat the event monthly. Spreiter's Livery, shown here, advertised itself as Mora's "pioneer livery stable."

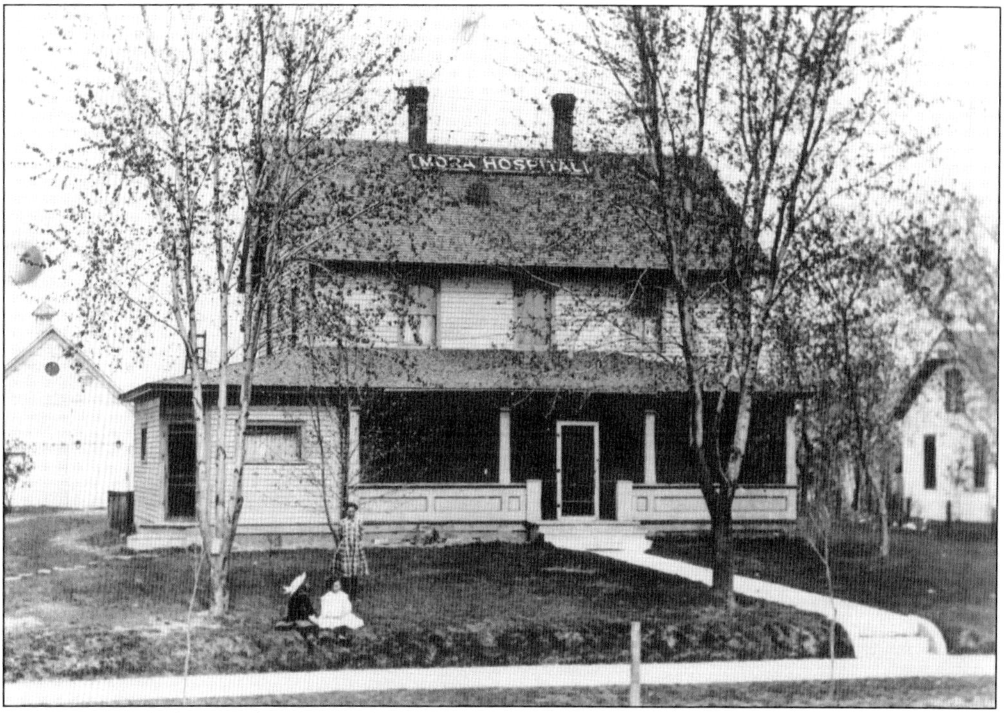

Dr. Titus founded Mora's first hospital in a house on Maple Avenue in 1906 and almost immediately performed an appendectomy on the hospital's first patient, Mrs. A.B. Trelstad of Comfort Township. Over the years, Drs. Bossert, Nordman, and Rhiem kept offices at the hospital. Dr. Bossert practiced medicine in Mora for 40 years and delivered 3,426 babies. The new Kanabec Hospital was built in 1945.

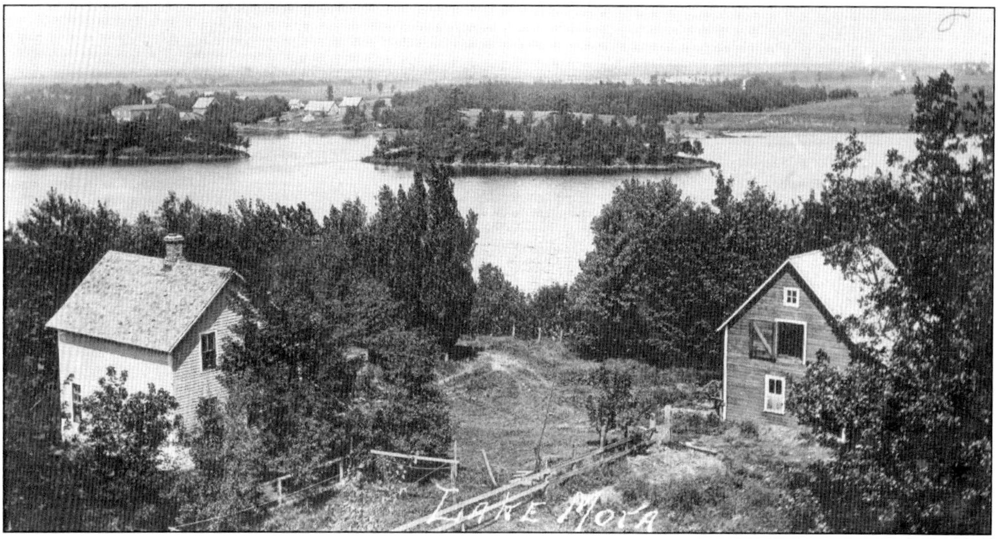

When Mora was founded in 1882, Lake Mora, on the village's northern edge, was a muddy swamp. In the spring of 1885, Mora citizens formed a committee to examine the possibility of raising Lake Mora's water level. The village offered to finance a project to connect the lake by canal to Spring Lake to the east. The plan worked, but Lake Mora's water level has fluctuated frequently throughout the years.

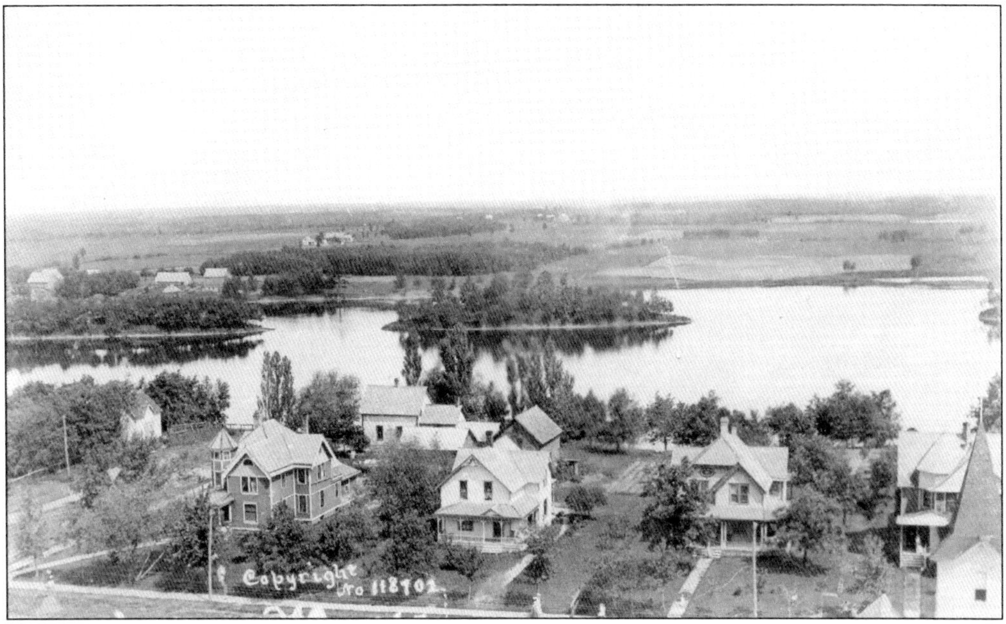

By 1909, a fashionable residential area had developed along Lake Mora's south shore. The C.E. Williams house, shown here in the left foreground, was one of the grandest residences in town. Charles F. Serline built the Queen Anne–style home in 1902 and sold it to Williams in 1909. The Williams family lived in the house for 55 years.

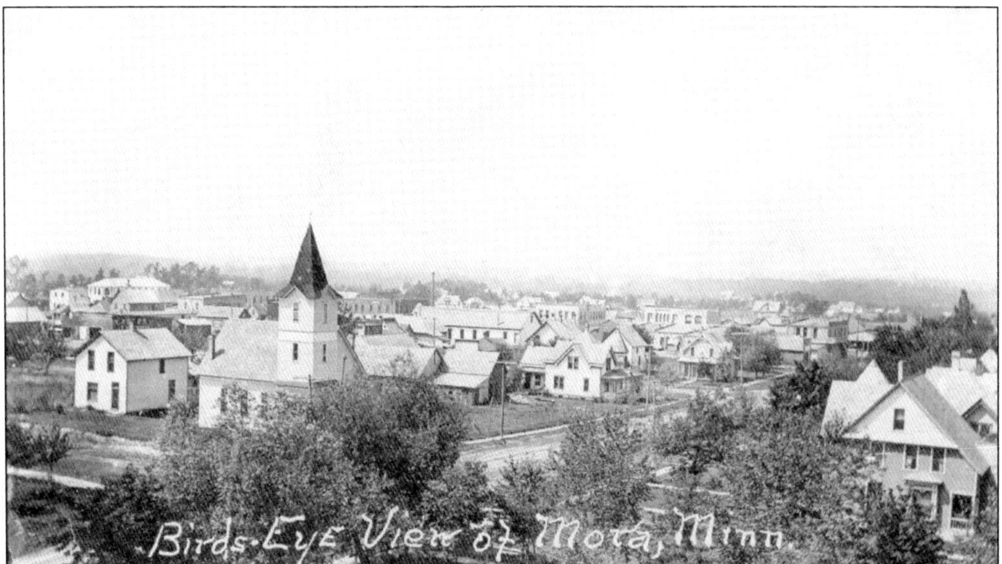

This 1910 bird's-eye photograph of Mora was taken from Maple Avenue looking southwest toward Union Street.

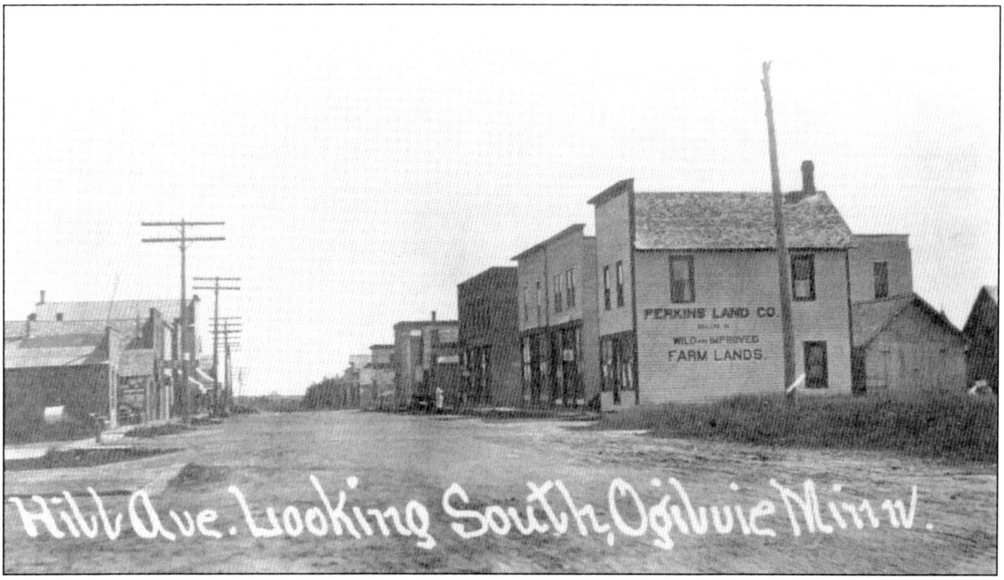

In 1882, the railroad established a shipping point called "Groundhouse" in western Kanabec County. The area had been the site of logging operations since the 1850s, but with the arrival of the railroad, a few settlers began to build homes and farms. Noah Adams founded a sawmill and post office, and J.W. Bragg opened a store. In 1889, Oric Ogilvie Whited purchased the townsite and renamed the little community Ogilvie.

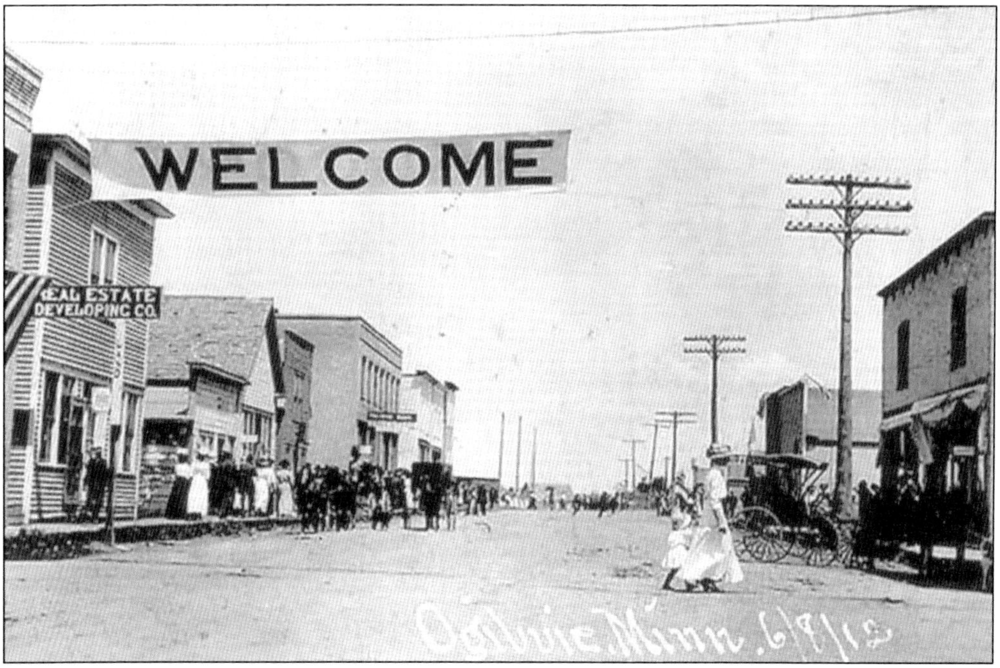

Ogilvie was officially incorporated on November 16, 1901, and the village continued to grow. Residents had already established a school in 1895, and J.S. Anderson had constructed a large store building in 1899. By 1904, Ogilvie could boast of several stores, a hotel, a feed mill, a bank, a funeral parlor, a shingle factory, and telephone service. This photograph of Ogilvie's main street was taken in 1912.

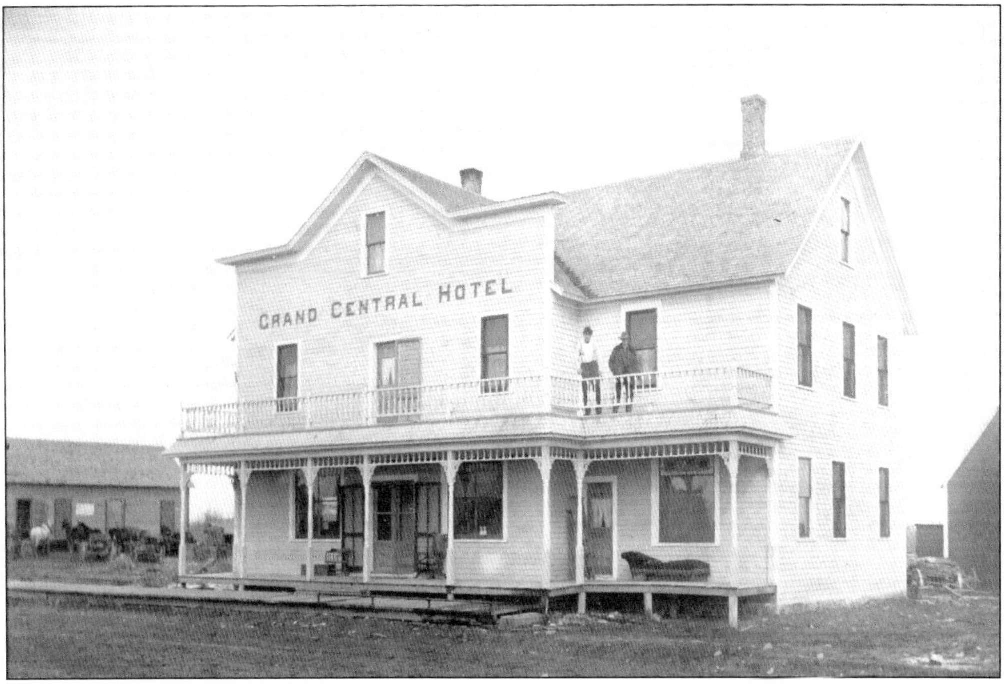

Railroad foreman Nels Bangson and his wife, Bessie, moved into Ogilvie's section house in 1900. They often housed travelers who had nowhere else to stay. In 1902, the couple opened the Grand Central Hotel. The establishment was considered luxurious with 12 sleeping rooms, a kitchen, a dining room, an owners' apartment, and daily rates of $1 or $2. Bessie was an excellent cook, so her guests never left hungry.

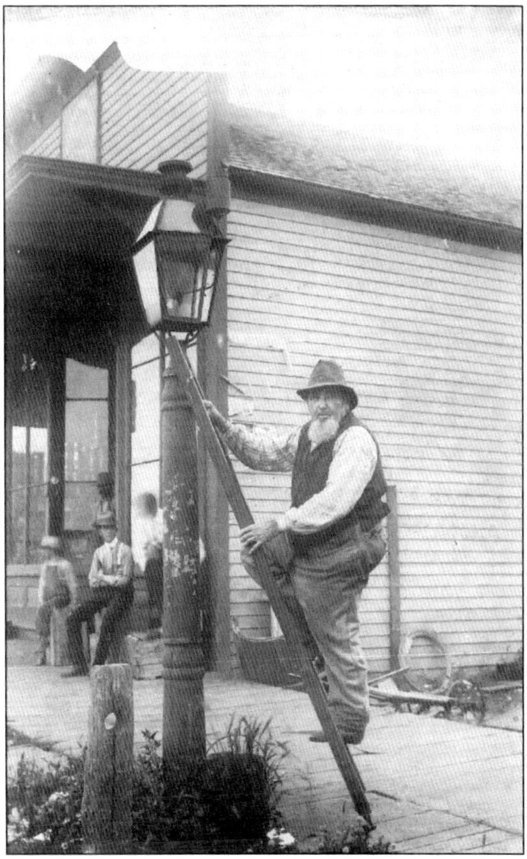

Ogilvie residents took great pride in their town, especially in such modern innovations as streetlights, which were added in 1903. The kerosene kitchen lamp inside each streetlight had to be lit every evening and extinguished every morning. This was the job of the town lamplighter. Although his name has been lost to history, this photograph survives to capture Ogilvie's lamplighter at work.

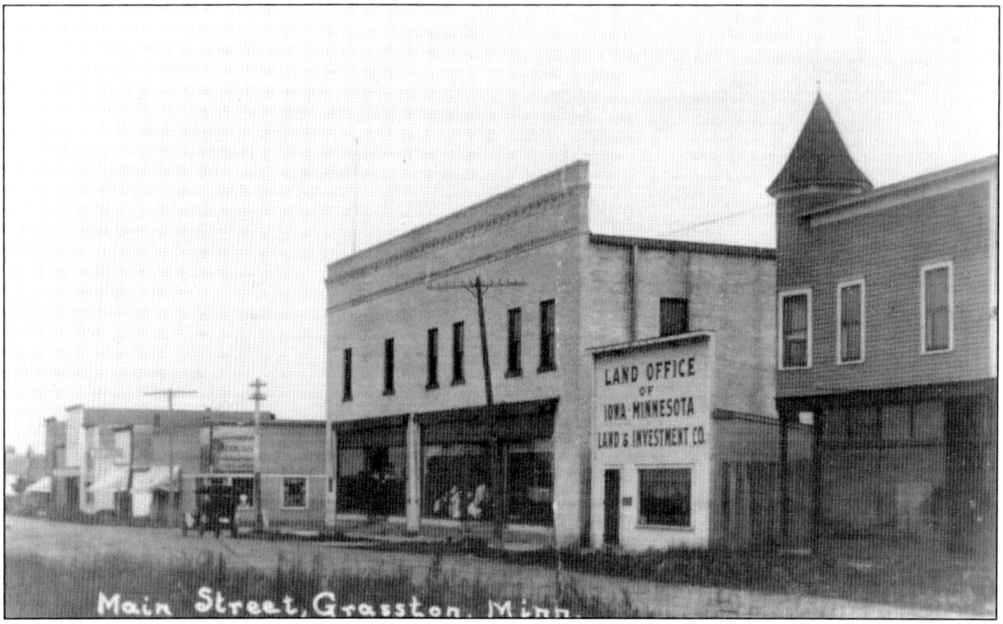

Grasston was founded in 1899 when the Great Northern Railway built a cutoff from Coon Rapids to Hinckley. Village planner and hotel owner John Swan wanted to name the new town Swanville, but since that moniker was already taken by a town in southern Minnesota, Swan decided on Oxenville instead. The railroad objected and suggested Grasston. The Runquist General Store was prominent in this Main Street photograph.

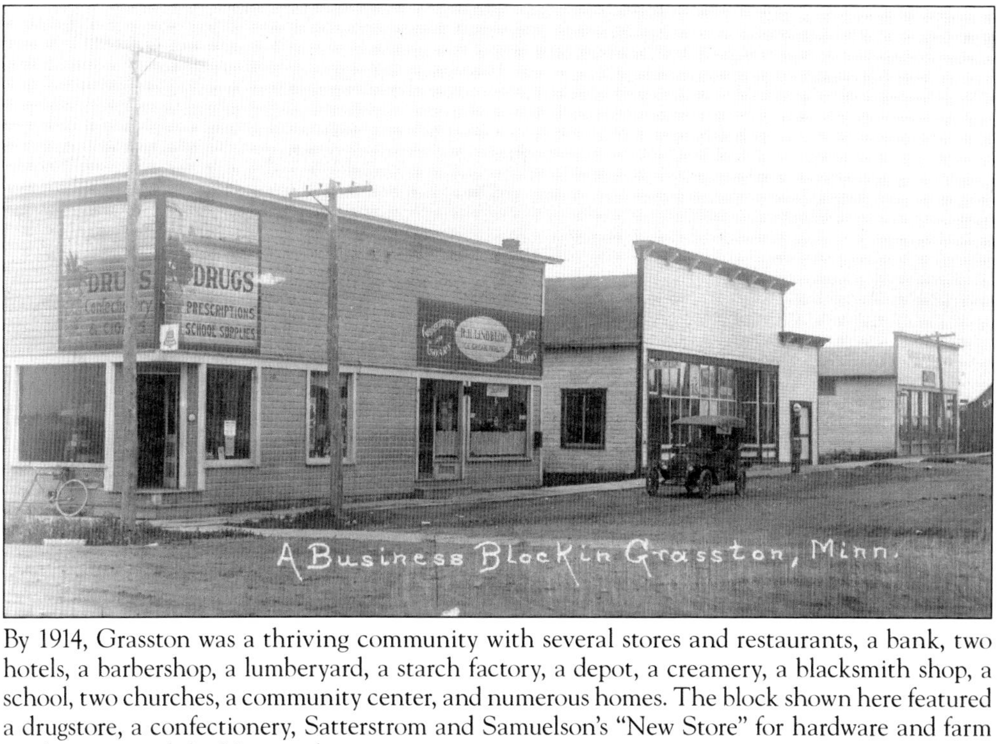

By 1914, Grasston was a thriving community with several stores and restaurants, a bank, two hotels, a barbershop, a lumberyard, a starch factory, a depot, a creamery, a blacksmith shop, a school, two churches, a community center, and numerous homes. The block shown here featured a drugstore, a confectionery, Satterstrom and Samuelson's "New Store" for hardware and farm implements, and the Mercantile.

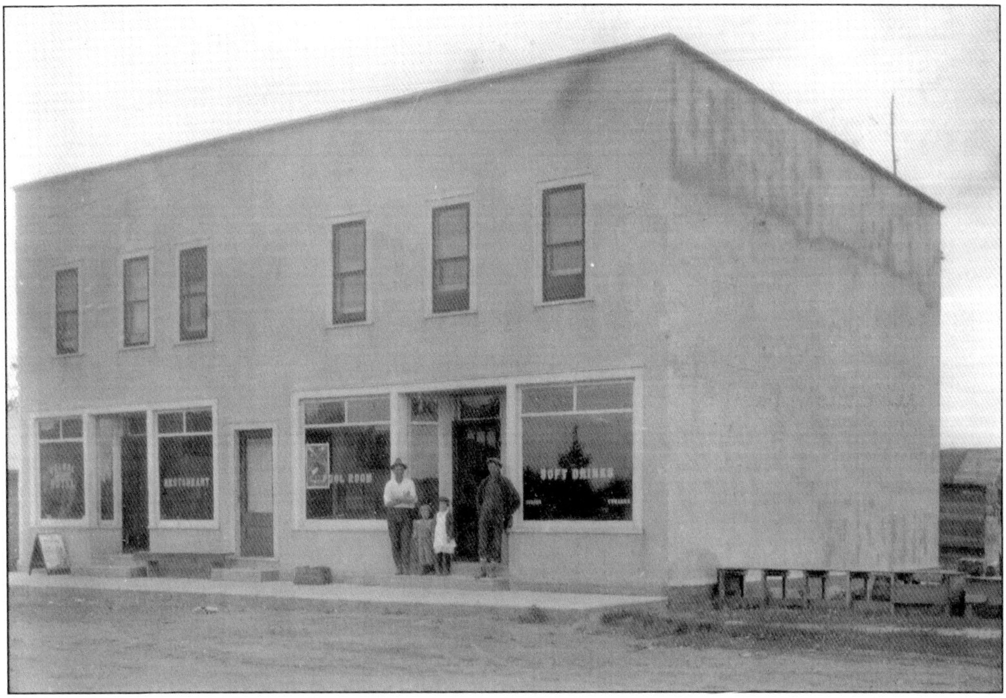

Quamba was platted by Oric Ogilvie Whited in 1901 but not officially incorporated until 1952. Over the years, the little village supported two general stores, a lumberyard, a bank, a hardware store, three potato warehouses, a school, a creamery, and a church. The Quamba Hotel, shown here, was built in 1923. Its first floor housed a restaurant, pool hall, bar, and barbershop. The sleeping rooms and recreation hall were upstairs.

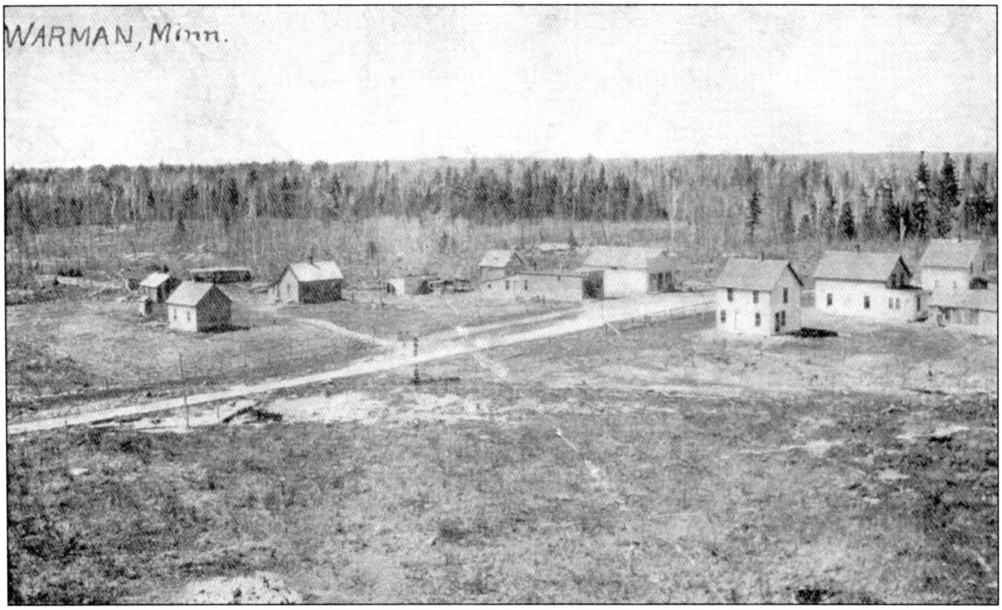

Samuel and Sarah Warman platted the town bearing their name on July 18, 1907. The original plat allowed for 42 fifty-foot lots and six streets. Most early Warman residents worked at the nearby granite quarry or provided merchandise and services to quarry workers.

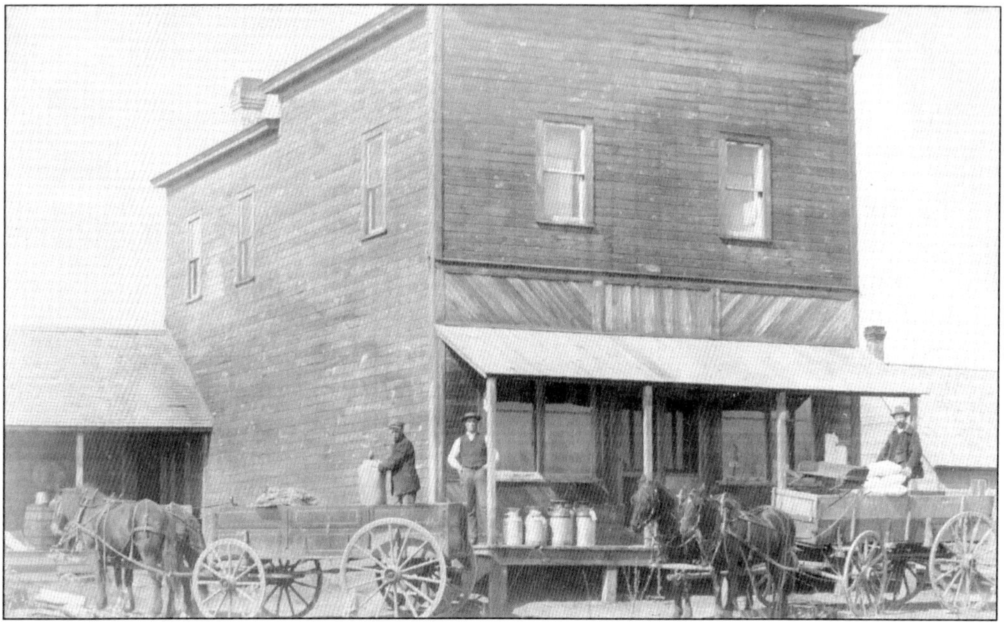

Kroschel Township, in northeastern Kanabec County, was organized in 1899. The village of Kroschel received its post office the following year. Village residents soon added two stores, a school, and a German Lutheran church. This photograph of George Skogen's store was taken in 1905. Since there were no roads between Kroschel and Mora, residents traveled to either Hinckley or Sandstone to purchase items or services their town could not offer.

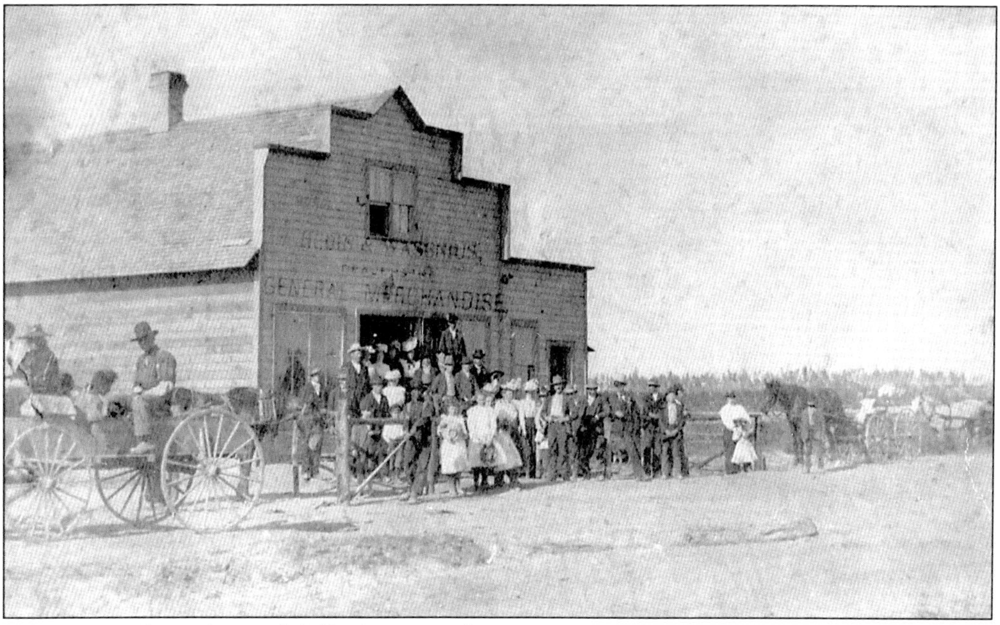

Because travel was slow and difficult in Kanabec County's early days, small communities sprung up throughout the county to serve nearby settlers. Usually, these little villages consisted of only a general store and post office where residents could buy necessary supplies and receive and send mail. Hedin in Knife Lake Township was one such village. It was established in 1901, but its post office was already discontinued in 1905.

Six

Shopping with Grandma and Grandpa

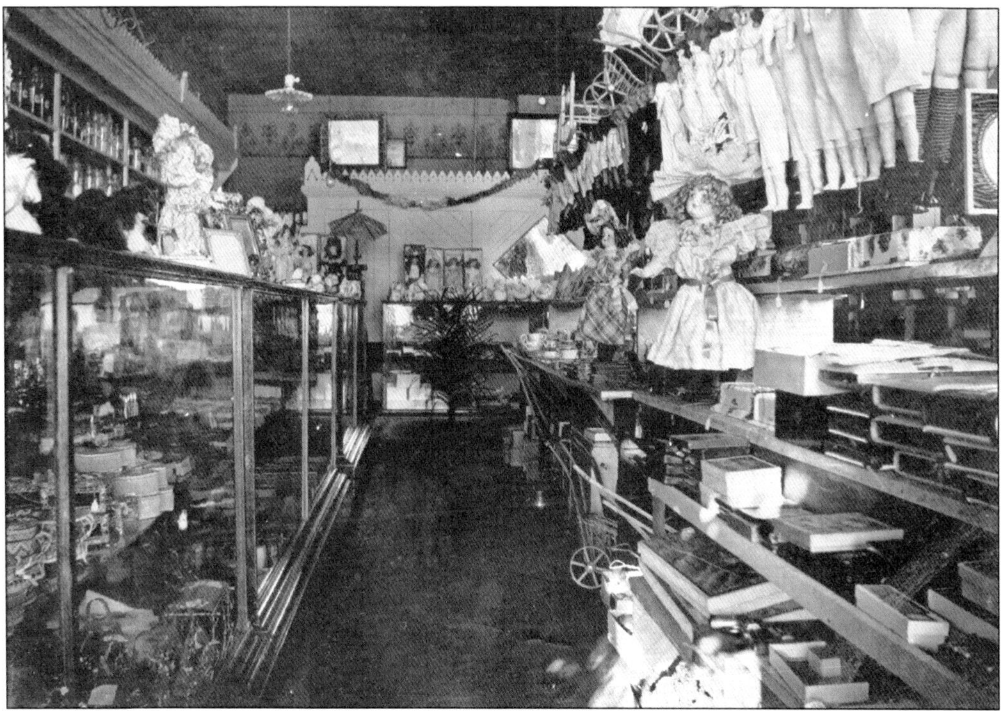

When early Kanabec County residents set out for a day of shopping, they could not visit their local supermarket or discount store and buy everything they needed. Instead, they headed for their town's main street, which was lined with small stores that specialized in groceries, meats, clothing, hats, medicines, hardware, or furniture. In this photograph, L.E. Conger's Drug Store in Mora looked ready for the Christmas shopping season.

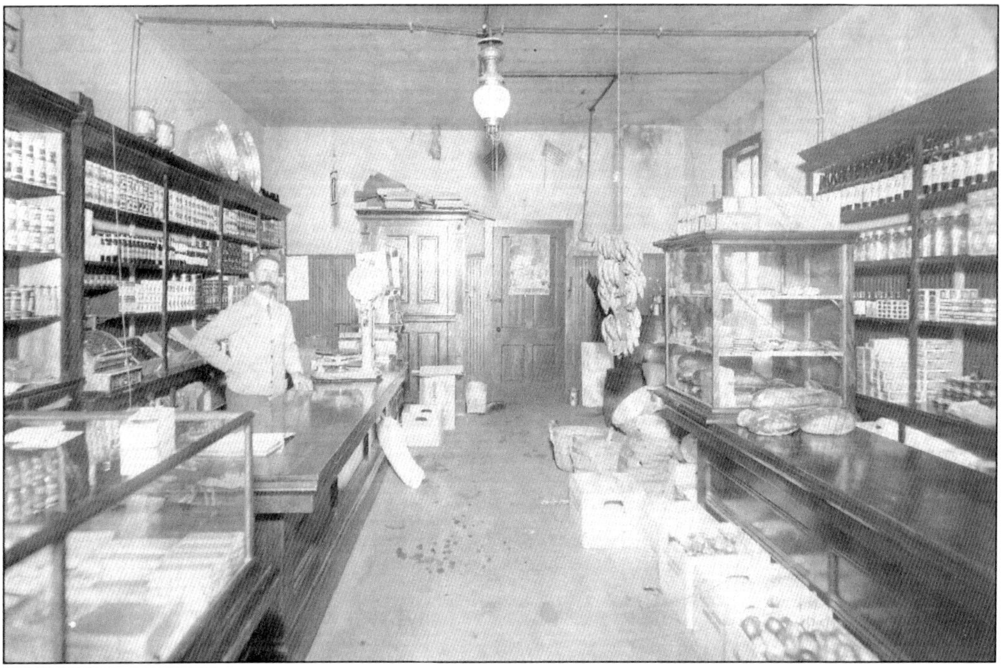

This 19th-century grocery store was typical for its era. Notice the bananas hanging from the ceiling, the case of freshly baked bread and cookies, the boxes of produce, the scale on the sales counter, and the cash register behind the clerk.

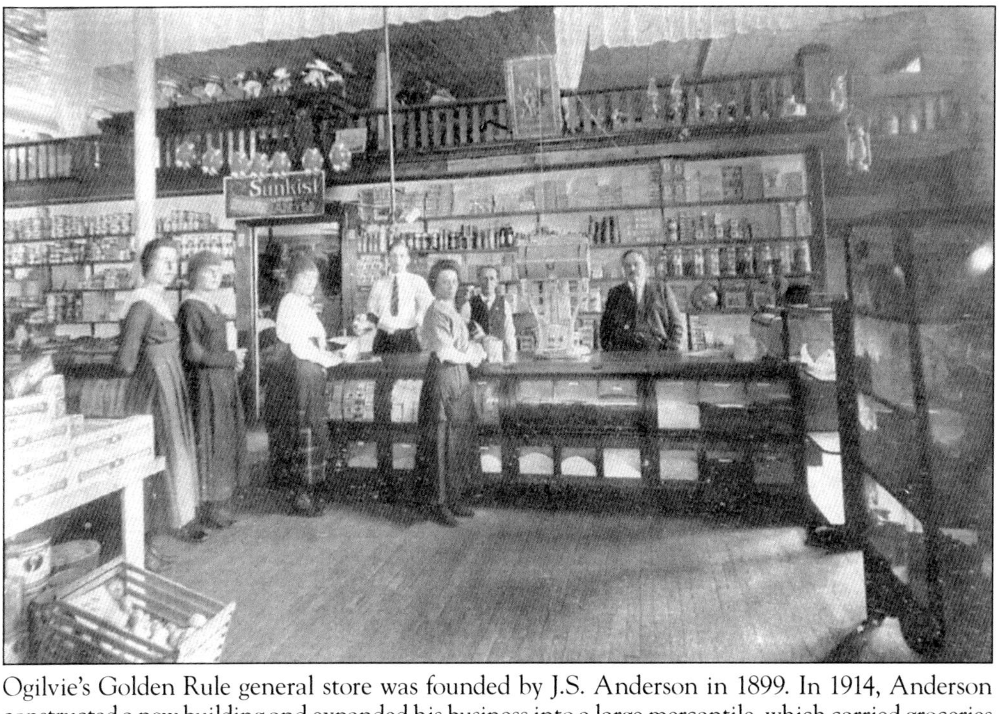

Ogilvie's Golden Rule general store was founded by J.S. Anderson in 1899. In 1914, Anderson constructed a new building and expanded his business into a large mercantile, which carried groceries and dry goods and featured a top-notch dress department. Ogilvie residents boasted that their town was home to the "most modern department store between the Twin Cities and Duluth."

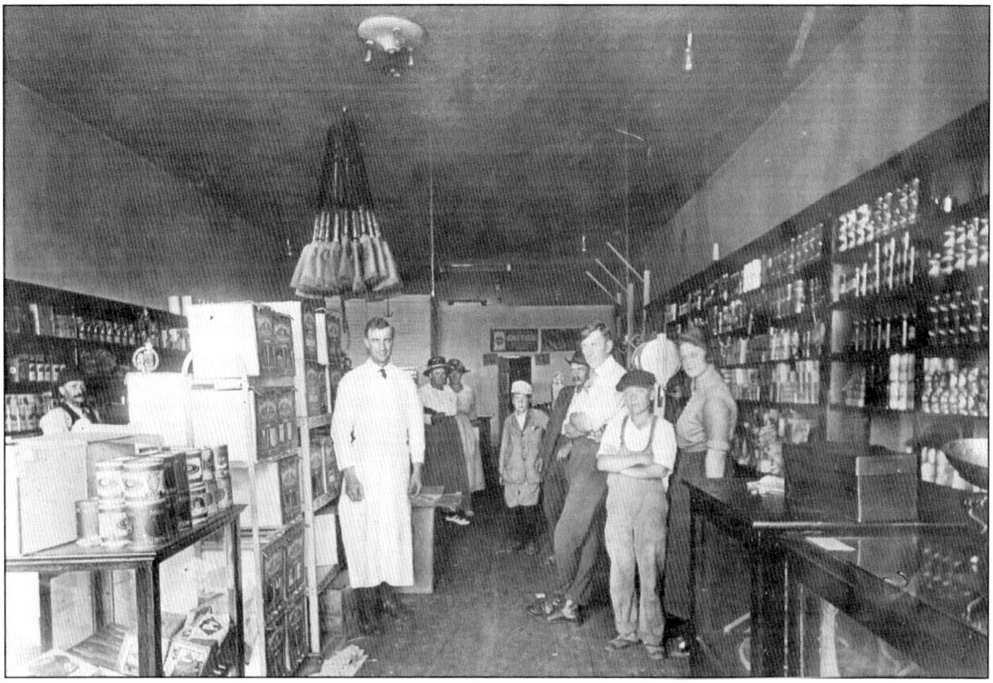

Grocery store owner L. Olson (in white) seemed to be chatting with his customers while he stocked shelves in this late-1910s photograph. Notice the brooms hanging from the ceiling and the stacks of canned pumpkin in the left foreground.

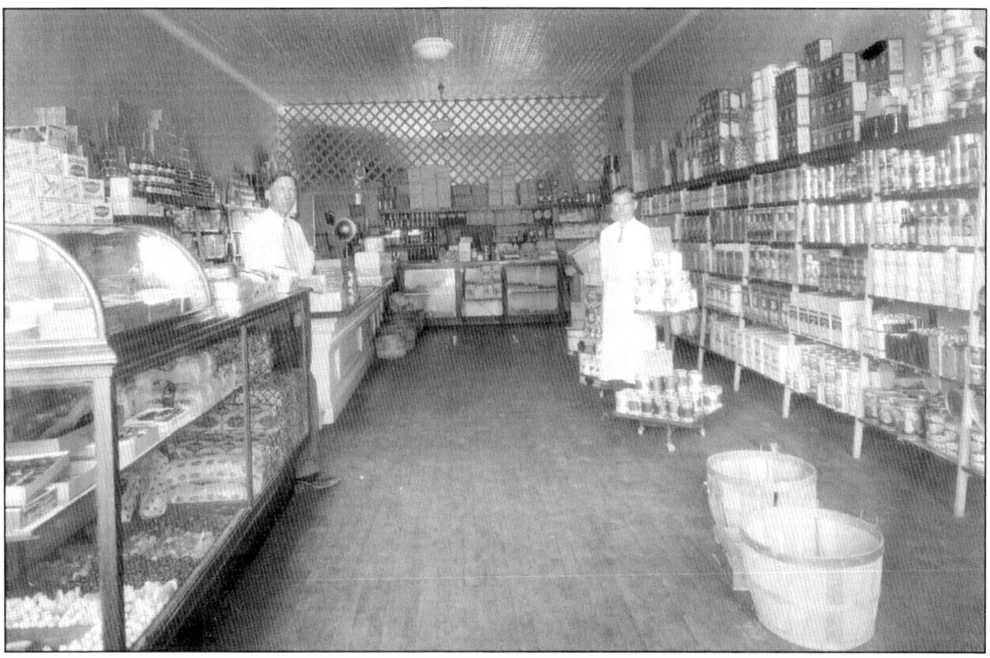

Clerk Gunnar Beckstrom (left) and his fellow employee Harold Stenstrom (right) proudly displayed merchandise at Mora's Fairway store. In 1932, Fairway shoppers could purchase a four-pound box of macaroni for 25¢, two packages of wheat cereal for 32¢, and a four-pound sack of pancake flour for 21¢.

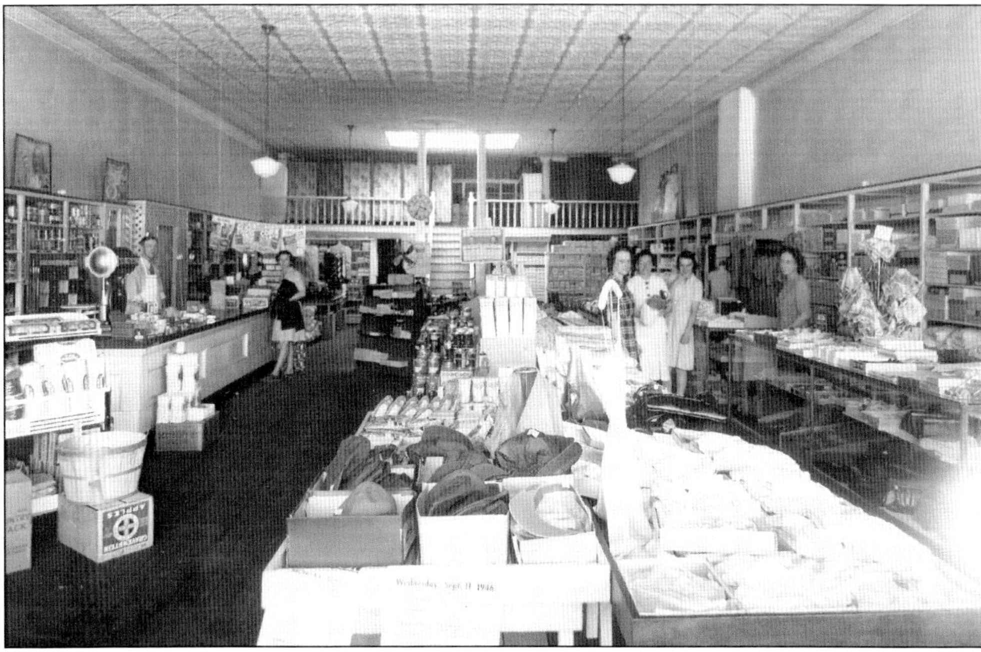

Gunnar Beckstrom (far left) also worked as clerk at Max and Florence Young's Red & White Store in Mora. The Youngs and their business partner Lillian Van Alstyne purchased their store from E.B. Anderson in 1916 and operated it together under the name Young & Van Alstyne. In 1928, the Youngs assumed sole ownership and reopened the store as a Red & White franchise.

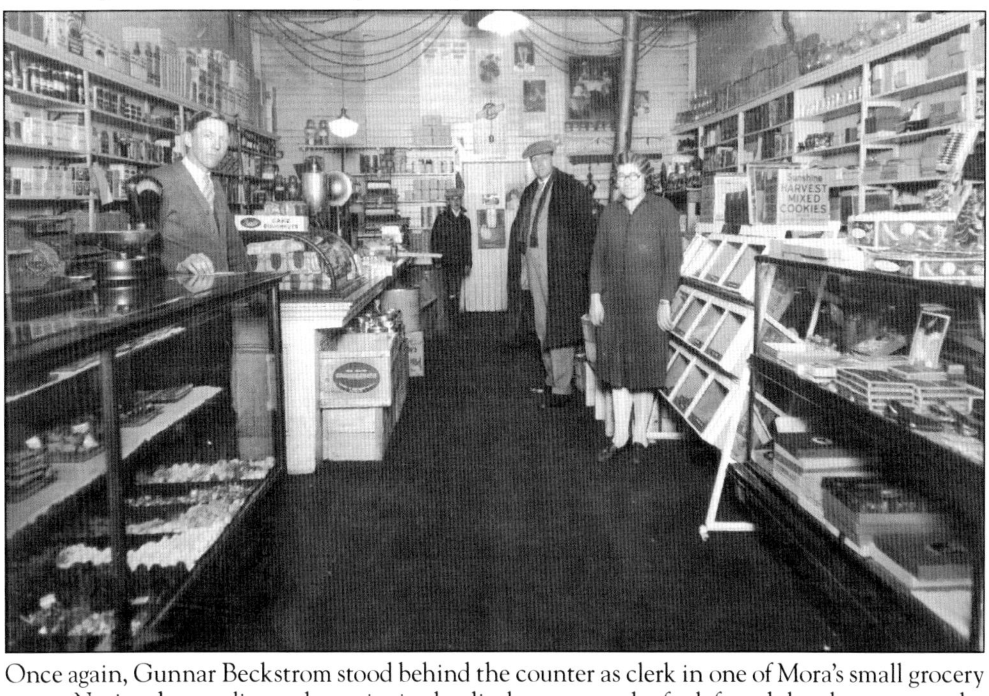

Once again, Gunnar Beckstrom stood behind the counter as clerk in one of Mora's small grocery stores. Notice the candies and pastries in the display case on the far left and the glassware on the shelves to the right. Grocery store operators tried to stock a little of everything their customers might want.

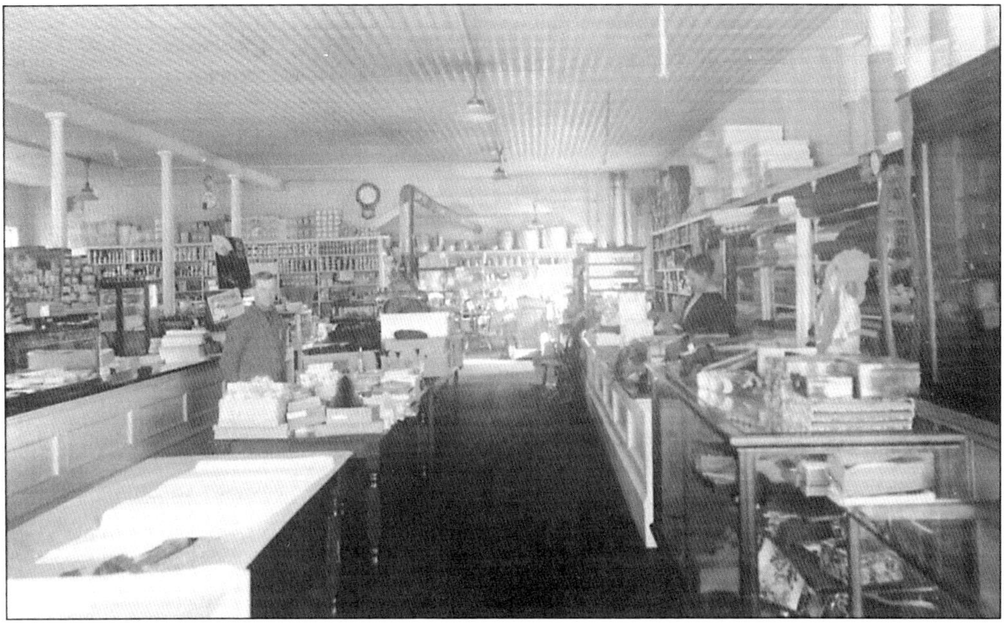

John Runquist established his general store in Grasston in 1902. While O.M. Nelson managed that business, Runquist ran his blacksmith shop, built a lumberyard and livery stable, served as president of the bank and starch factory, and platted village additions. By 1909, Runquist's newly expanded store building housed the bank, a confectionery shop, a pool hall, a casket company, an opera house, and a doctor's office.

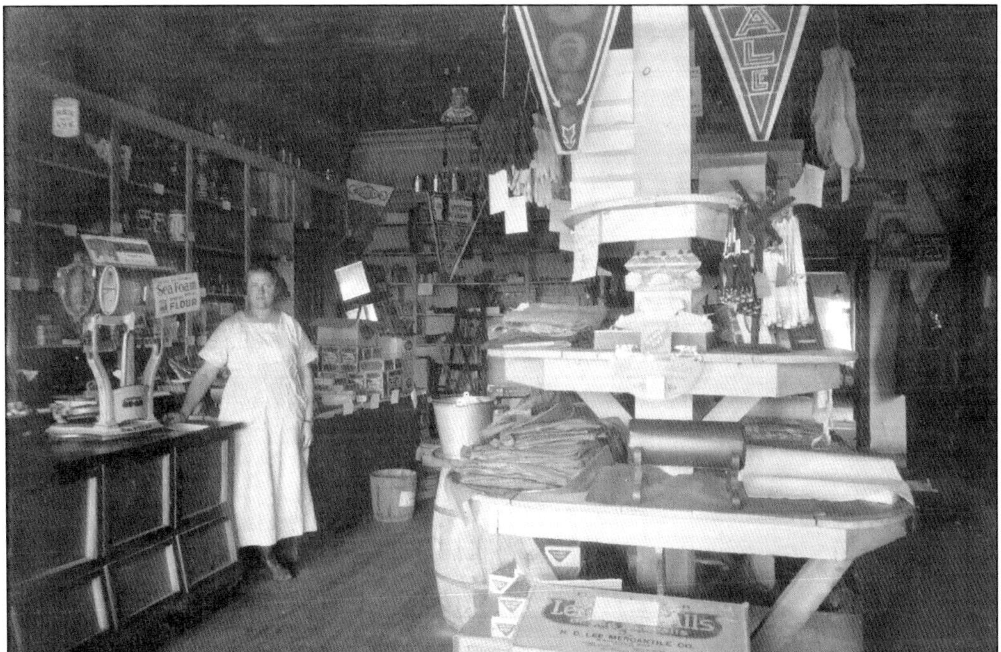

P.W. Peterson opened his grocery store in Quamba about 1920. He later sold the business to Ole Edstrom. Victoria Peterson Johnson was minding the store in this photograph from the early 1920s.

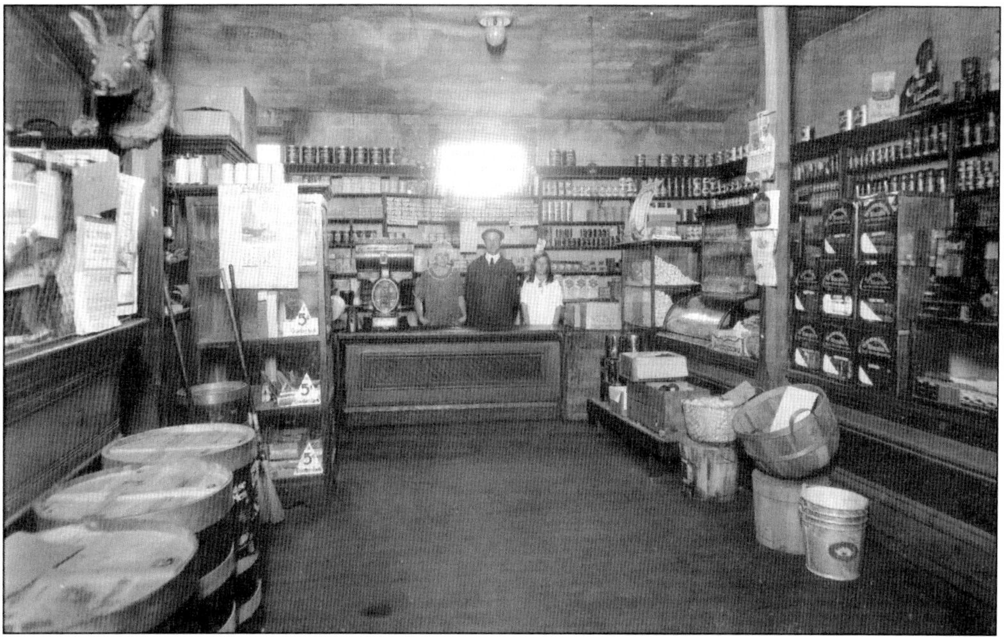

In 1889, Andrew Skoglund of Brunswick opened a store in a small frame building. A few years later, he built a larger structure with his store on the ground floor and living quarters for his family upstairs. As the business continued to grow, Skoglund needed more space and, in 1901, he erected an even larger building, shown here. The first store building was converted into a wood shed.

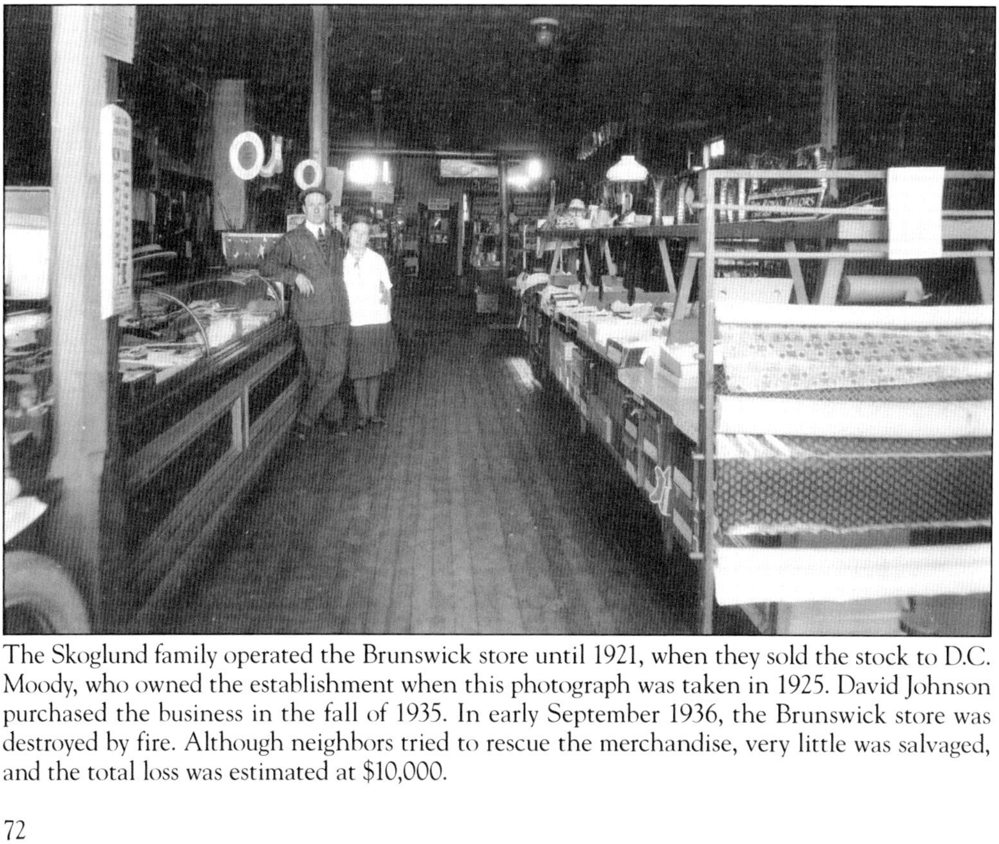

The Skoglund family operated the Brunswick store until 1921, when they sold the stock to D.C. Moody, who owned the establishment when this photograph was taken in 1925. David Johnson purchased the business in the fall of 1935. In early September 1936, the Brunswick store was destroyed by fire. Although neighbors tried to rescue the merchandise, very little was salvaged, and the total loss was estimated at $10,000.

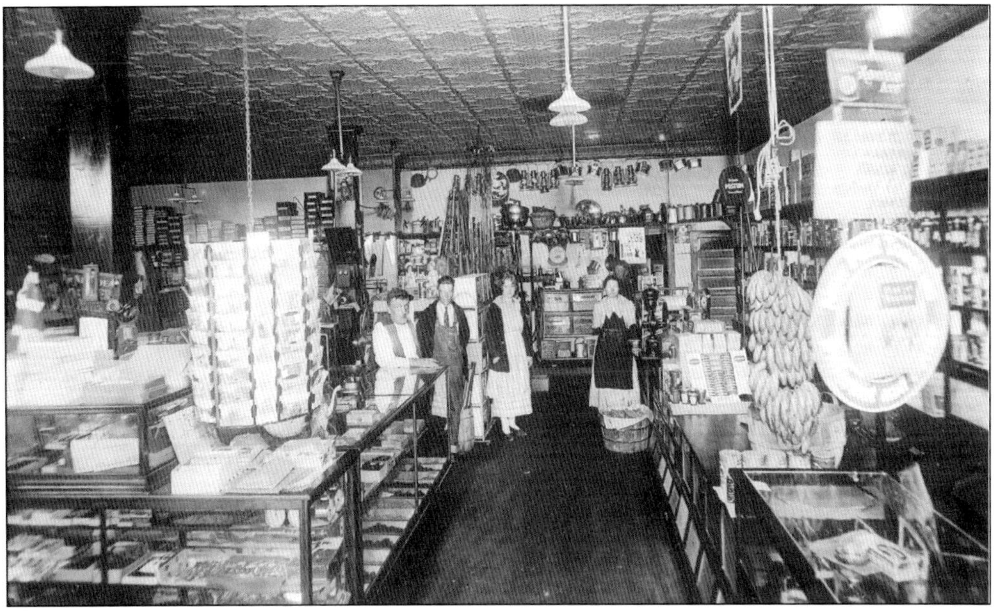

Mora's Zetterberg & Co. store carried a little bit of everything. Old-timers often remarked, "If you couldn't get it at Zetterberg's, you probably didn't need it anyway." This photograph of Zetterberg's was taken in 1913. Pictured from left to right are Peter Zetterberg, Joe O'Donnell, Alice Dahlin, and Clara Schoon.

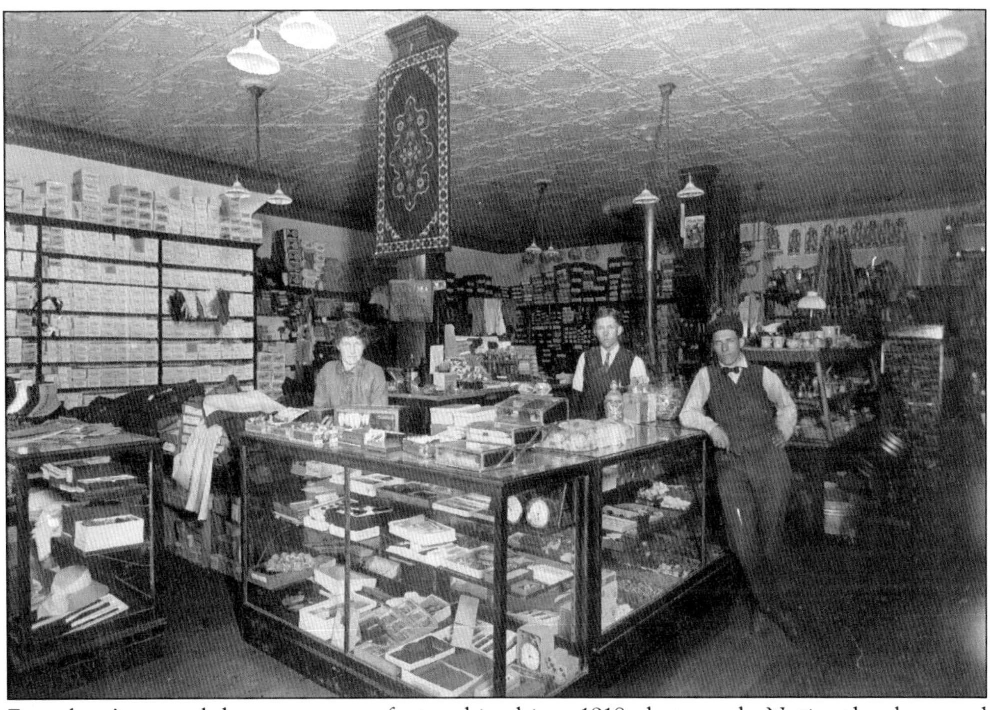

Zetterberg's apparel department was featured in this c. 1918 photograph. Notice the shoes and hats in the display case on the far left, the gloves hanging from the shelves in the background, and the clocks in the center case. Clerk Gunnar Beckstrom, center, must have worked at nearly every store in Mora during his sales career.

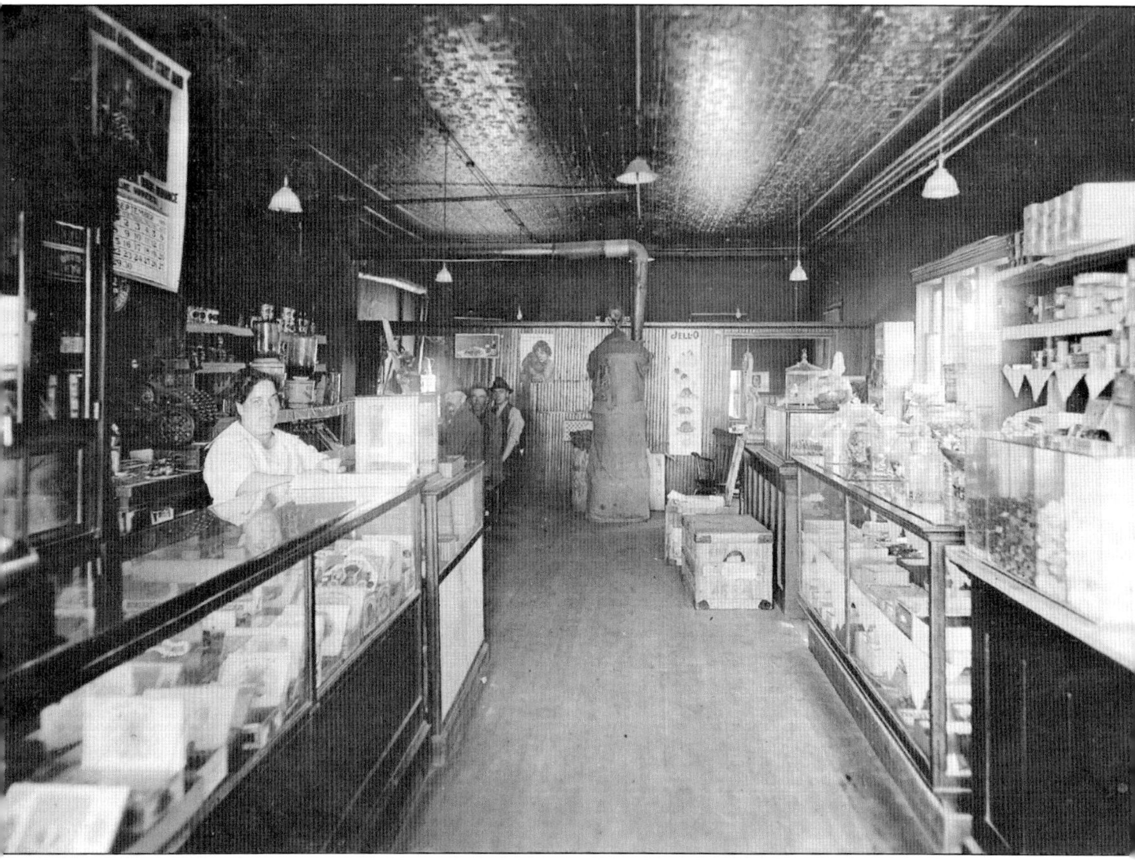

Nearly every Kanabec County town boasted a confectionery shop. Confectioneries sold bulk candy, gum, sweets of all kinds, and sometimes even tobacco. Dora Marquart was minding her confectionery shop in Ogilvie in this 1920s photograph. Notice the cigar boxes in the case on the left, the stove in the back of the building, and the boxes and jars of candy in the display on the right. Popular candy choices in the 1920s included Bit-O-Honey; Hershey, O Henry, and Baby Ruth bars; Abba-Zaba taffy; Slo Pokes; Reese's Peanut Butter Cups; Double Bubble, Clove, and Teaberry gum; Chuckles; Goobers; Jujubes; Squirrel Nut Zippers; and Dum Dum Pops.

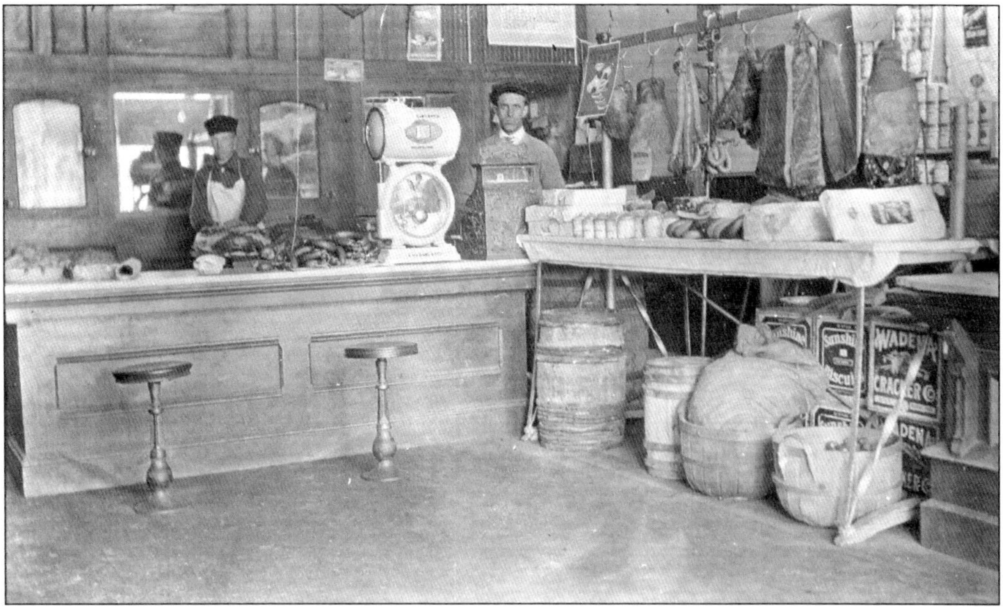

Meat markets were a standard feature in small town business districts. Grocery stores typically did not stock meats, so shoppers had to visit the local butcher to purchase their meal's main course. Eddie Olson, left, and Louis Stolle, right, posed in their Mora meat market in this 1910 photograph.

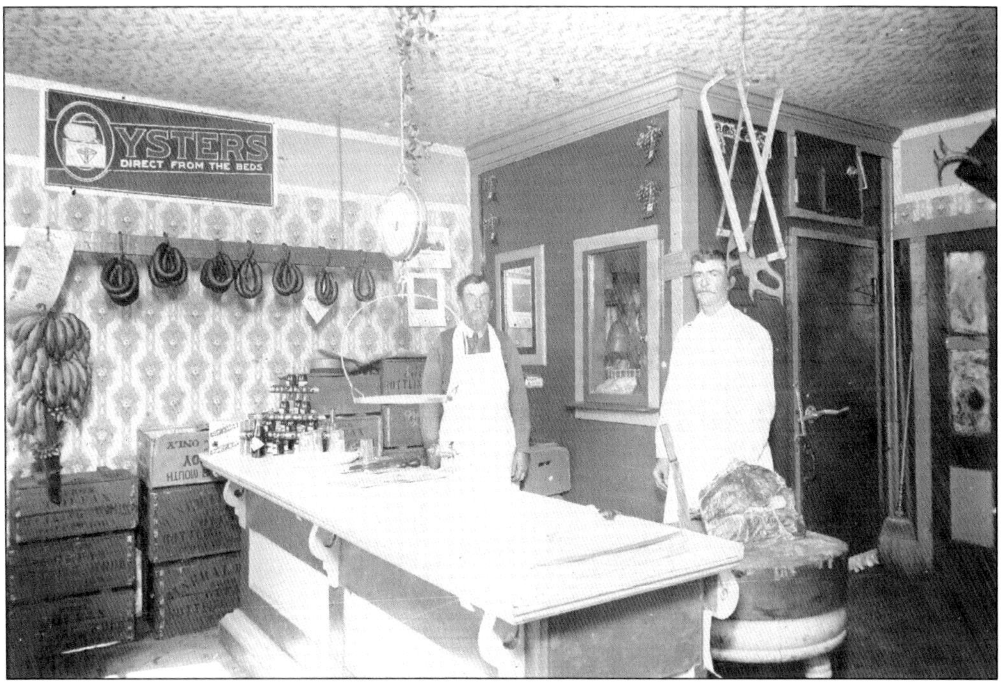

Meat markets generally carried fresh and salted meats, fish and oysters, poultry, and wild game. Meat was prepared and cut to order in the store. This early meat market, probably in Mora, expanded its merchandise line to include mineral water and bananas.

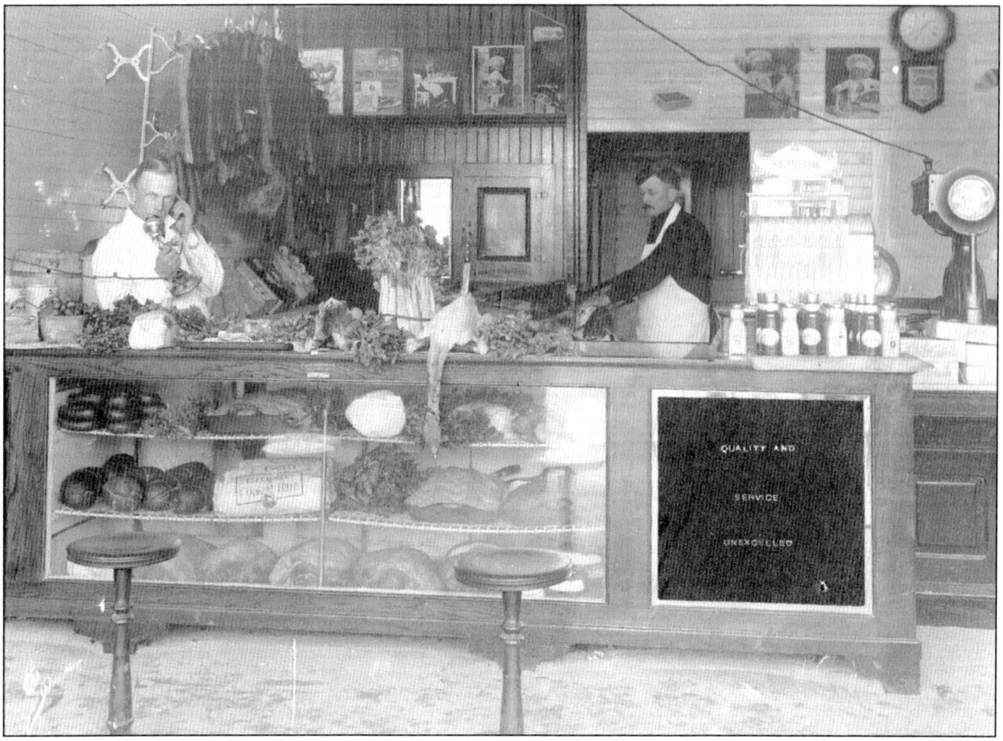

This meat market announced right on its front counter that its quality and service were unexcelled. Notice the butcher hard at work, the clerk taking an order by telephone, the display case filled with fresh meats, the posters along the back wall, and the goose dangling over the counter.

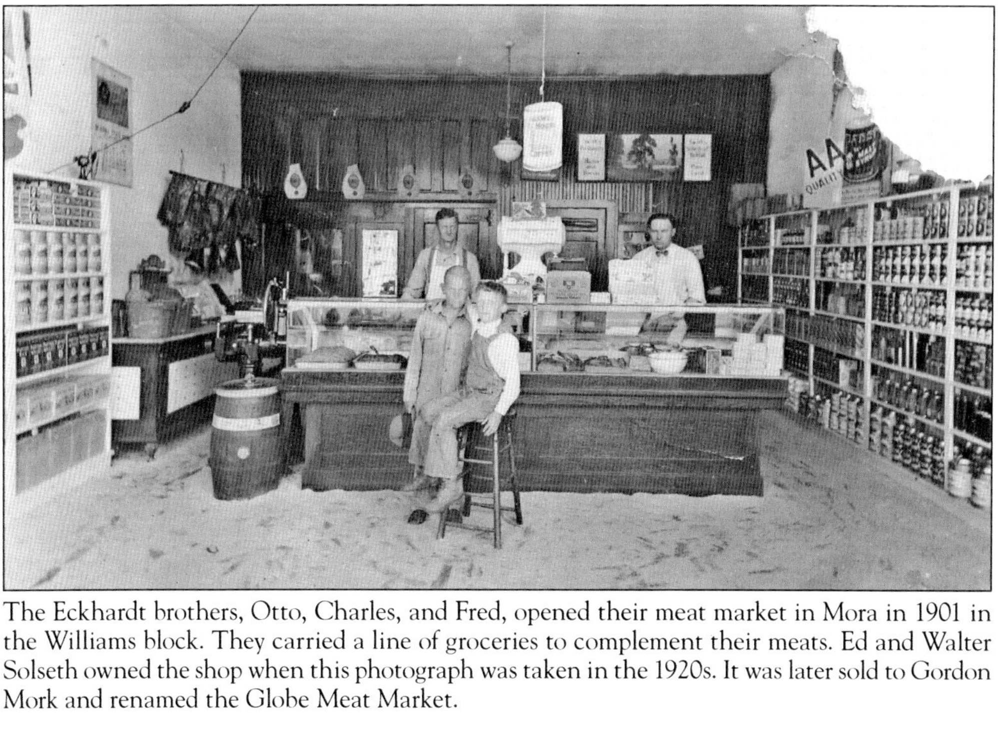

The Eckhardt brothers, Otto, Charles, and Fred, opened their meat market in Mora in 1901 in the Williams block. They carried a line of groceries to complement their meats. Ed and Walter Solseth owned the shop when this photograph was taken in the 1920s. It was later sold to Gordon Mork and renamed the Globe Meat Market.

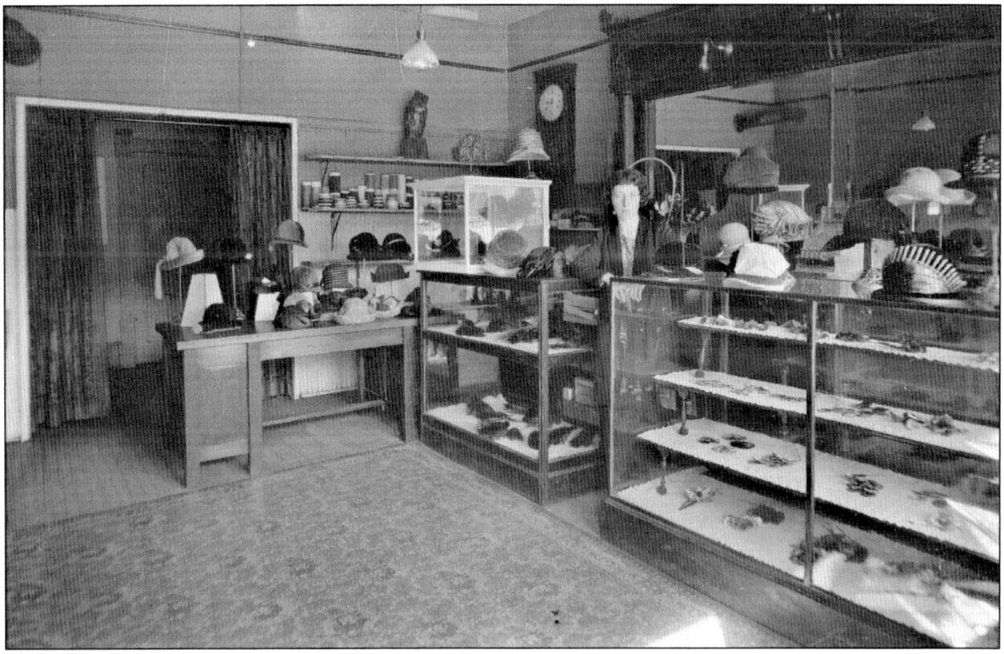

On October 3, 1923, Ivy Erickson proudly debuted her millinery shop on Union Street in Mora. Erickson had just completed a month-long course in hat making at Rothchild's Wholesale House in St. Paul and was excited to demonstrate her new skills. The millinery shop carried a complete line of women's and children's hats, filled custom orders, and offered a wide selection of trimmings to give old hats a fresh look.

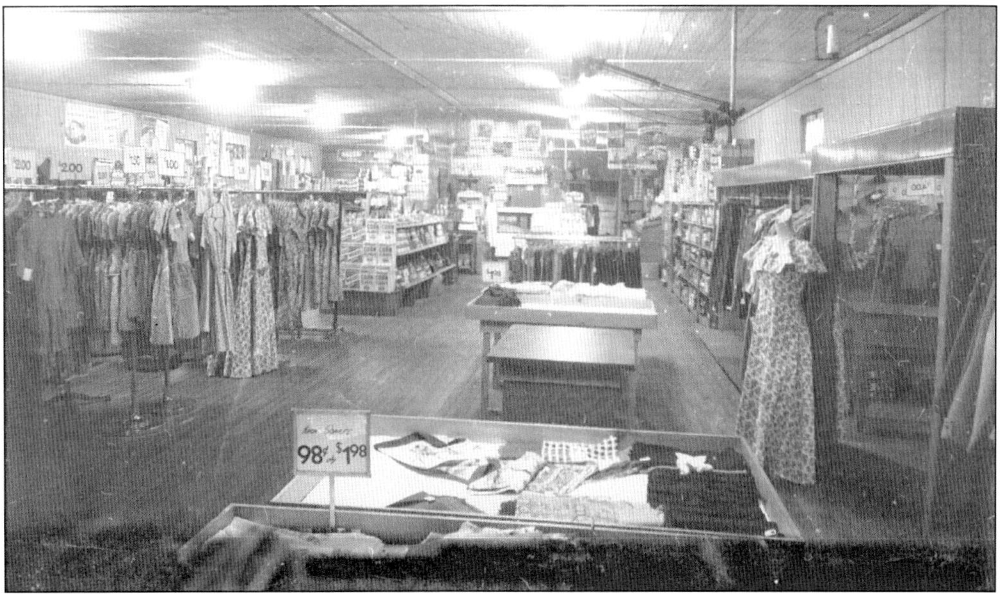

Mora's Hall Mercantile sold clothing, shoes, and dry goods. In March 1942, the Union Street store burned, destroying the mercantile's $25,000 worth of stock and gutting the second-floor meeting spaces of the Odd Fellows, Modern Woodmen of America, and American Legion. The store's owners secured temporary quarters, ordered new stock, and reopened for business one week after the fire.

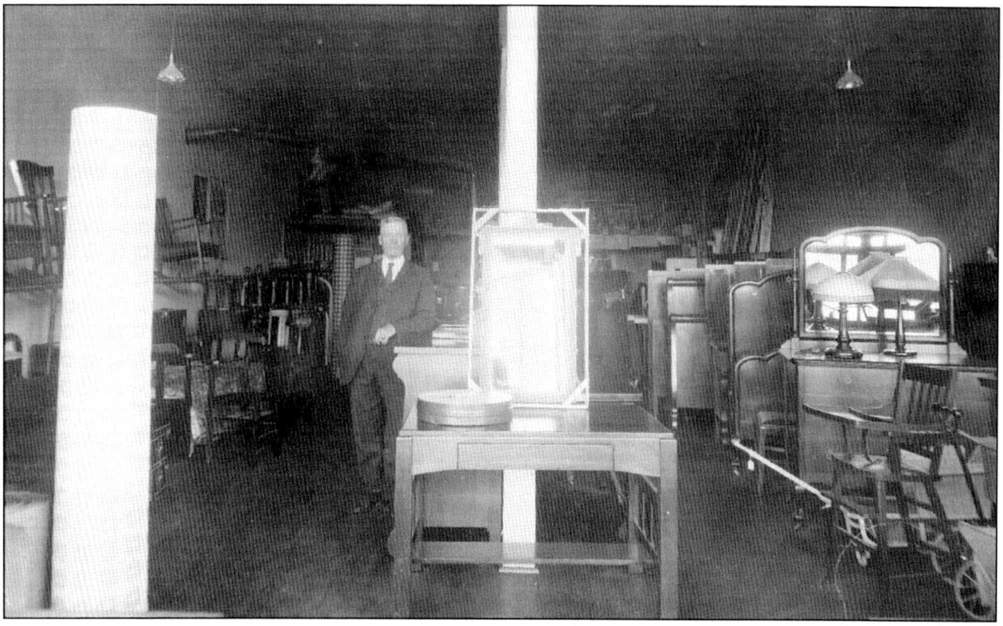

Andrew Erickson established his furniture store in Mora in 1909. The store sold caskets, so Erickson provided funeral services along with furniture sales. By 1934, he was also operating an ambulance. Perhaps Erickson figured that he might as well keep his hearse in action even when there were no funerals.

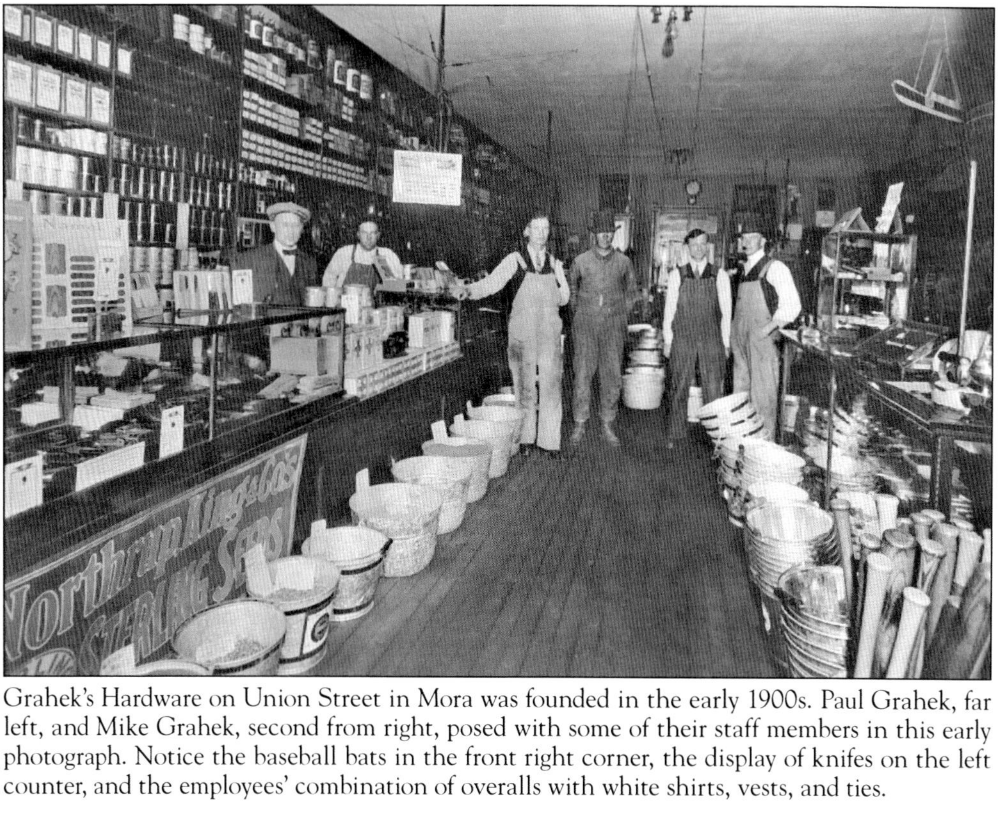

Grahek's Hardware on Union Street in Mora was founded in the early 1900s. Paul Grahek, far left, and Mike Grahek, second from right, posed with some of their staff members in this early photograph. Notice the baseball bats in the front right corner, the display of knifes on the left counter, and the employees' combination of overalls with white shirts, vests, and ties.

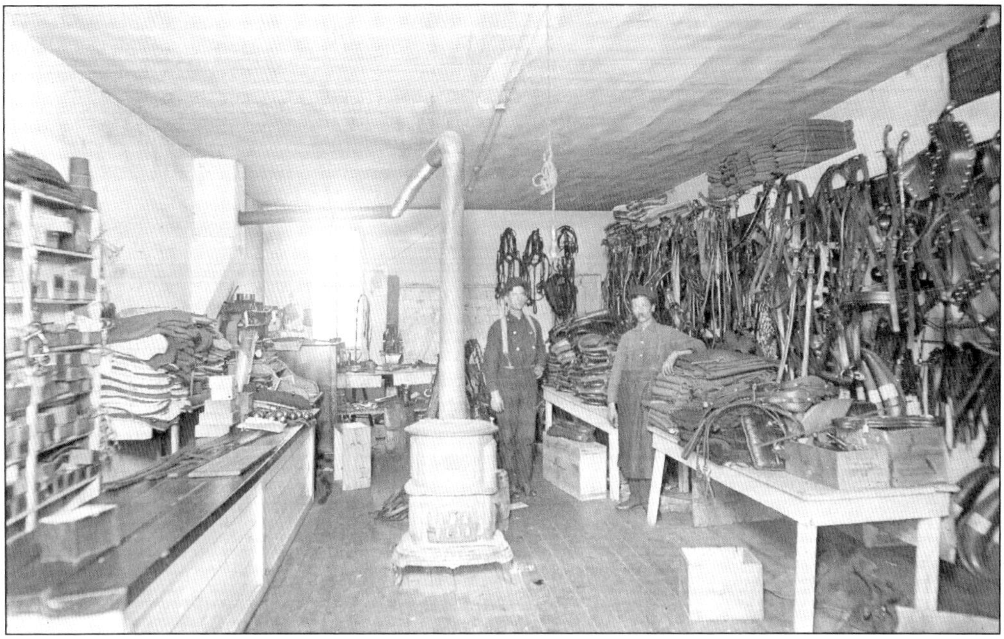

Ole Sundstrom's harness shop and bootery opened in Mora in 1907 to sell quality, handmade leather gear to Kanabec County's loggers, farmers, and workmen. Sundstrom's son Helmer took over the family business in 1932. In 1936, Helmer added a line of work clothing. Over the years, he continued to offer new merchandise and eventually changed the store's name to Sundstrom Shoe and Clothing.

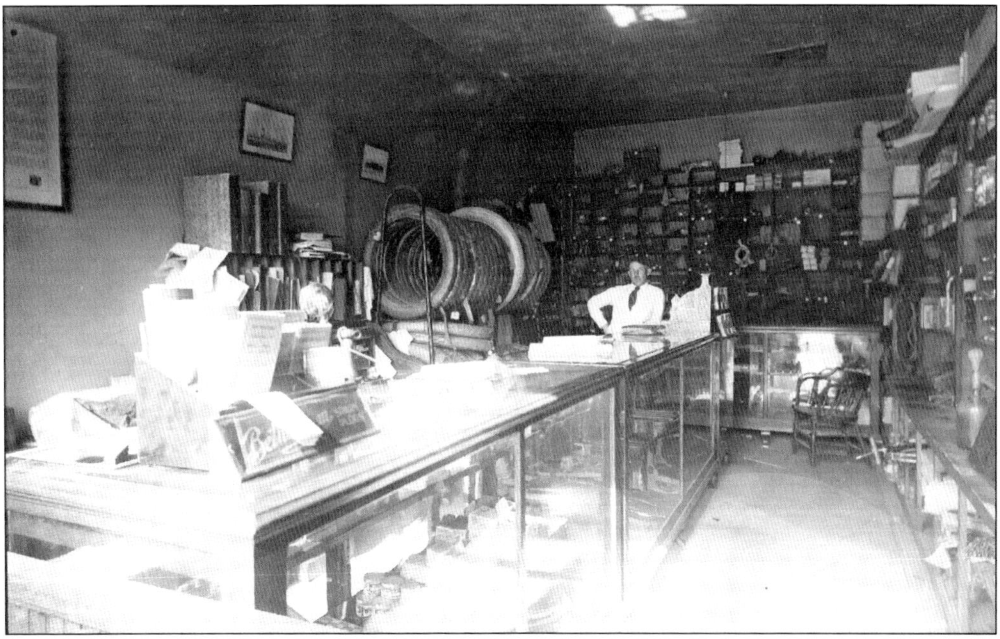

In the 1910s and 1920s, Kanabec County's primary means of transportation shifted from the horse and buggy to the automobile. Enterprising businessmen established auto parts stores, gas stations, and repair shops to serve owners of the horseless carriage. Mac's Auto Company, shown here in 1916, was one such business. It was also Mora's first oil transport company.

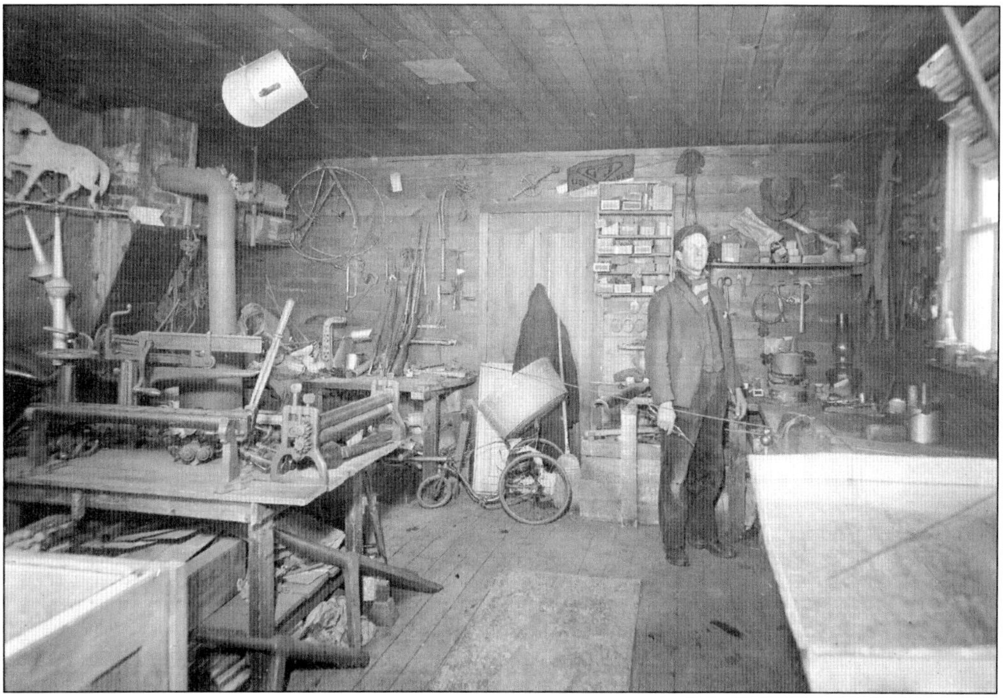

C.J. Abbe took a break from working in his tin shop to pose for this c. 1910 photograph. Abbe purchased his business on East Forest Avenue in Mora from Israel Anderson in 1905. He made and repaired all sorts of metal goods. One of his specialties was "Abbe's Strictly Hot Water Brooders," which sold for $20 apiece and were used to keep baby chickens nice and warm.

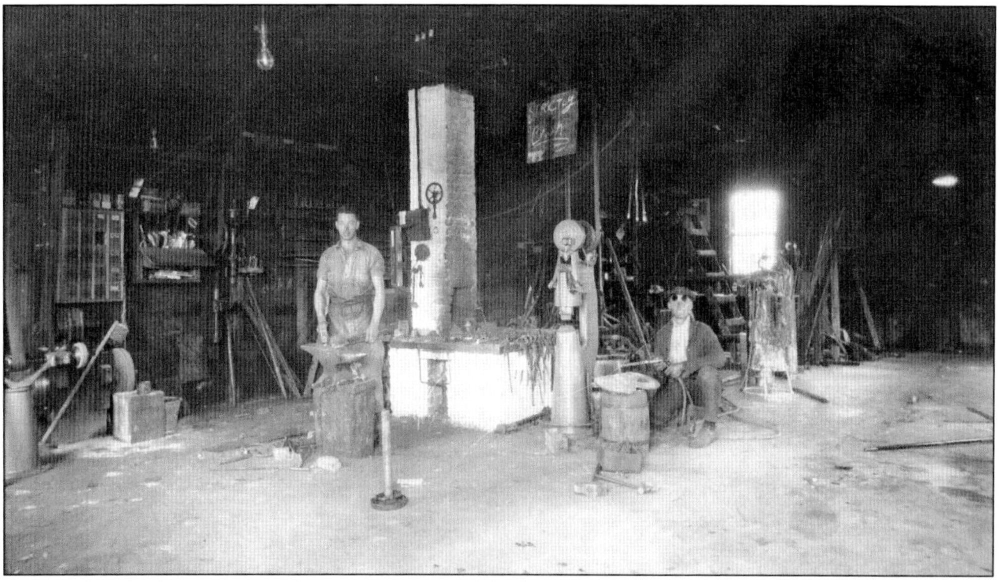

In the days before motorized transportation, blacksmiths were necessary members of Kanabec County communities. Along with forging horseshoes and wagon parts, they made and repaired farm implements, hardware, iron tools, and household necessities. Early area blacksmiths included McPherson and Tidd, John Toberg, E. Wickstrom, A.J. Lindsten, the Hanson brothers, Andrew Hogberg, and Henry Streightiff.

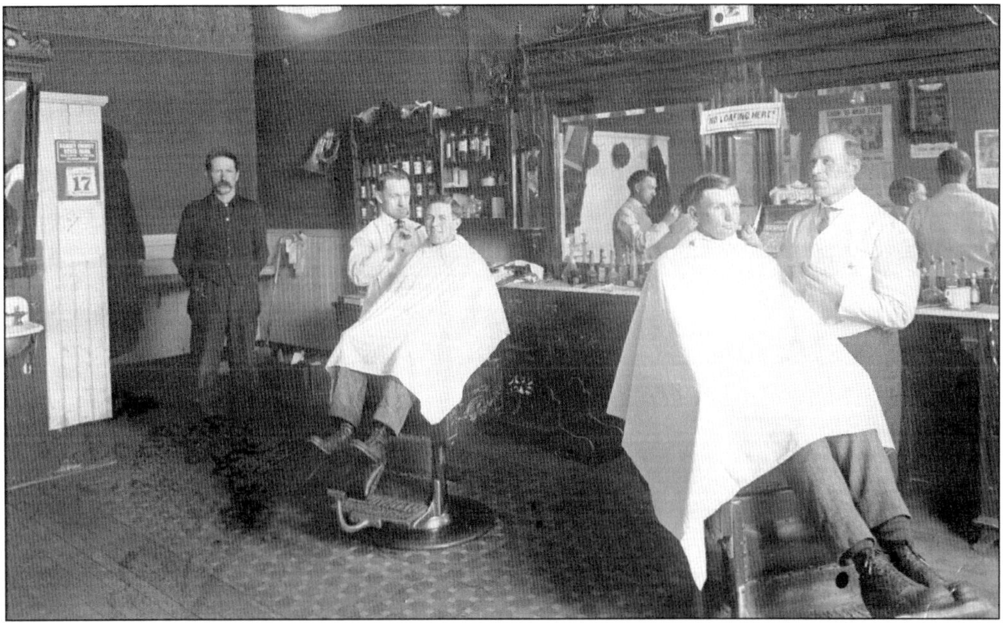

Glen Goldsmith, the barber on the left, began barbering in 1906 at age 16 for Mora barber Mose Jessmer. Two years later, with business partner Charles Naumann, Goldsmith purchased Jessmer's establishment. After several moves, the business settled into a shop in the Williams block, where it remained for several decades. Goldsmith offered haircuts and shaves for men, and, beginning in the 1920s, haircuts and styling for women.

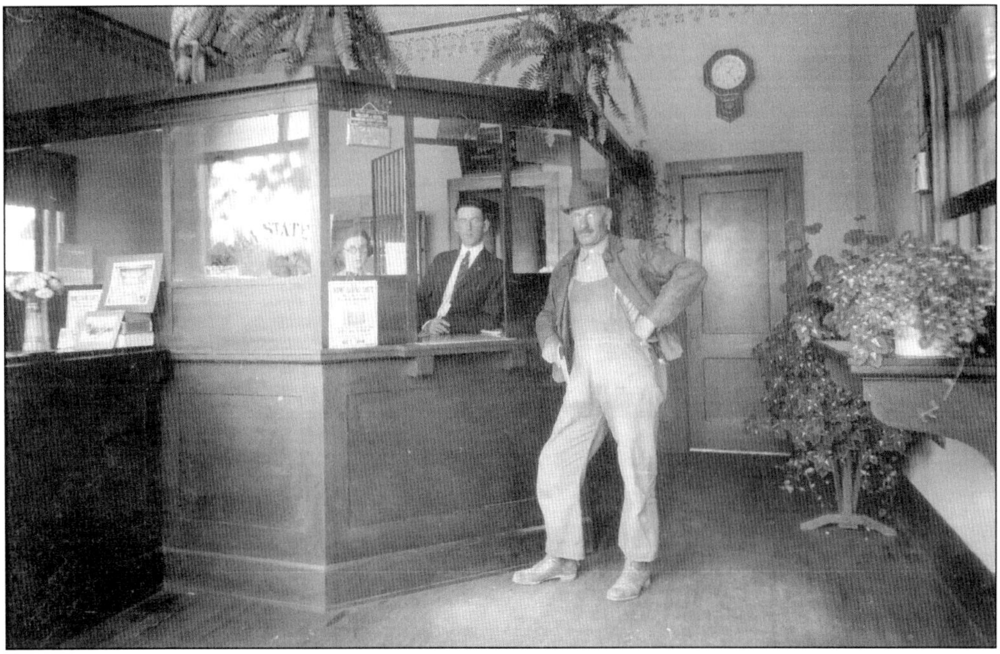

The Quamba State Bank organized in 1917 under the management of Frank Powers. Powers and his sister Mary Powers Woodbeck were visiting with customer Hjalmar Obarius when this photograph was taken about 1920. The Quamba State Bank moved to Mora in 1932 and reorganized as the Kanabec State Bank.

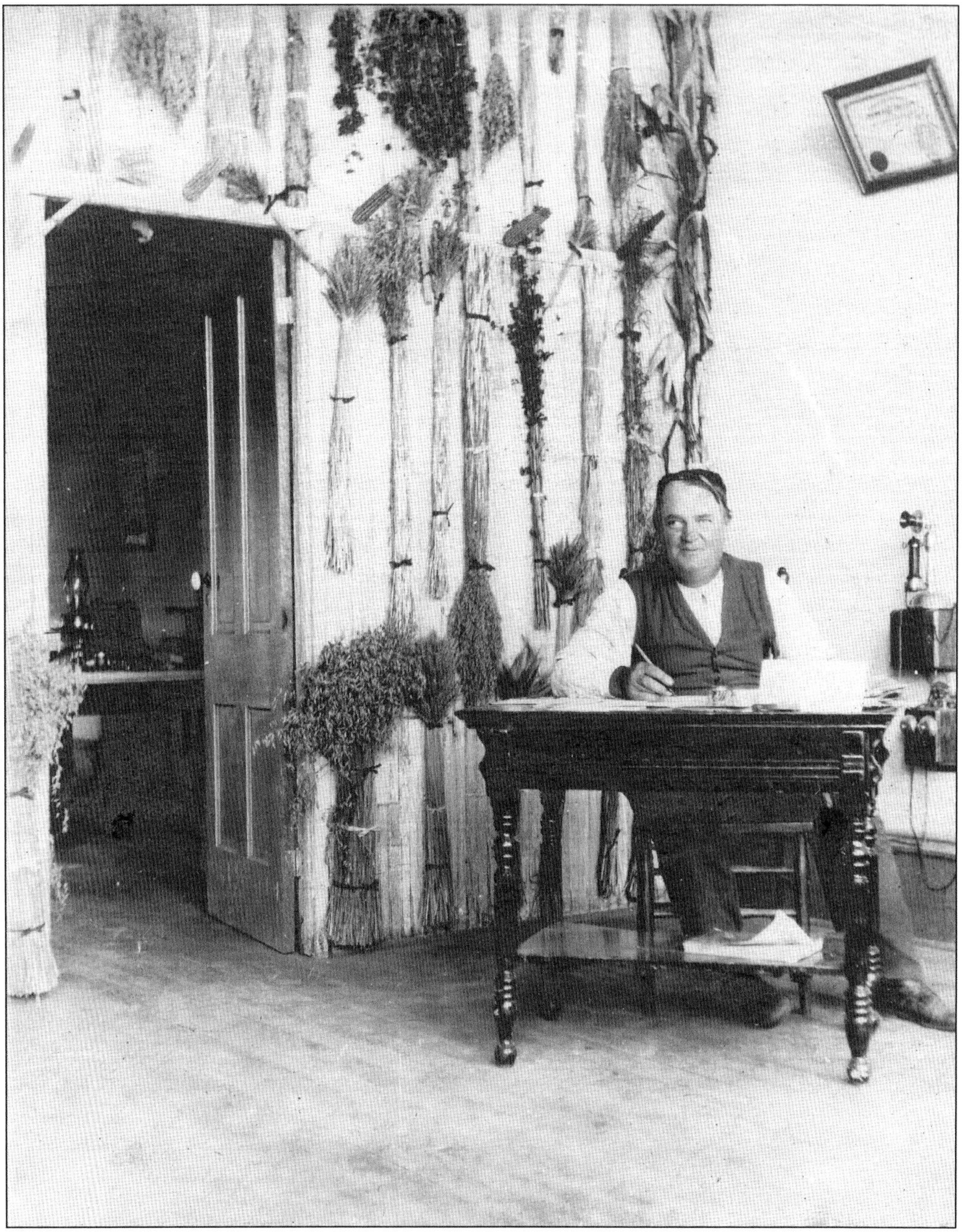

Land offices, like this one in Ogilvie, were Kanabec County's early real estate agencies. Land offices often published laudatory pamphlets to attract new settlers, especially farmers, to the area. One such pamphlet announced, "Central Eastern Minnesota is no second-rate country . . . to which settlers are flocking in desperation because good land in the older settled farming regions is no longer available. On the contrary, it is not only as fertile as any section in the Union, but one that proudly offers its products for comparison with the best produced in the highly developed farming sections of all states in the north temperate zone. Acre for acre its soil has been demonstrated time and again to be capable of equaling and even surpassing in productiveness land that is commonly held at a price of $150 to $200 per acre."

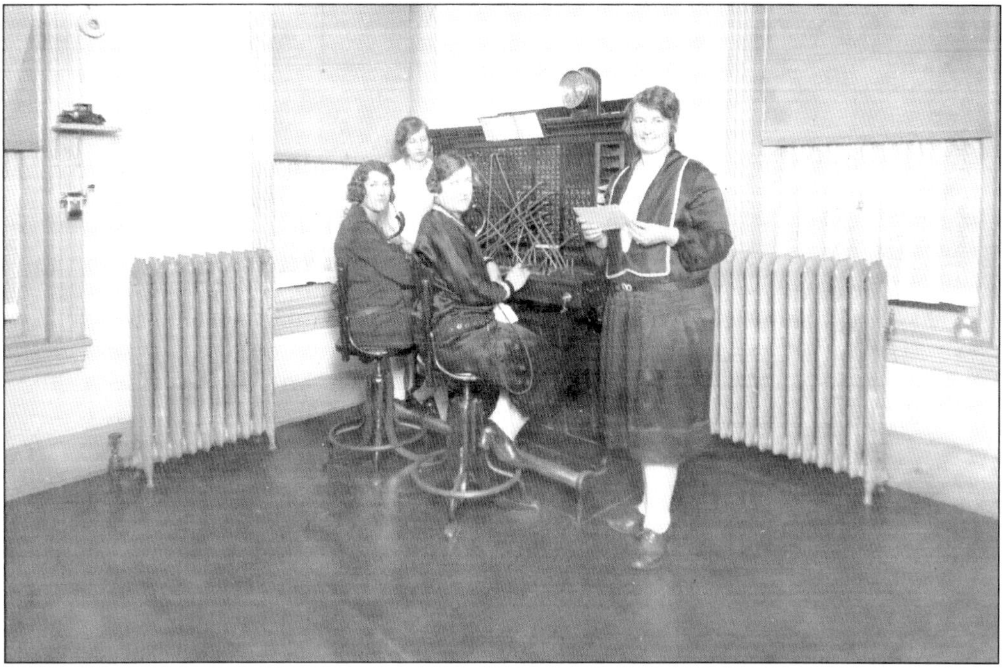

Kanabec County's first telephones were installed in Mora in 1895 and operated over a private line from Hans Peterson's general store to the Great Northern depot. Andrew Skoglund of Brunswick tied into the line the following year, and other county residents, like Henry Rines and Hugo Naumann, soon acquired their own lines. In 1899, a few businessmen installed a small switchboard in Julius Anderson's jewelry store.

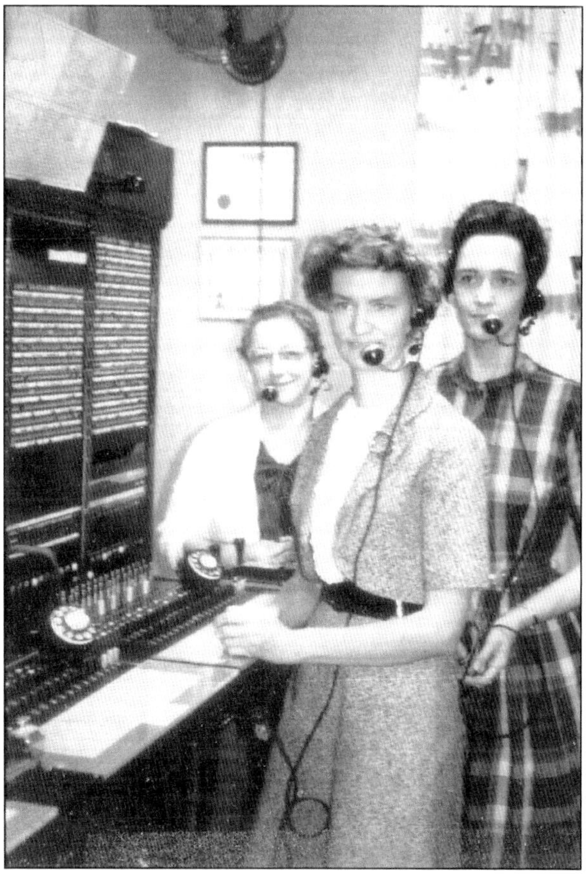

As telephone service expanded, the Maple Leaf Telephone Company purchased the Mora system. Over the years, the company became Tri-State and then Northwestern. Rural residents established their own networks, which consolidated into the Kanabec County Mutual Telephone Company. By 1949, Mora could boast 659 telephones in town and 549 in rural areas, and Ogilvie claimed 110 town and 147 rural telephones.

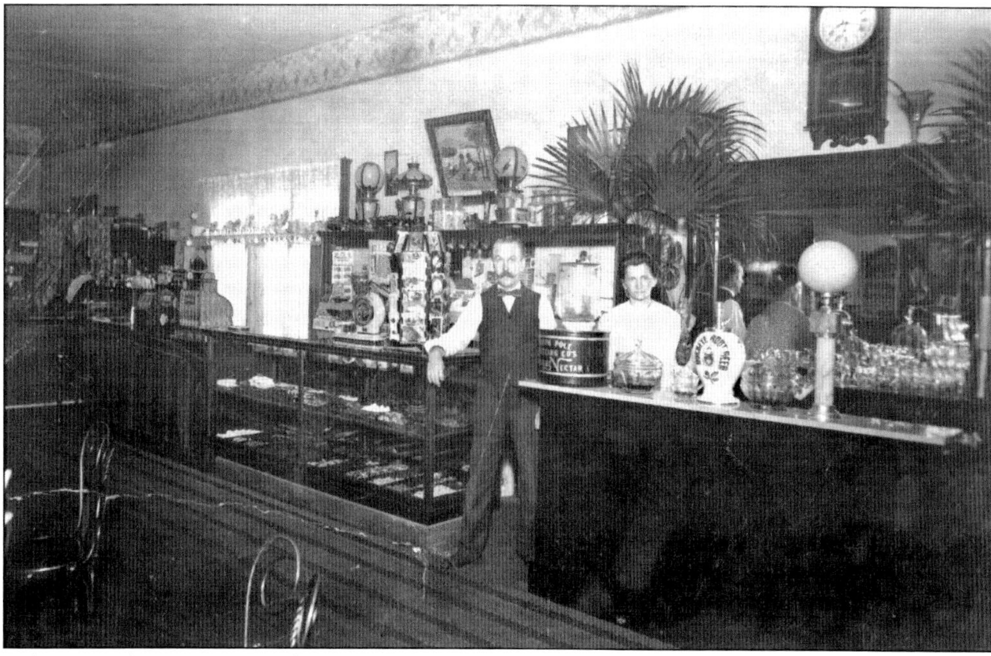

When Kanabec County residents wanted to take a break from their errands and enjoy something tasty to eat or drink, they had plenty of options. Each town offered at least one restaurant, café, and saloon. In this 1910 photograph, Leonard and Hildur Westlund posed behind the counter at their Comet Restaurant in Ogilvie. Notice the Buckeye Root Beer tap and North Pole Bottling Company nectar dispenser on the counter.

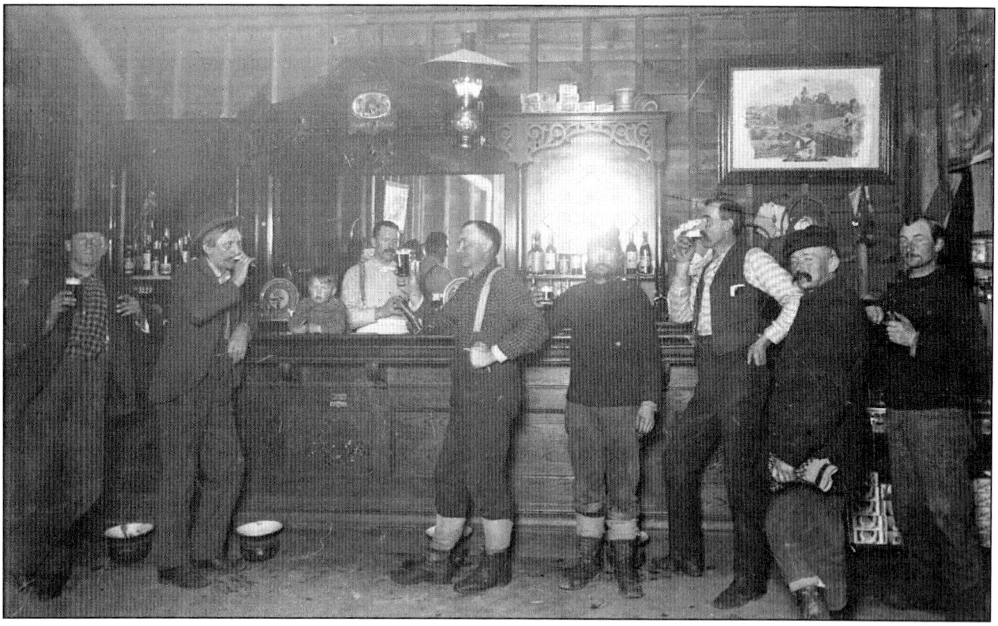

These men were certainly drinking something stronger than root beer or nectar. Many of Kanabec County's early settlers liked their liquor. Loggers and homesteaders worked hard during the day and often drank hard at night. The county sheriff sometimes had his hands full when fights broke out between men who had imbibed a bit too much.

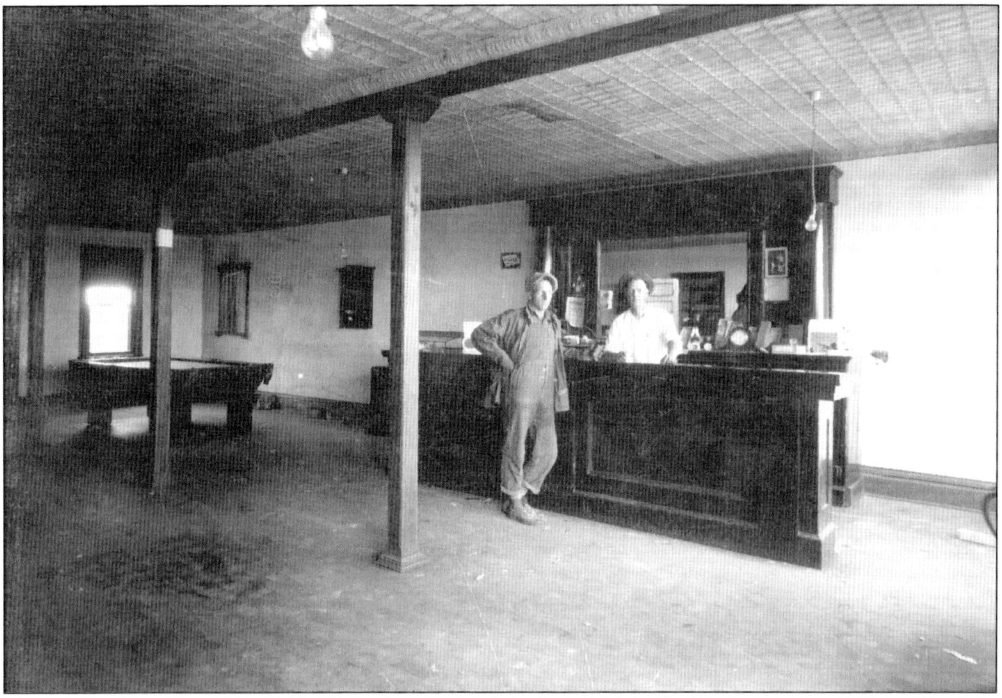

Quamba's pool hall was located on the first floor of the Quamba hotel. Men gathered there in the evenings to shoot a few games of pool, drink, and visit. Walter Peterson and Aleck Oslin were probably preparing for another busy evening.

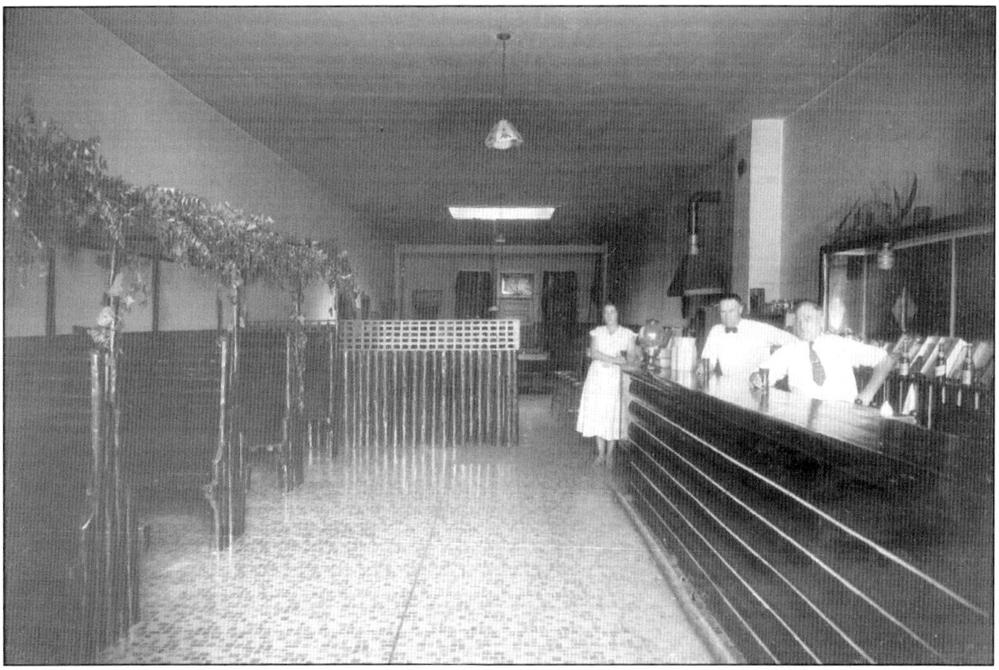

At Jack's Billiard Parlor on Union Street in Mora, customers could play a game of pool for 10¢. Winners received 10¢ in pool hall chips that were good for anything in the place. Owner Jack Kramer (left) and Ed Solseth stood behind the bar in this 1934 photograph.

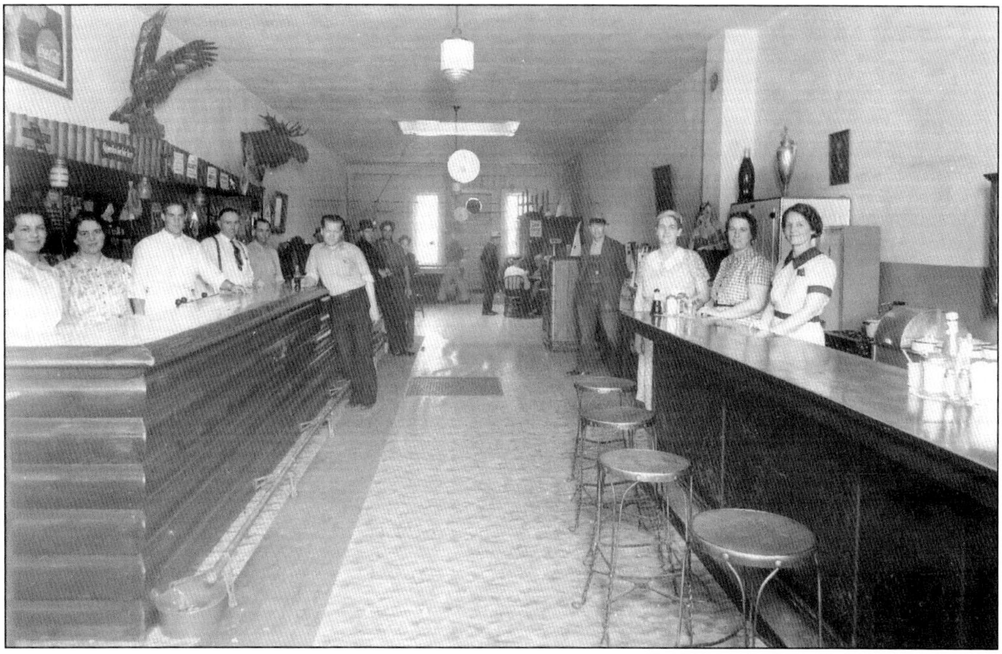

Jack Kramer sold his billiard parlor to O.B. Luloff in the late 1930s. Luloff had done some remodeling before this photograph was taken in 1940.

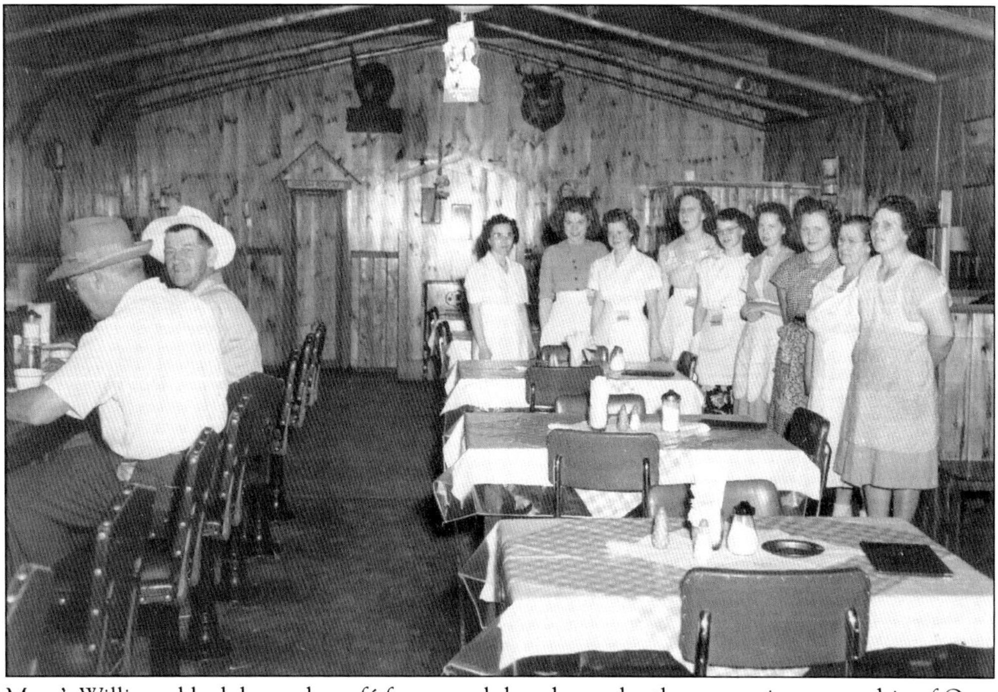

Mora's Williams block housed a café for several decades under the successive ownership of Otto Jensen, the Whitney family, Emmet Hageman, Bert Nordquist, and Don Kemp. Octer Beck and Mrs. Austin Cassman joined the series of owners in 1947 when they opened the DeLuxe Café, shown here. Beck and Cassman often advertised that they proudly served Folgers coffee and none other.

Seven

Feeding the Mind and Soul

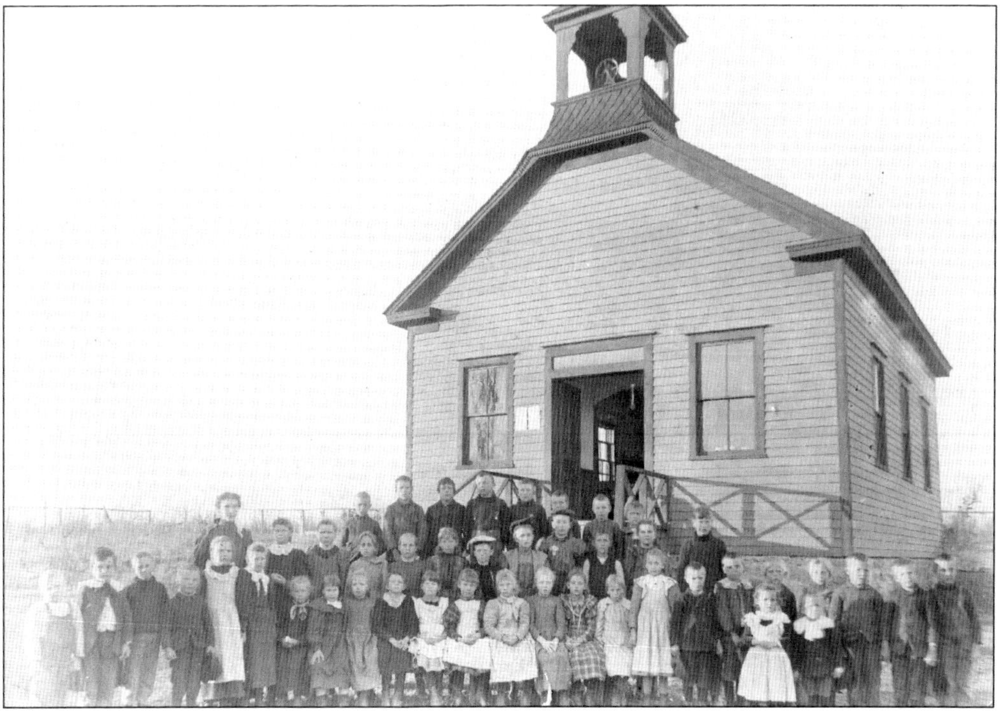

In 1856, Charlotte Pennington became Kanabec County's first schoolteacher when a small class of settlers' children gathered for instruction at a Brunswick home. Three years later, the Windom School, District No. 1, was officially created, and eight pupils attended the first three-month term. The schoolhouse pictured here was the Washington School, District No. 3, in Brunswick until it burned in 1903 under mysterious circumstances.

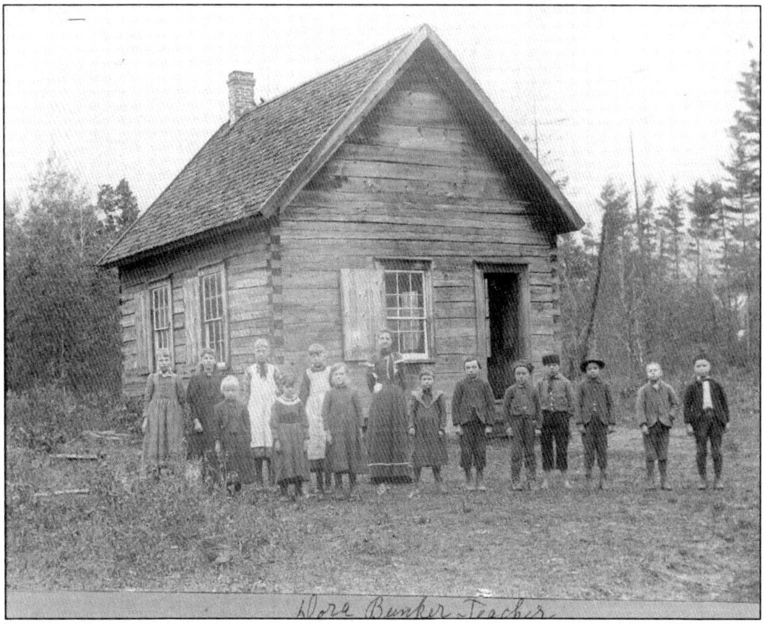

The Calhone School, District No. 8, was established in 1881 near the village of Coin in Brunswick Township. Teacher Etta Bunker posed with her class outside their first schoolhouse in this early photograph. Notice the dovetail joints on the rough plank building.

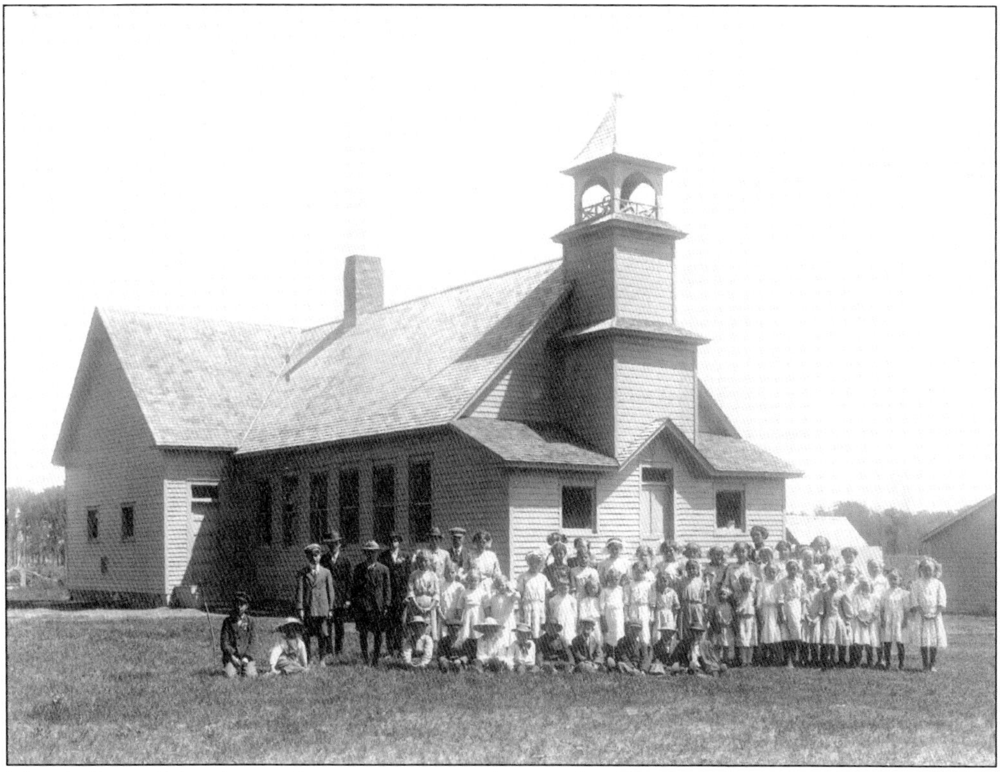

The Calhone School moved into a one-room frame schoolhouse in 1899. A second room was added in 1911. In 1913, the school was renamed the Coin School. In the 1960s, the Minnesota legislature required all schools without a high school program to consolidate with a school that offered upper-level classes. The Coin School was the last in the county to do so when it consolidated with Mora in 1971.

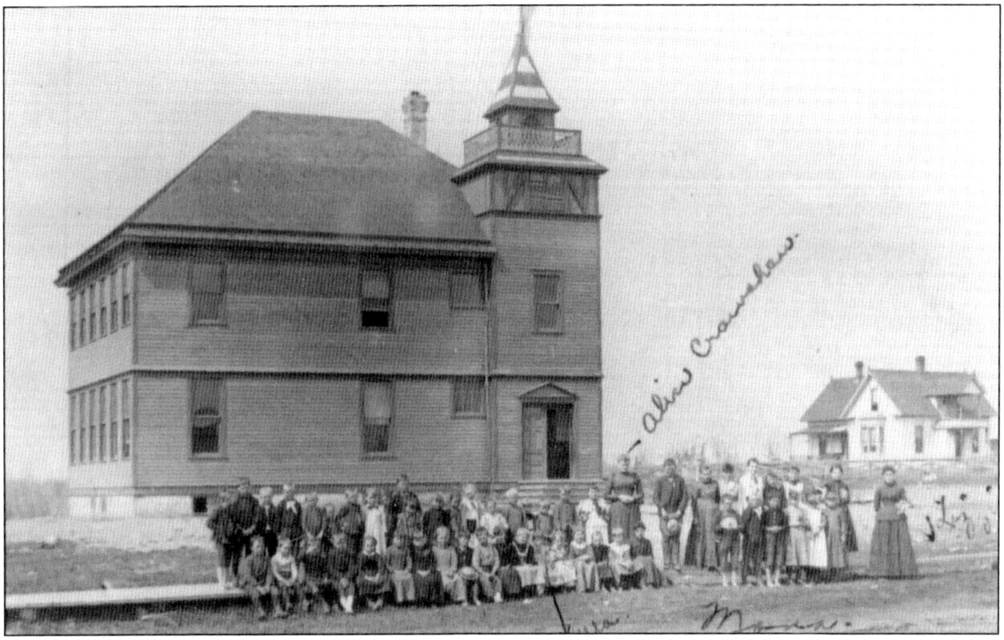

Mora School, District No. 9, was organized in 1883. The first school board, consisting of Myron Kent, F.H. Danforth, and M.B. Myrick, rented temporary quarters from C.E. Williams so May Tallman, age 16, could teach her 10 pupils. A one-room schoolhouse was constructed later that year, but as the school population grew, the board built a new school, the one shown here, in 1890 for a total cost of $2,390.

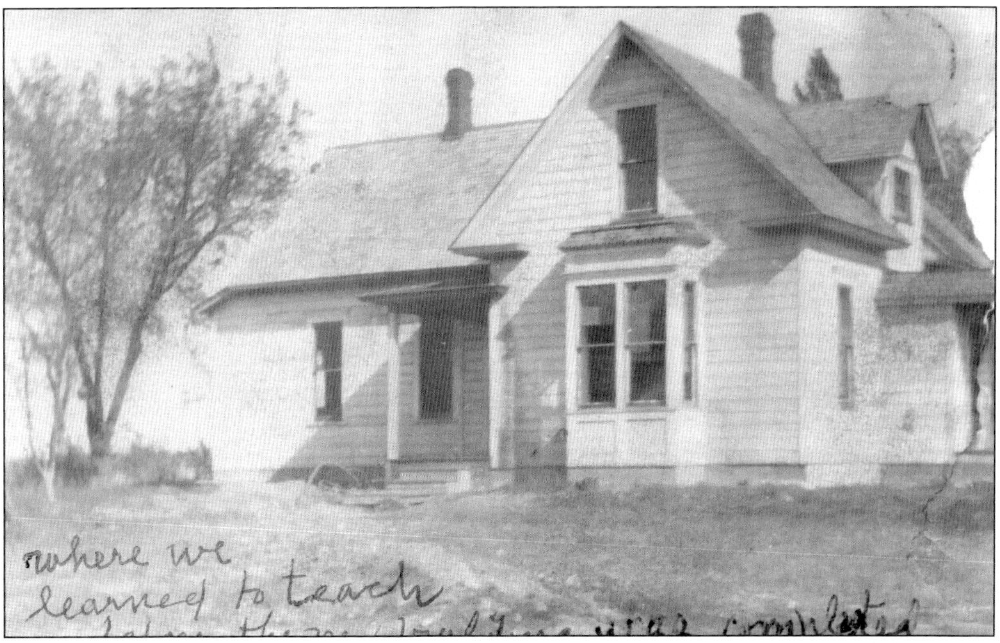

Mora's early schools never seemed to have quite enough space. Board members rented this nearby house to accommodate the normal school program. Normal schools trained high school graduates to be teachers. Students studied a variety of subjects, learned pedagogical methods, and worked toward certificates that allowed them to teach grades one through eight in country schools.

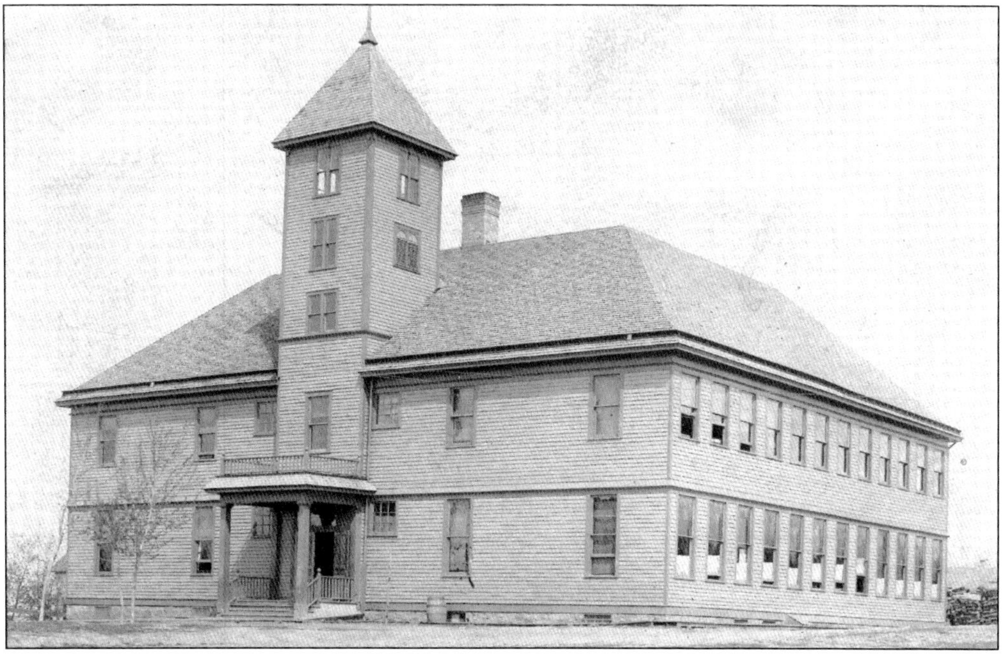

In 1901, a two-room addition was added to the Mora school, followed by a four-room addition in 1904 as enrollment continued to grow. In 1911, Mora Public School became Independent District No. 1 with its own superintendent apart from the rural school system.

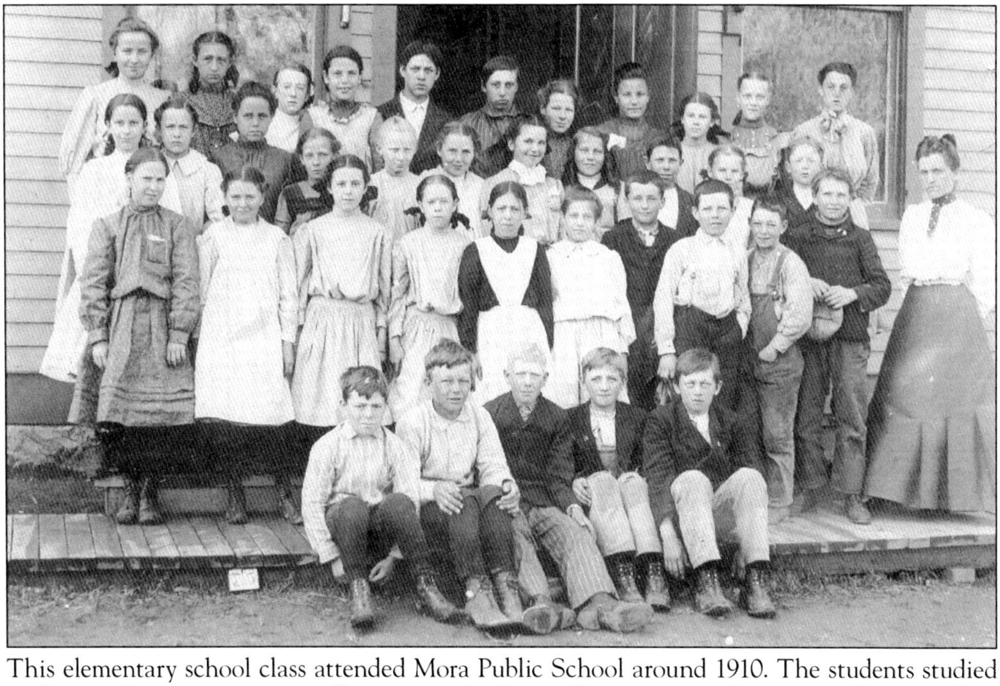

This elementary school class attended Mora Public School around 1910. The students studied reading, arithmetic, grammar, spelling, geography, history, hygiene, natural science, and penmanship. Pupils were also expected to learn how to recite literary pieces and master the basics of drawing and singing. Even with all these subjects, children still had plenty of time for games like tag and kittenball at recess.

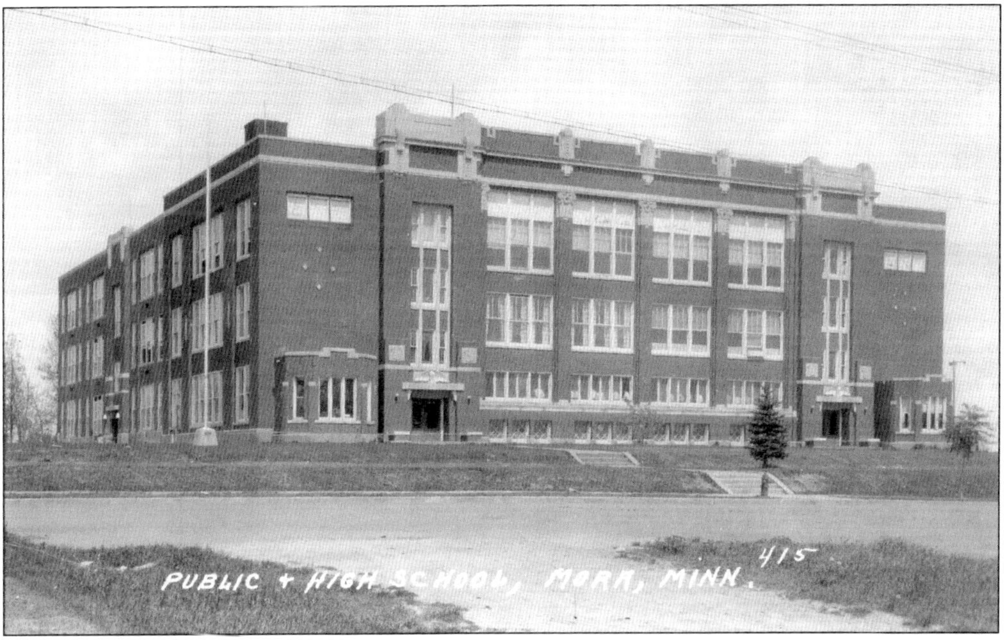

By 1917, the Mora school board decided that the town could support a new high school building, shown here after its dedication in 1918. Most high school students followed a course of studies designed to lead them into the working world of business or agriculture. Only a few signed up for the college preparation course and learned subjects like advanced mathematics and Latin.

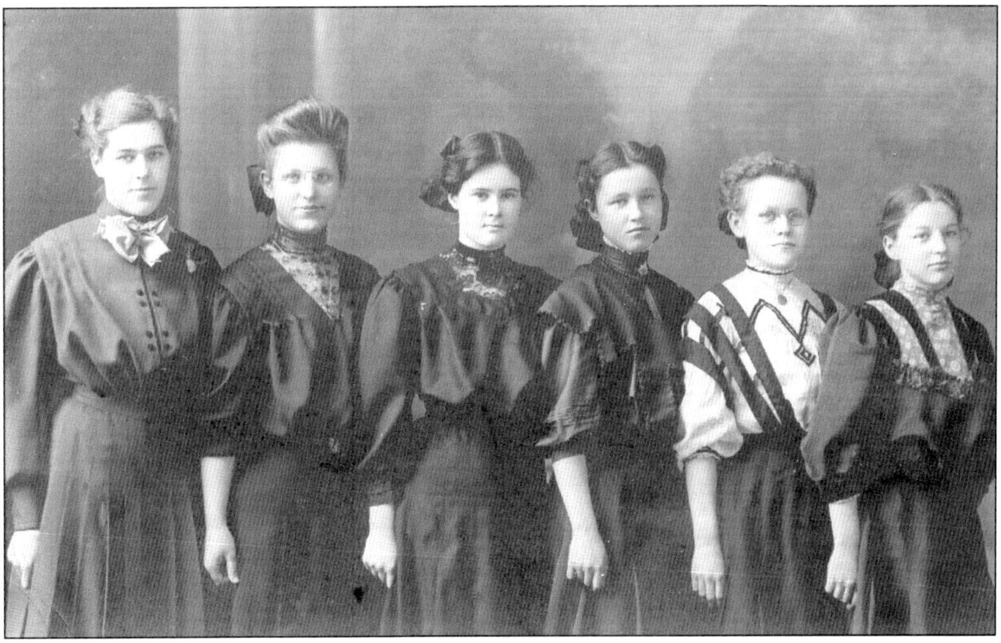

Early Mora schoolteachers Dora Williams, Clara Hoffert, Inez Hayes, Wanda Cupp, Bessie Goldsmith, and Beatrice Larson posed for this photograph in the late 19th century. Even in relatively large schools like Mora, teachers often taught more than one grade at a time. They were also expected to continue their own studies through summer classes, independent reading, and teachers' institutes.

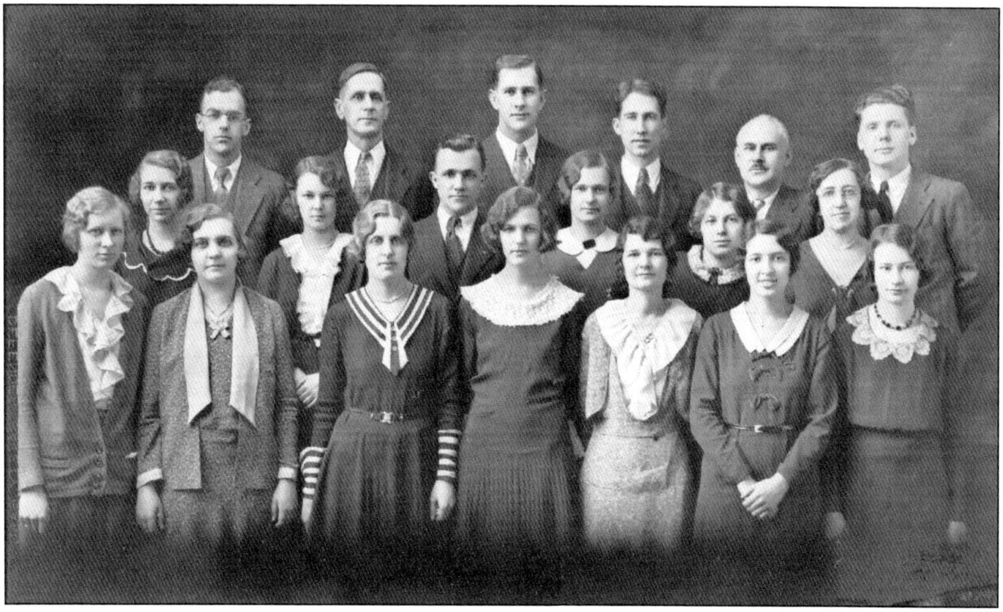

The Mora elementary and high school faculty gathered for a group photograph in 1931. By 1936, some of these teachers would be teaching in the brand new Mora Elementary School that replaced the deteriorating 1890 building.

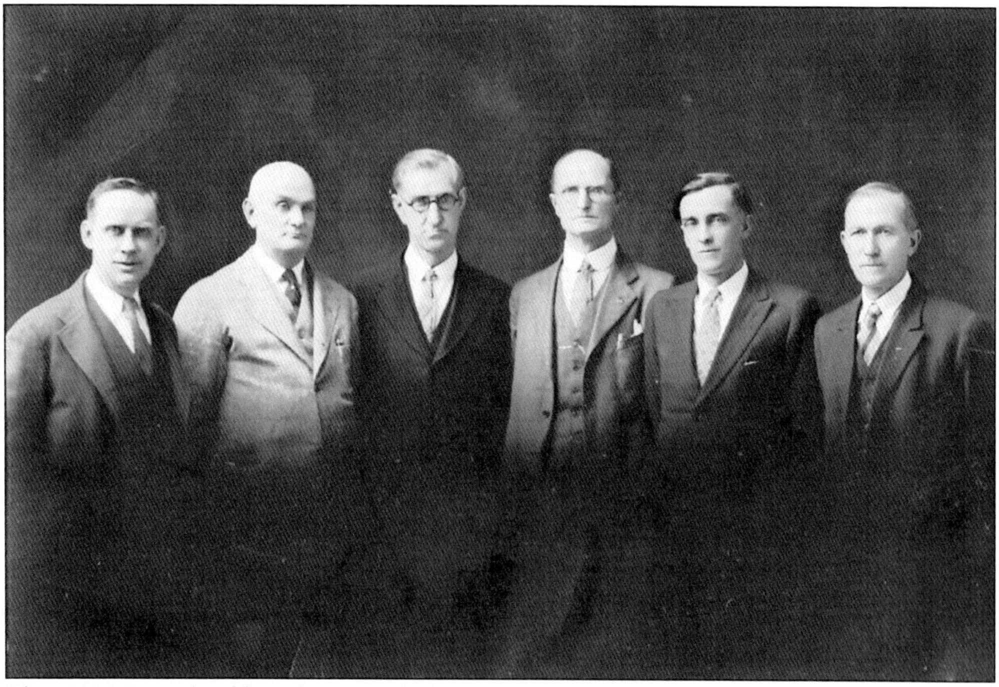

The 1930 Mora school board consisted of Mr. McFarland, Mr. Newbert, Dr. Bossert, Mr. Olson, Mr. Gorham, and Mr. Swanson. The board members, who were leading local businessmen, took their duties very seriously. They managed school property, oversaw district employment and curriculum, and made sure that Mora public schools offered students the best possible educational opportunities.

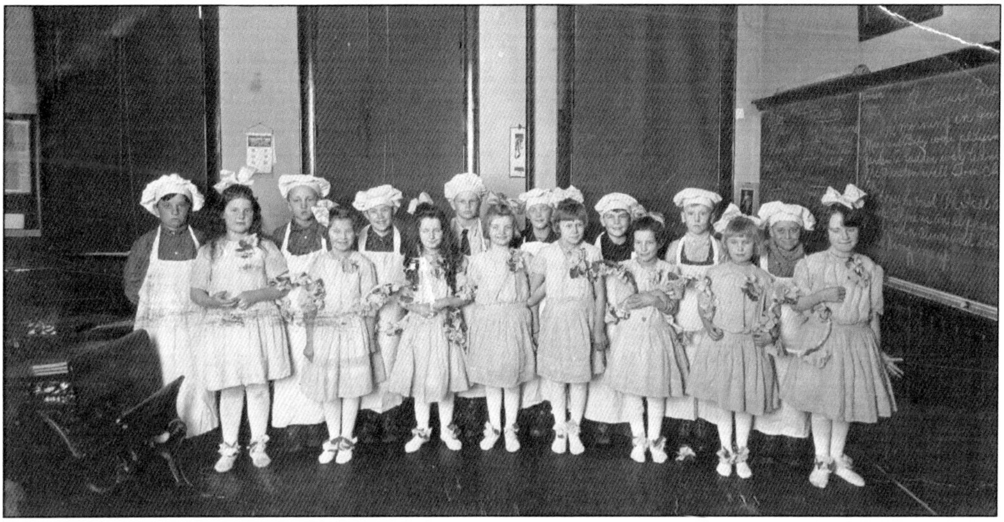

Mora's 1913–1914 fourth-grade class must have been performing a play or skit when this photograph was taken. Teachers tried to make studies as interesting as possible by interspersing fun activities that reinforced lesson materials.

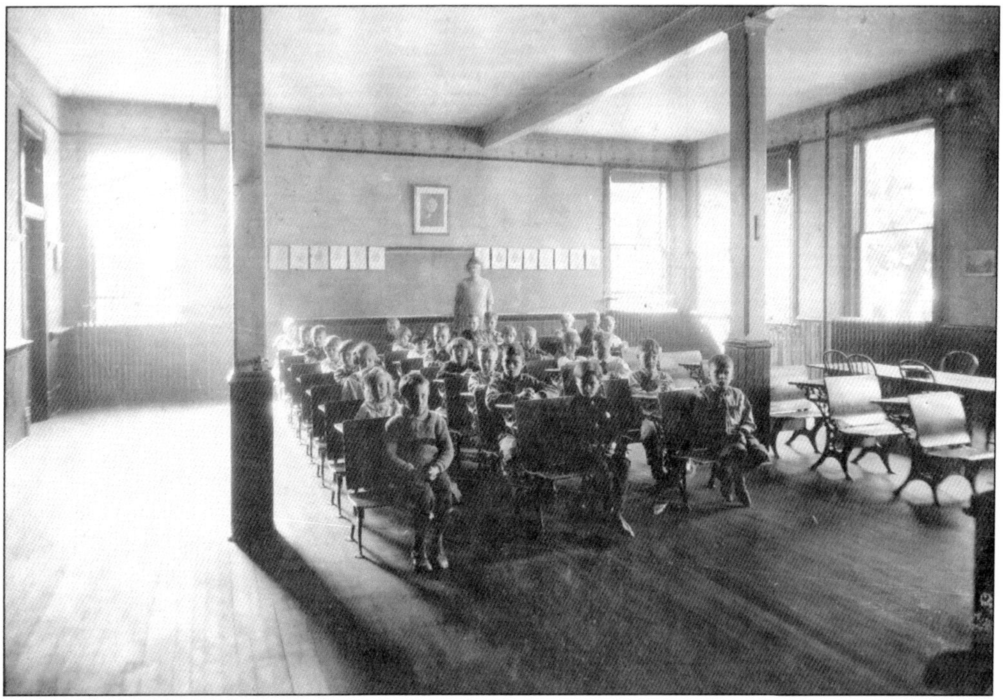

Mora's second-grade class sat primly at their desks for this 1923 photograph. Notice the wrought-iron and wood school desks, the table on the right where students probably met for reading groups, and the row of class work on display in the back of the room.

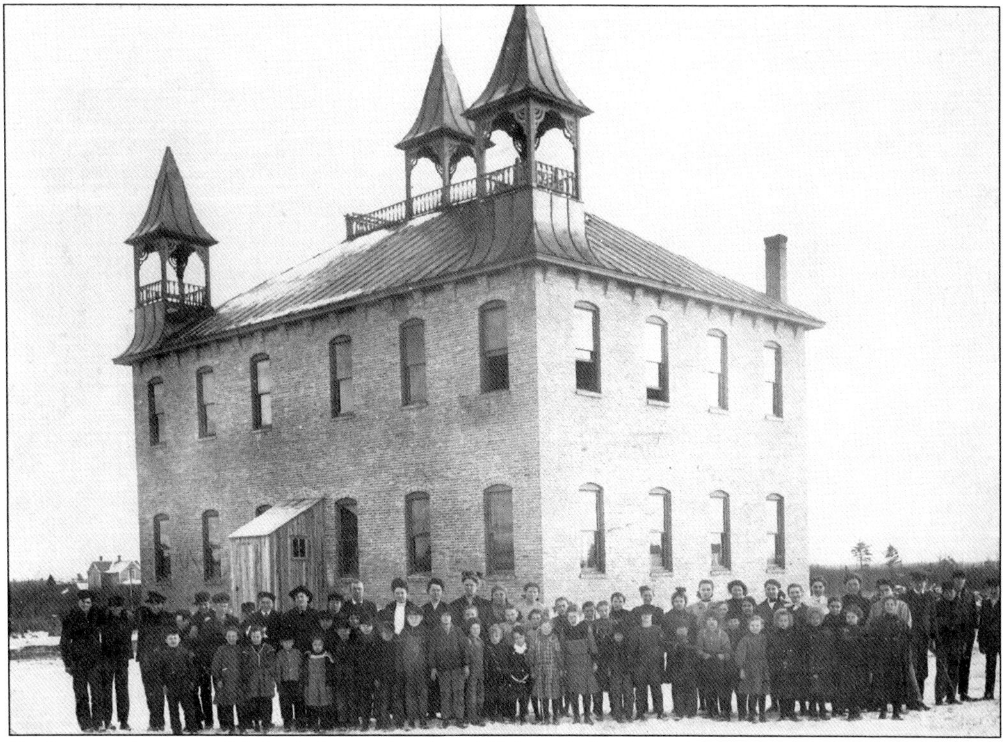

Ogilvie residents established their school in 1895, and the first class, with only seven students, met in a tar paper shack. The two-story brick-veneer schoolhouse shown here was built in 1902. It provided four classrooms and a library. Ogilvie's high school program began in 1911, and the first senior class of Bertha Gadola, Stella Neimann, and William Neimann graduated in 1915.

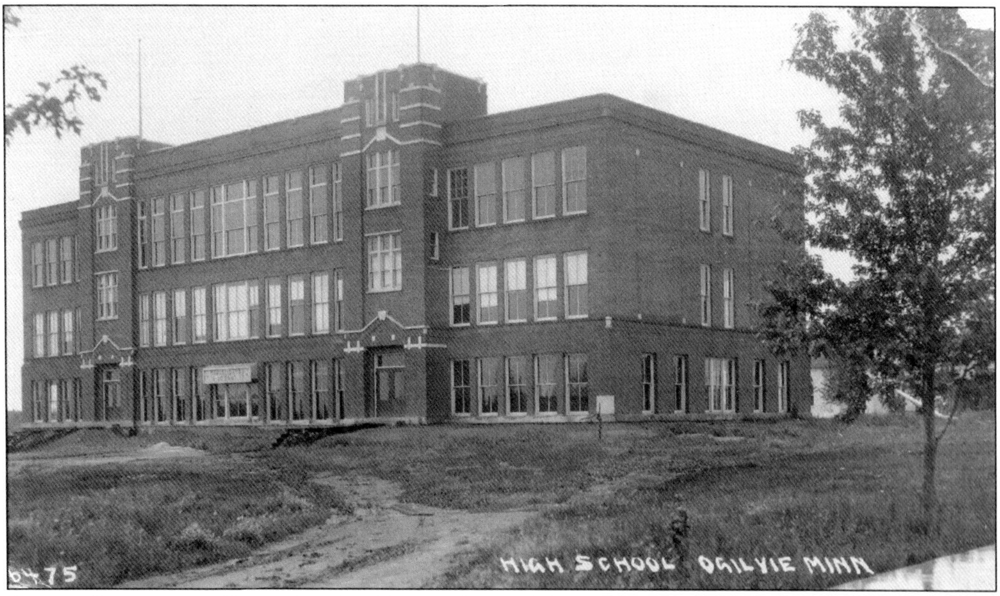

As enrollment grew, Ogilvie's school board decided that its town needed a new school. By 1917, the first two floors of Ogilvie's brick-and-stone, three-story school building were completed for a cost of $100,000.

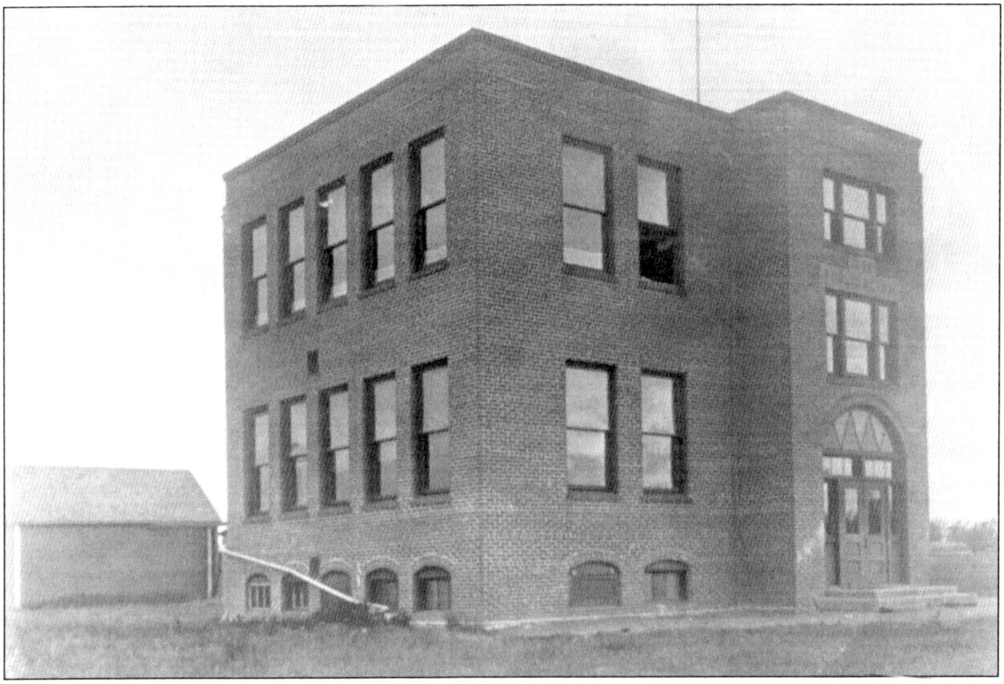

The first school in Grasston was held in a log cabin on the Runquist farm in 1896. By 1909, the town could boast of the two-story brick schoolhouse shown here. A 1919 addition to make room for a high school program cost $33,000, but Grasston residents were proud to say that their school was one of the finest in the county.

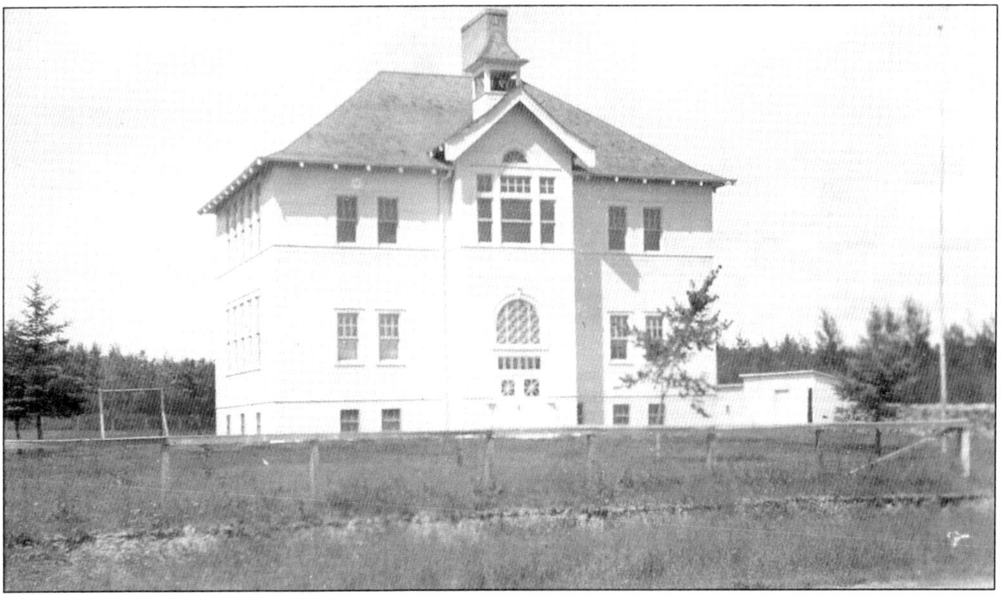

The Jefferson School in Warman was built in 1908 for $6,000. In the winter of 1916–1917, seventy students spent the night at school when a blizzard made travel impossible. Their two teachers, who lived on the school's upper floor, made biscuits for supper, and the children, wrapped up in their coats, slept on the floor. They all reached home safely the next day even with two feet of new snow.

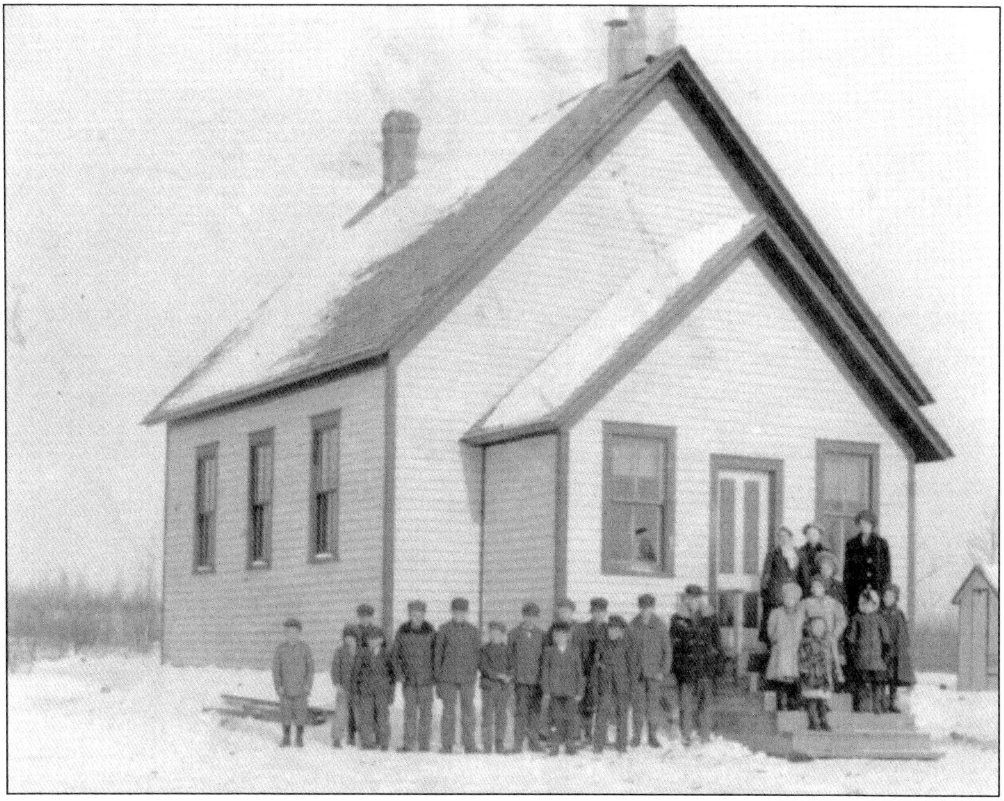

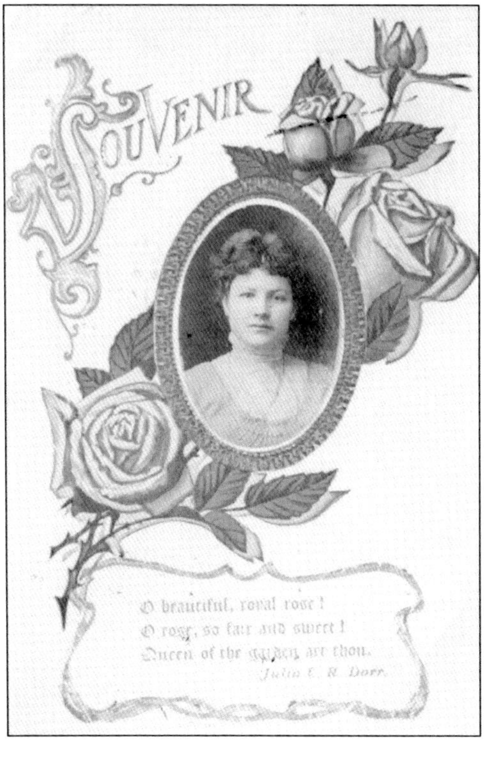

In 1901, several Quamba residents held a meeting to establish the village's first school. They cleaned out an old sawmill bunkhouse and furnished it with school desks, a teacher's desk, an armchair, and some books. Darwina Seymour opened the school term with 11 pupils. Two years later, the village sold $500 worth of bonds to pay for a new schoolhouse, the one shown here in 1911.

Country schoolteachers often handed out souvenir postcards at the end of each school term. Frances Bongaarts distributed this card to her Quamba pupils between 1909 and 1911. Bongaarts was a very courageous woman. When sparks from a passing train started a fire that threatened the schoolhouse, she and her students pulled a burning woodpile away from the school, beat out the fire, and saved the building.

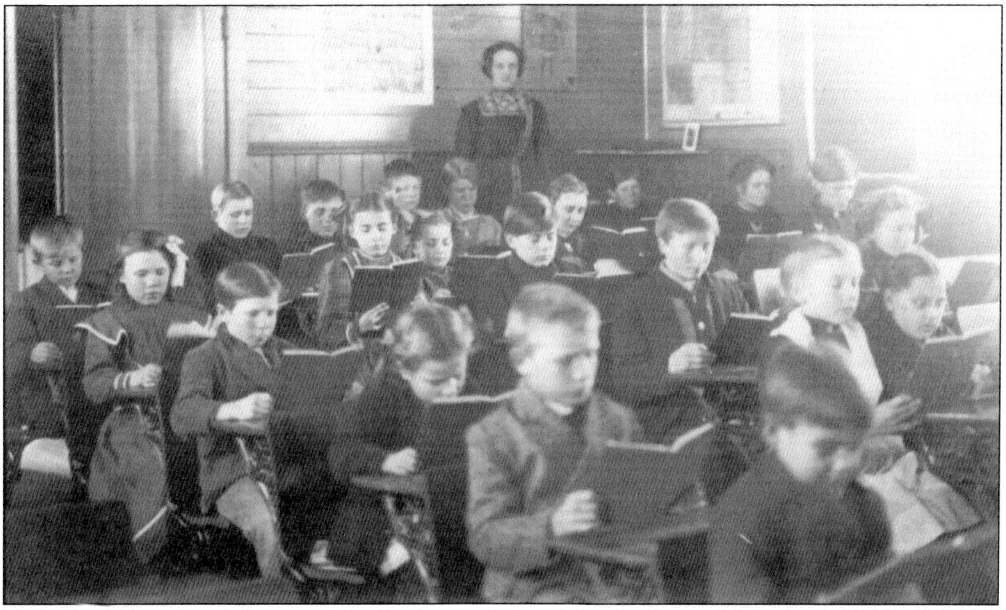

These Quamba students were busy with their studies when this photograph was taken about 1912.

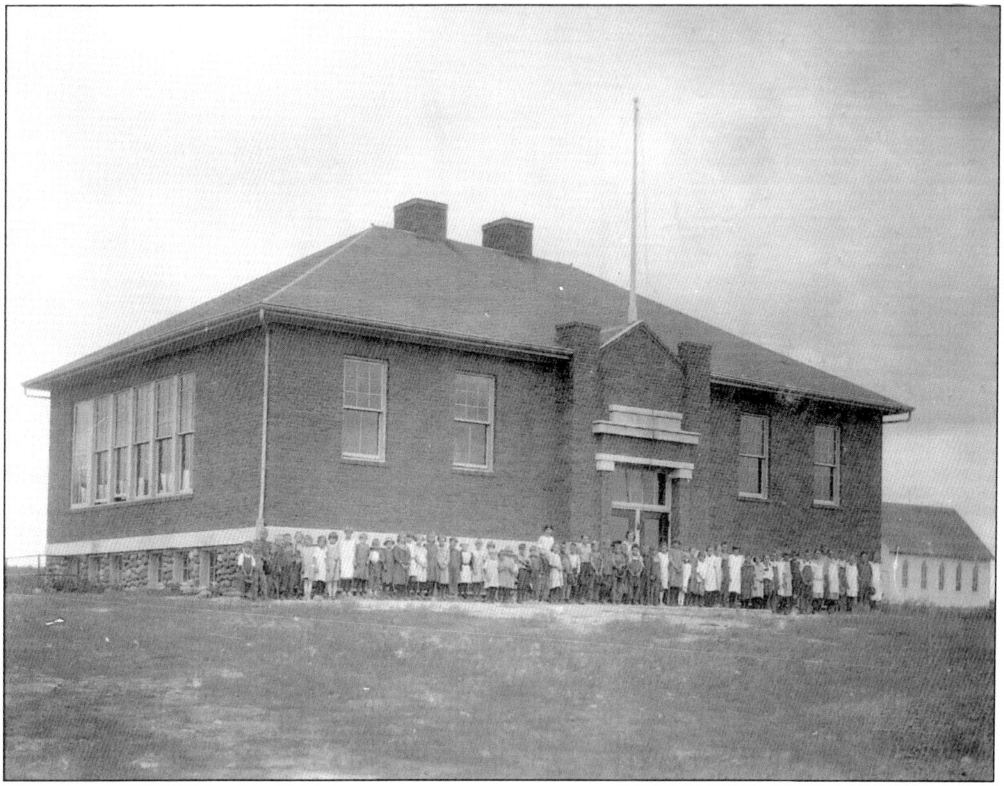

Quamba residents met in February 1919 to discuss building a new schoolhouse, which would be financed through bond sales. The brick building, which was completed in 1920, cost $10,750. The old frame school was purchased by the Farmer's Store for $550.

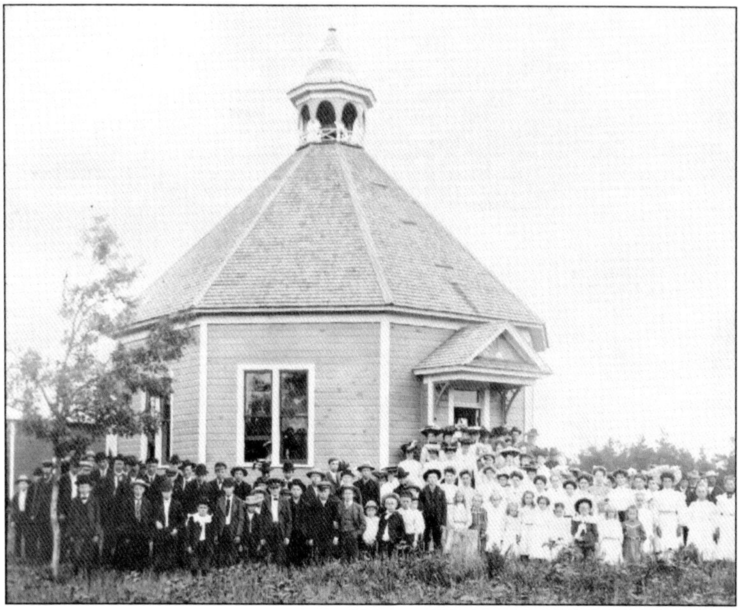

The Monroe School, District No. 32, near Lewis Lake was organized in the spring of 1902. Community members wanted to build a unique schoolhouse and designed the octagonal structure shown here. Each side measured 12 feet. Two cloakrooms flanked the front door, and the teacher's desk and blackboards stood opposite the entrance. Notice the decorative cupola at the top of the building.

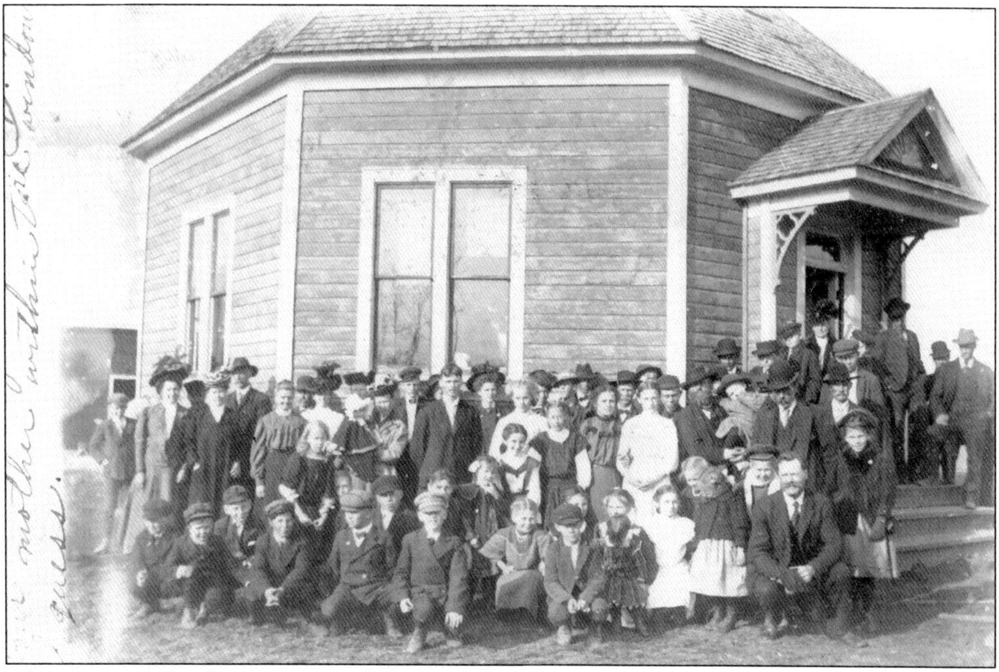

The Monroe School was overcrowded almost from the beginning. Desks meant for two students often accommodated three or four, and enrollment soared to 60 pupils. In 1918, the school board voted to abandon its unique schoolhouse for something larger and more practical. This photograph was taken in 1909.

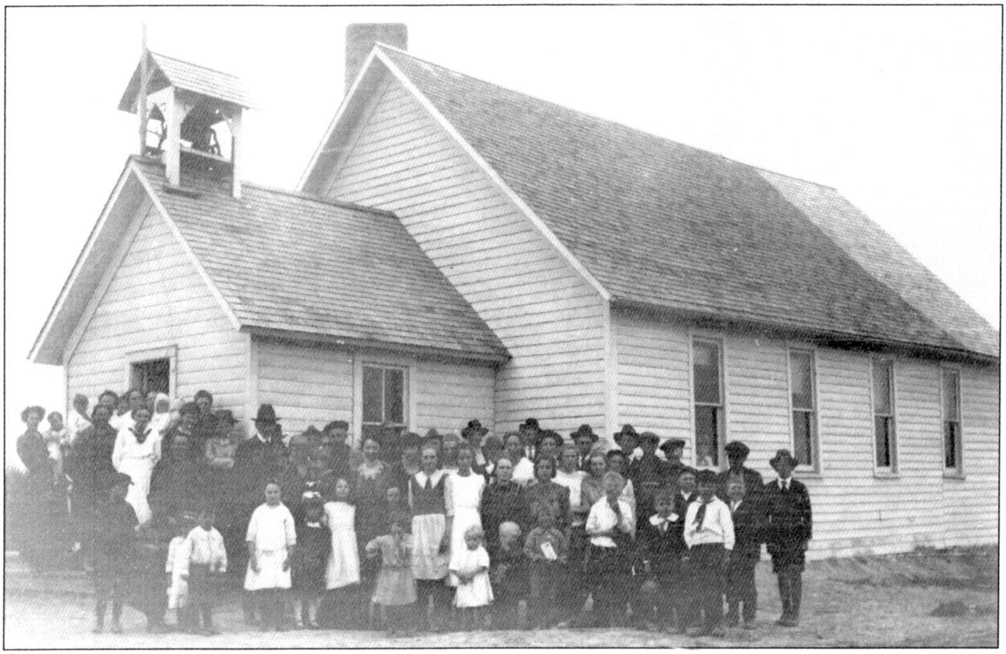

Blaine School, District No. 17, was located in Knife Lake Township. Organized in 1889, the district's first classes were held in the John Nord home with Lizzie Black as teacher. A year later, area residents built a small school and hired Lucy Naumann to teach. A larger school was constructed in 1900. Esther Boyd, who served as county school superintendent for many years, attended the Blaine School.

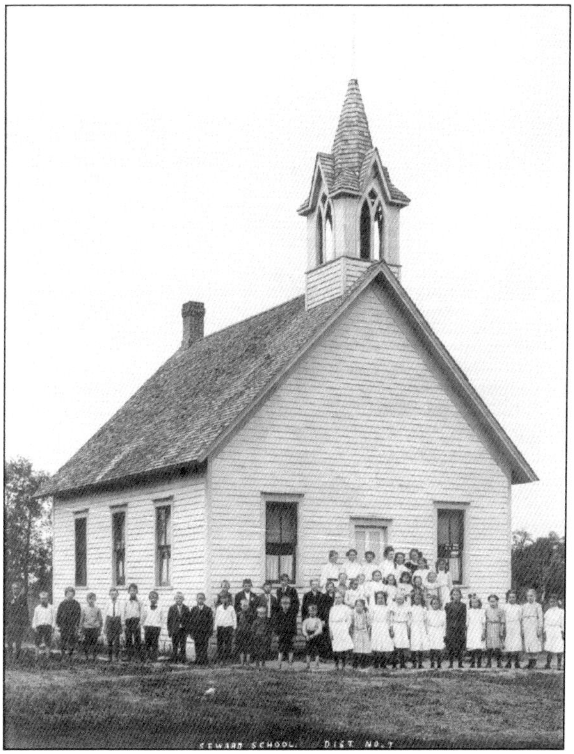

Pupils of Seward School, District No. 7, attended classes at the home of Magnus Eliason in Grass Lake Township from 1878 to 1883 before transferring to a small, one-room building furnished with homemade desks. School was in session for three months in the fall and three in the spring. The schoolhouse shown here was built in 1898 by carpenter Olaf Nelson, who charged $73.50 for labor and $161.22 for materials.

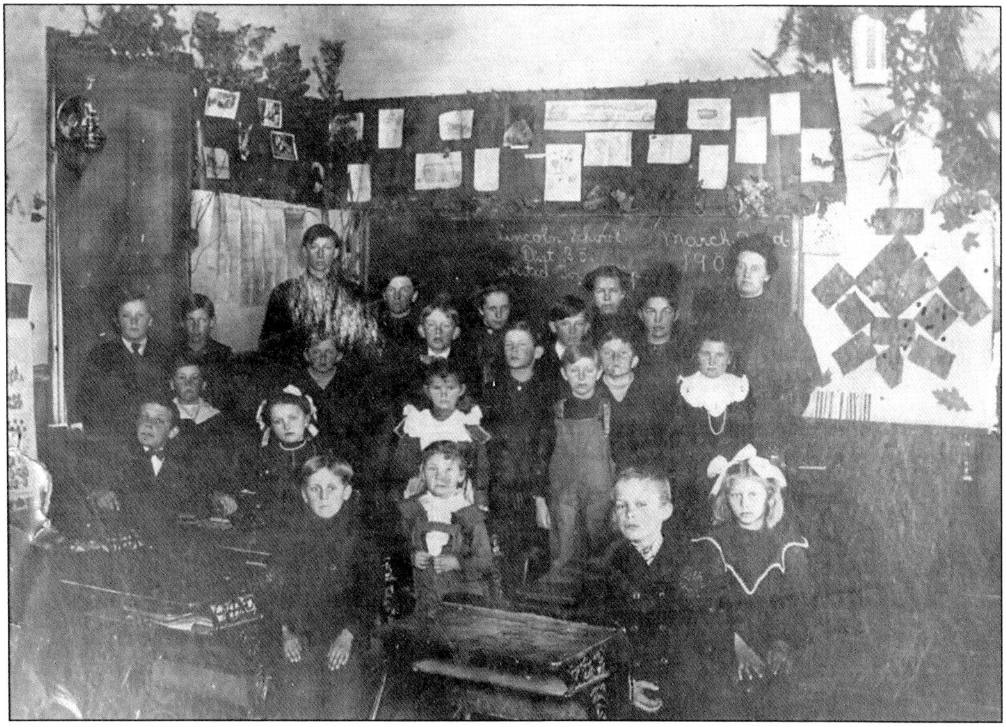

The pupils of Lincoln School, District No. 35, posed for their photograph with teacher Jeanette Jenks during the 1907–1908 school year. Jenks earned $40 per month to teach 30 students. The schoolhouse, a 24-by-32-foot building in Whited Township, had been constructed in 1903 for $100 plus $7 for the land. Notice the pictures, posters, and plants that decorated the schoolroom.

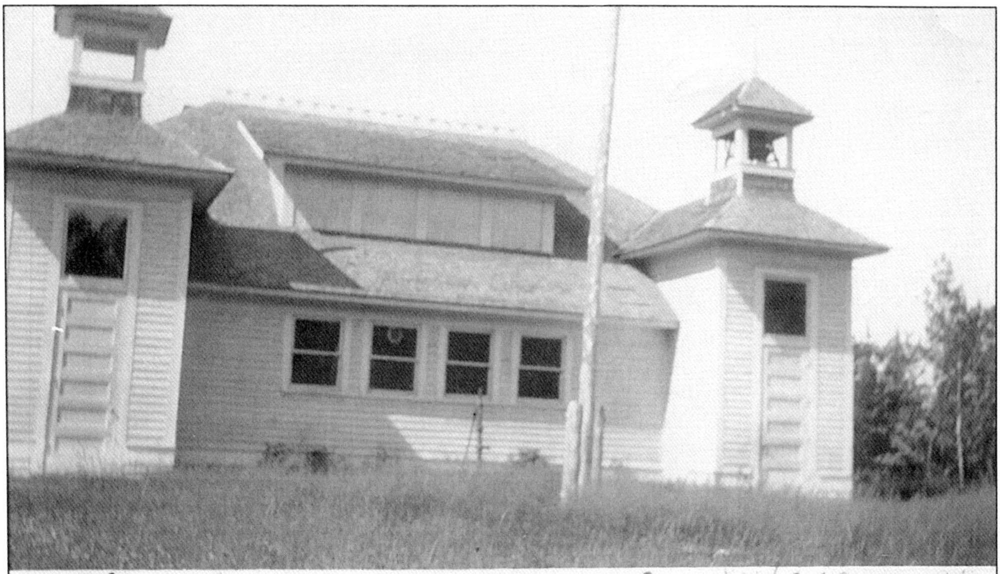

The Clay School, District No. 54, was organized in Hillman Township on October 25, 1910. It was also called the Trudell School after a local landowner. This picture, taken in 1925, shows the Clay School's distinctive architecture with its double doors and cupolas.

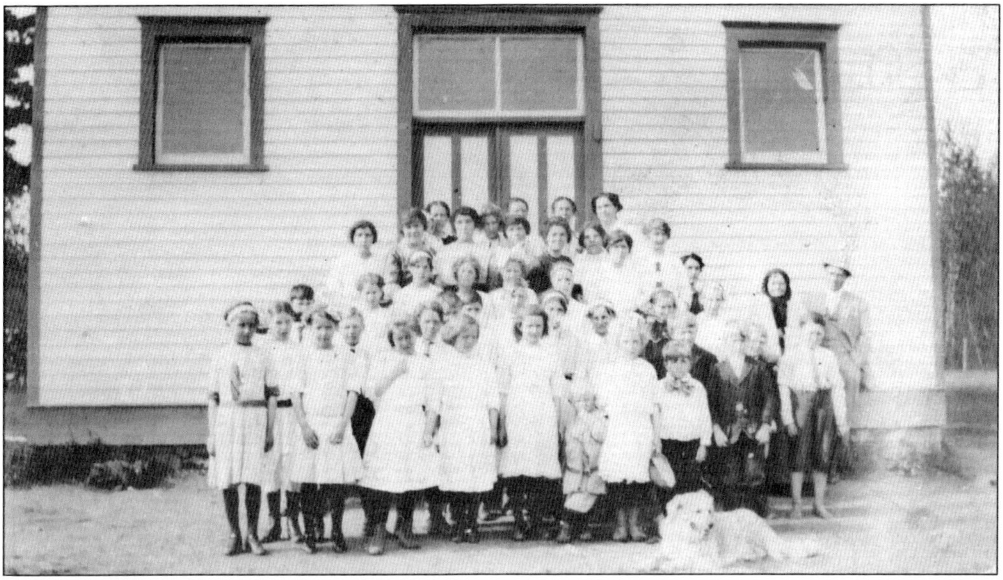

The students of Roosevelt School, District No. 6, in Arthur Township were enjoying their picnic day when this photograph was taken in 1914. Picnic day, with its games, contests, and delicious food, was a much-anticipated break from studies. The schoolhouse in the background was built in 1882 on land donated by the St. Paul & Duluth Railway. It was furnished with handmade desks and blackboards.

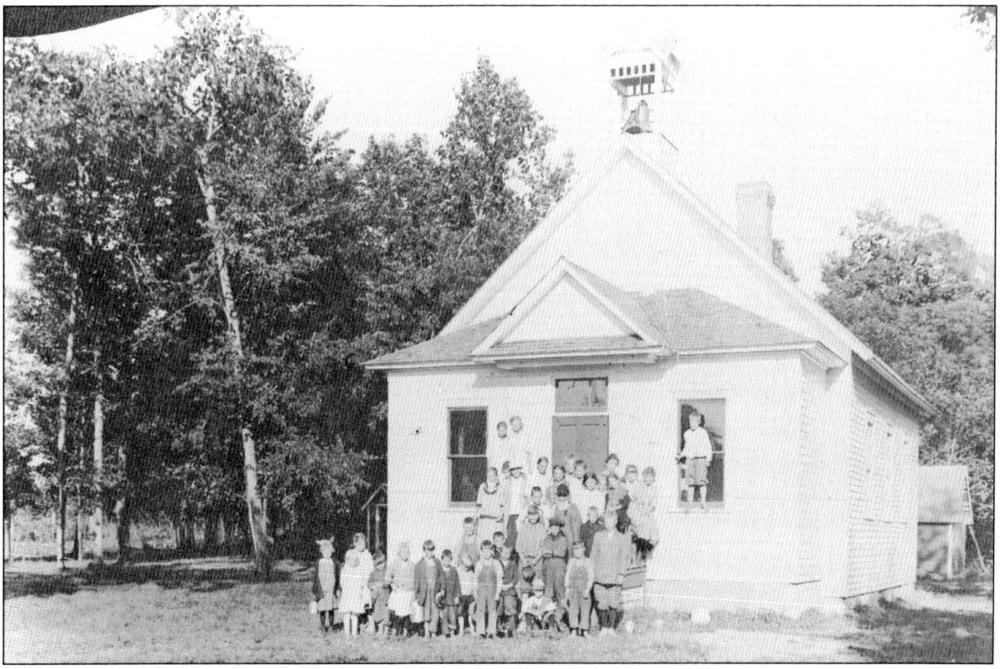

Ida Wickstrom was the first teacher at Hawthorne School, District No. 15, which was organized in 1890 in Brunswick Township. Wickstrom was required to be at the school at least one hour before classes started, serve as janitor and keep the school clean, ring the bell every morning to announce the start of the school day, and hand write copies of any work she required her students to complete.

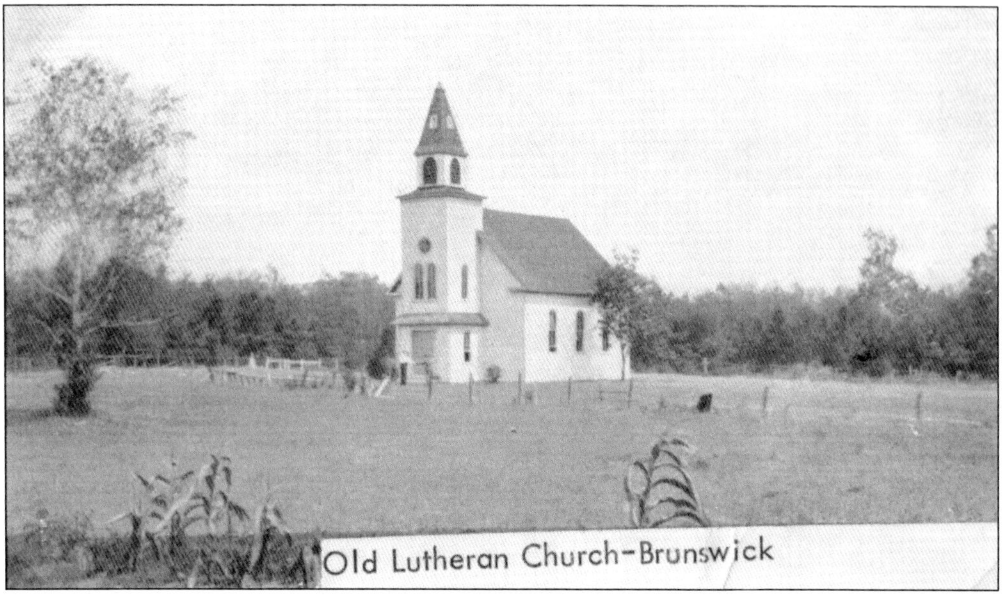

Brunswick's Lutheran church was founded in 1885 as the "Swedish Evangelical Lutheran Congregation of Brunswick." J.P. Leaf served as the congregation's first pastor, and worshippers met at the local schoolhouse until their first church building was completed in 1889. This photograph was taken after the tower was added in 1898. The church eventually became known as Immanuel Lutheran.

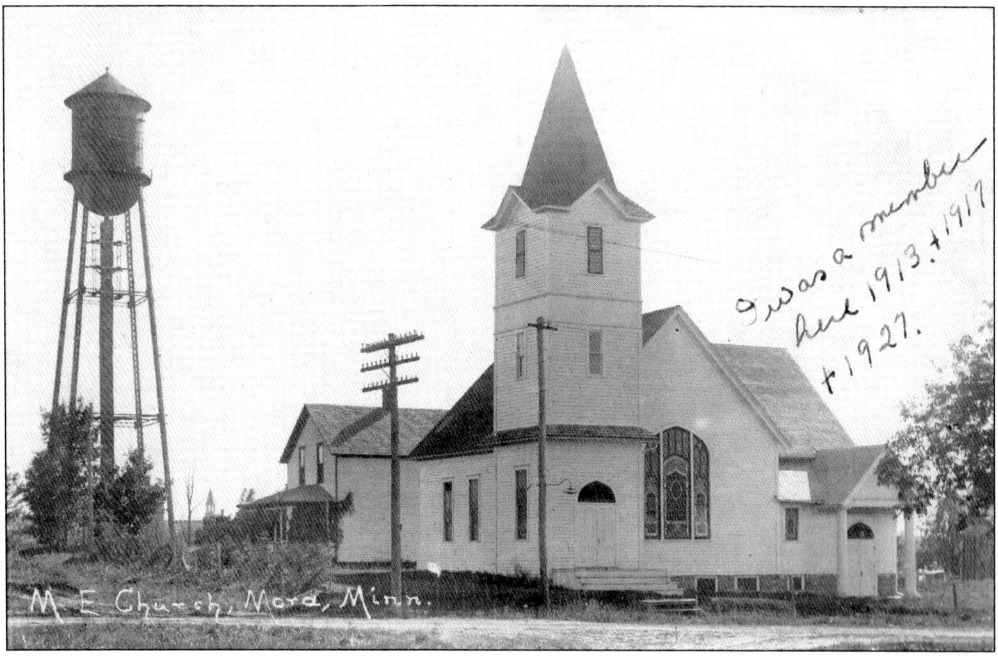

The first church services in Mora were held in the Conger hotel's meeting hall. Local residents took turns reading sermons to the small congregation and conducting Sunday school classes. In 1889, G.C. Parker came to Mora to organize the Methodist Episcopal church and serve as pastor. The first church building in Mora, shown here, was dedicated in September 1889 and housed the Methodist congregation.

On November 25, 1891, twenty-three people met at the home of N.P. Burgeson to discuss the organization of a Swedish Lutheran church in Mora. They called J.P. Leaf to serve as their pastor and met in homes until their church was constructed in 1902. Construction of the 32-by-40-foot building was supervised by P.G. Billstrom, who charged $165 for his services along with the cost of materials.

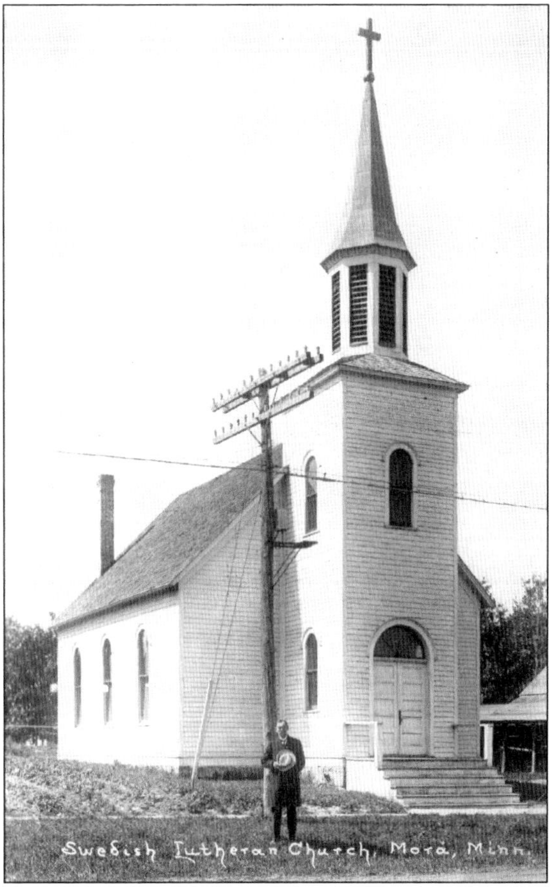

In 1898, Mrs. C.F. Griffin of Mora told her friend Mrs. E.E. Hughes that she would give almost anything to hear a good Presbyterian sermon. Her wish came true when S.A. Jamieson came from Duluth and preached at the courthouse on October 16. After the service, Jamieson led a meeting at the Griffin home to organize Mora's Presbyterian congregation. Their church building was dedicated on October 14, 1900.

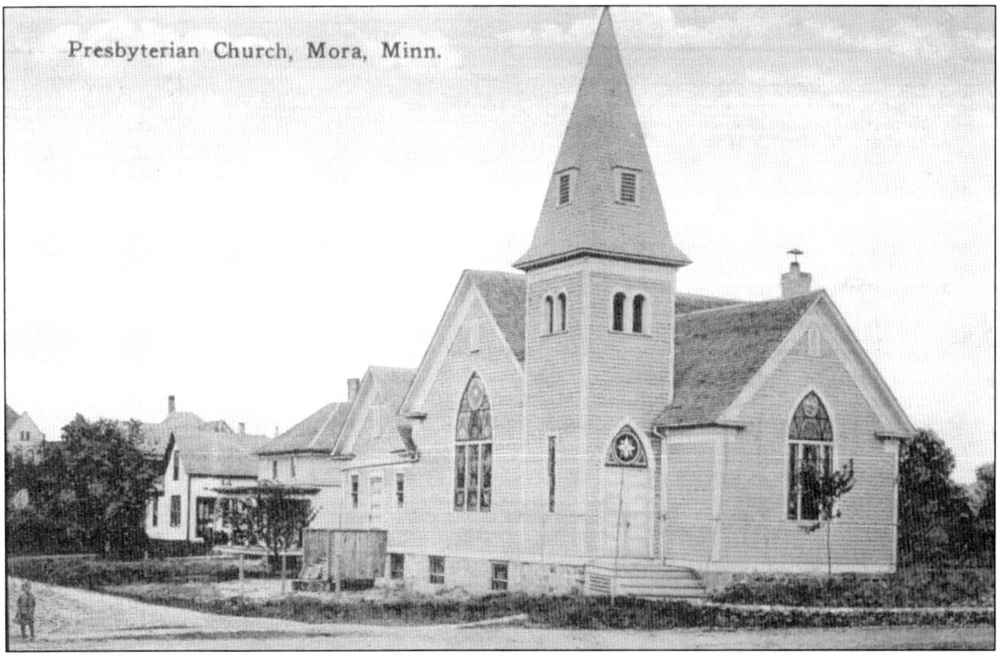

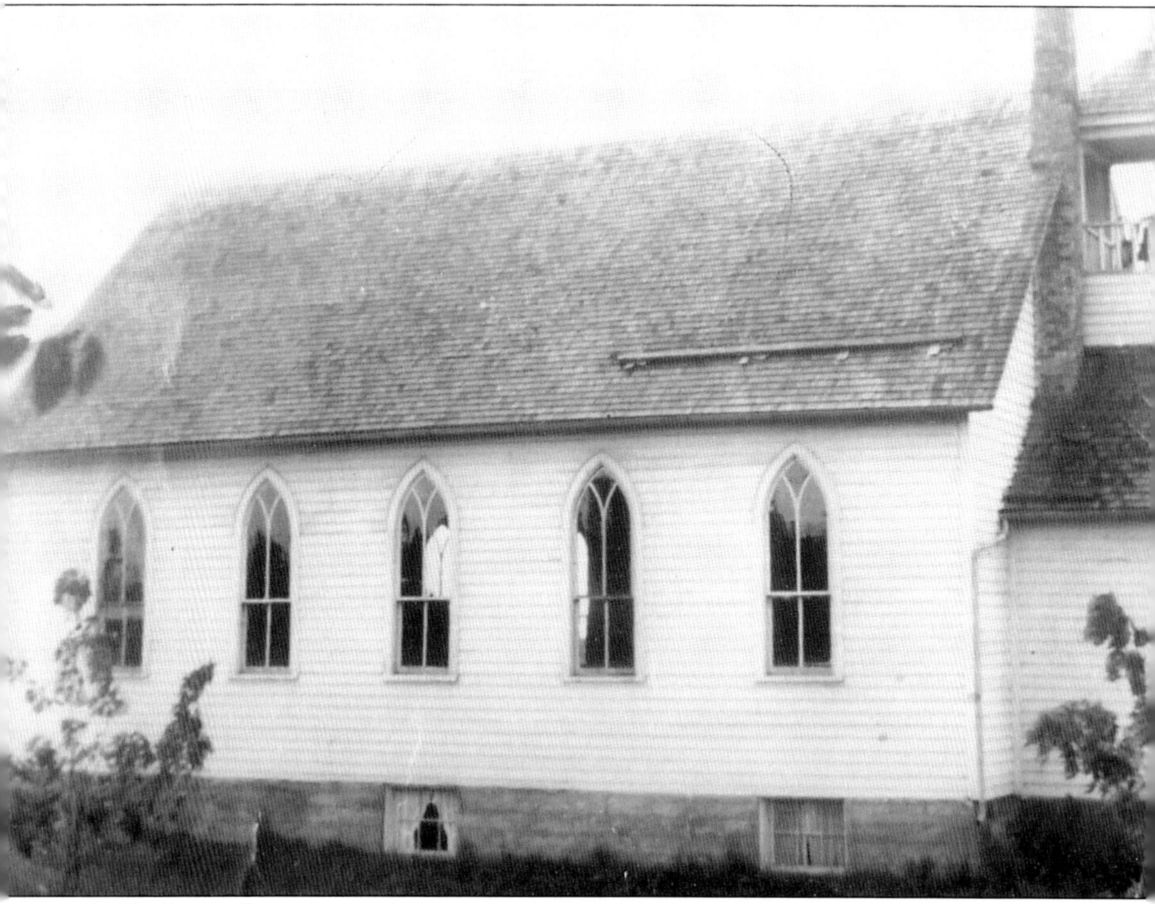

The Baptist denomination began in Sweden in 1848 when a Danish minister baptized five adults near Gothenburg. Because Lutheranism was Sweden's official state religion, Swedish Baptists lacked religious freedom and experienced persecution that made working and supporting their families difficult. Beginning in the 1850s, many Swedish Baptists immigrated to America, and some settled in Kanabec County. On November 20, 1892, a group of eight Swedish Baptists, assisted by Rev. A. Blomgren of Stanchfield, met at the John Sundstrom home near Quamba to form a church. For a few years, the small congregation met in homes, and Sundstrom served as pastor, chairman, and Sunday school superintendent. In 1897, Reverend Blomgren agreed to be Quamba Baptist Church's regular pastor, and by 1902, the congregation had constructed its own church building, shown here, on land donated by Jonas Svenson.

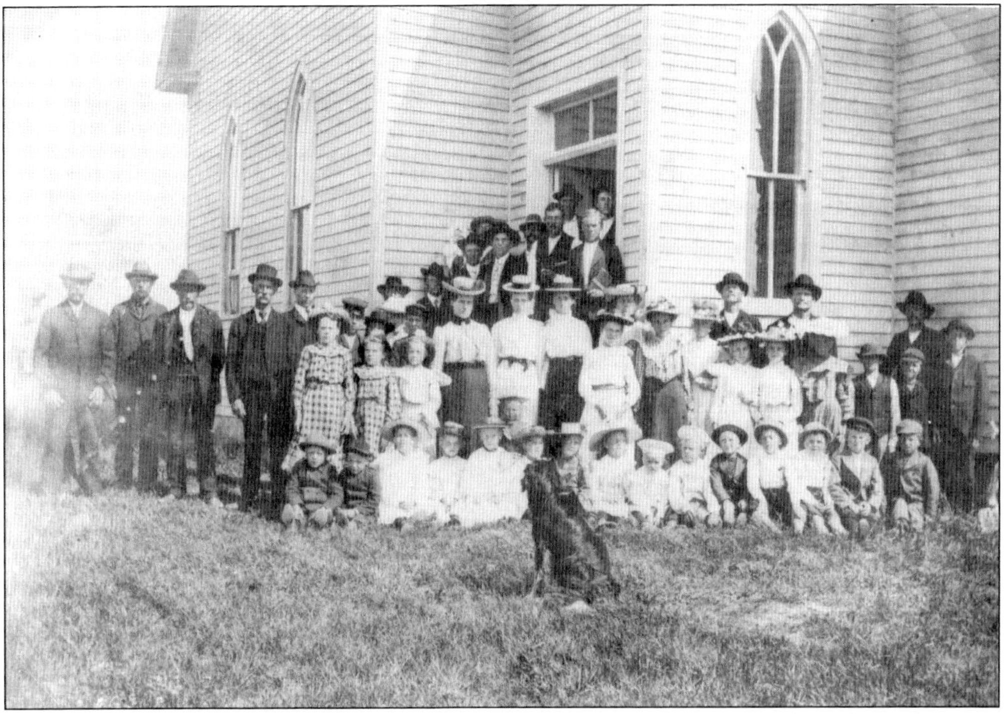

The congregation of the Comfort Baptist Church gathered for its photograph in the early 1900s. Most of the church's members transferred to Knife Lake Baptist in the first decades of the 20th century. When Knife Lake Baptist dissolved in 1937, its congregation began attending services at Emmanuel Baptist in Mora.

Ogilvie's first Sunday school, led by Mrs. Lockwood, met in empty railroad boxcars. When the Ogilvie schoolhouse was built, the Sunday school transferred there. Parents attended classes alongside their children. In 1900, Oric Ogilvie Whited donated two village lots for a church, and by 1902, the building was complete. The church, shown here, began as a community church but later elected to follow the Methodist denomination.

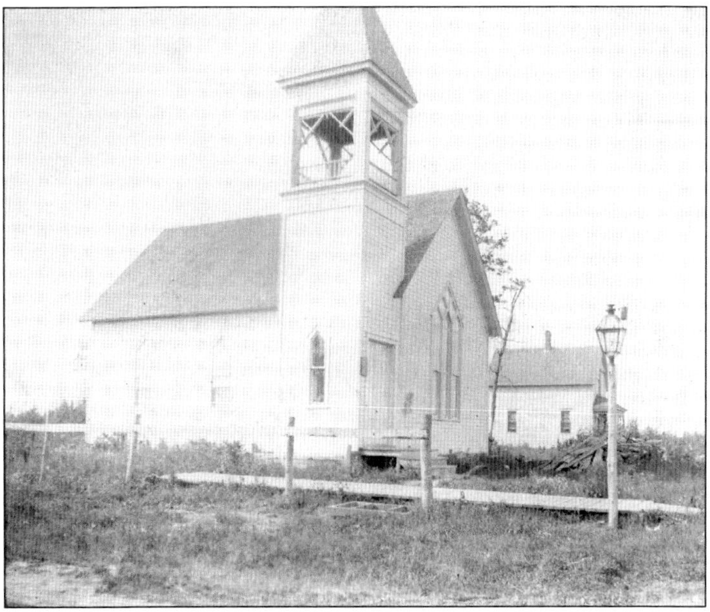

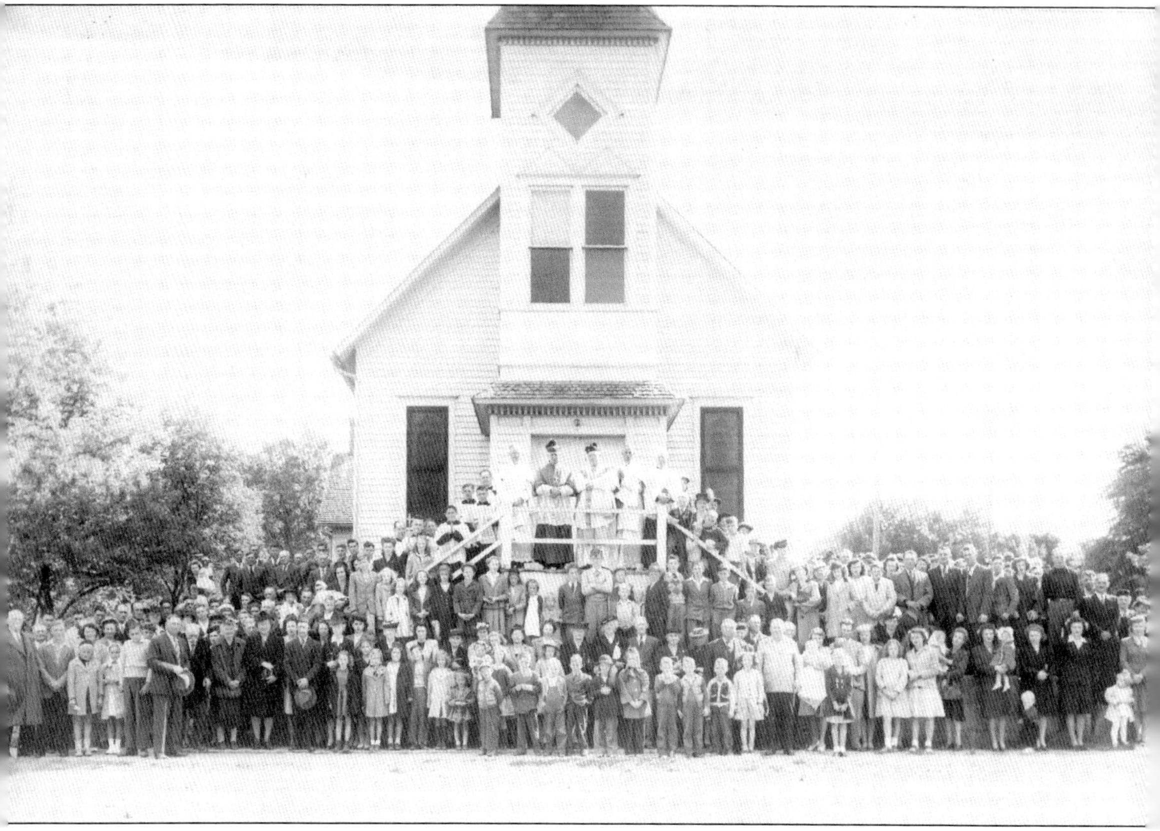

St. Mary's Catholic Church in Mora was incorporated on April 23, 1895. Mass was celebrated in the home of parish trustee James Golden until the first St. Mary's Church building, shown here, was completed in early December. The church was a modest, wooden structure, 26 by 60 feet, but it was large enough to accommodate Mora's small Catholic community. Fr. Patrick Mooney was the parish's first pastor, and founding members included Ambrose Crusoe, John Hayes, Moses Mayhew, James Walsh, W.J. Lawler, John Keenan, Henry Harrison, Mary Hayes, Patrick Glynn, Martin Murphy, Andrew McMahn, Christine Cooper, Michael Regan, Thomas Powers, John Bongaarts, Peter Zetterberg, John O'Donnell, and Alexander Burnett. This photograph was taken 50 years later, in 1945, at a parish anniversary celebration. In 1953, the first St. Mary's Church was torn down to make way for a modern, brick building.

Eight

Entertainment before Television

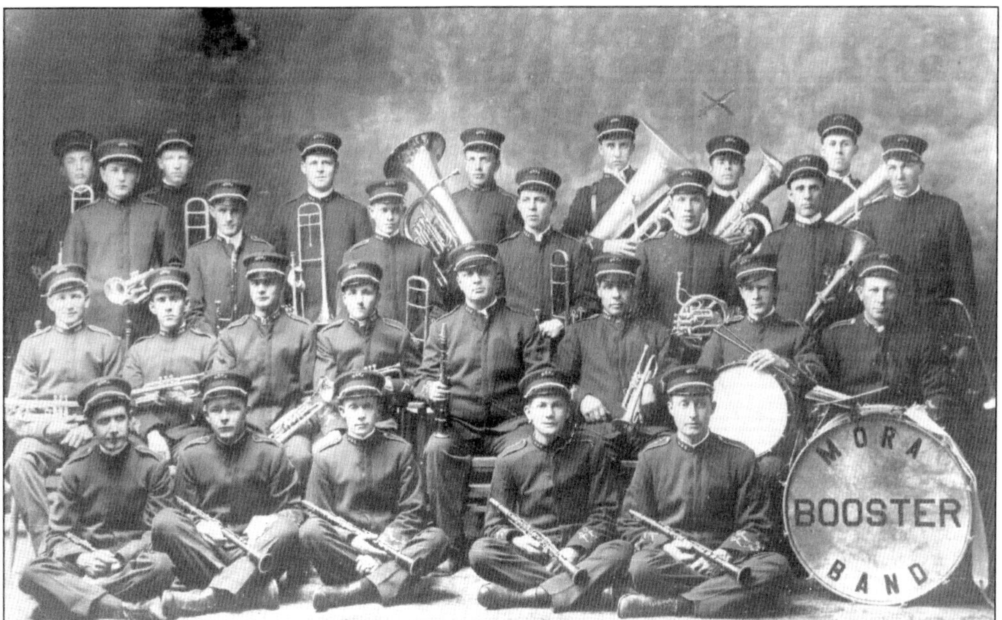

No matter how hard Kanabec County residents worked at their farms, businesses, and schools, they always found plenty of time for fun. Community bands provided enjoyable learning opportunities for aspiring musicians, who entertained their fellow citizens in parades and concerts. The Mora Booster Band posed for this photograph in 1914.

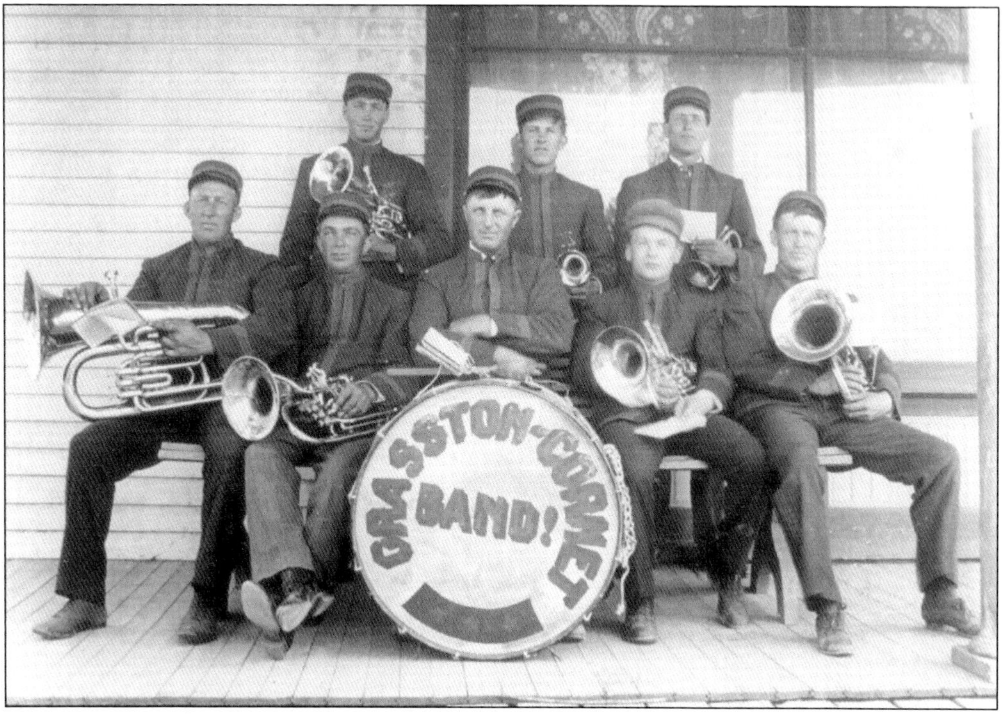

Communities took great pride in their local bands and often organized fundraisers to earn money for instruments, uniforms, and music. Band members practiced long and hard to live up to their communities' expectations. The Grasston Cornet Band posed on the porch of a local business for this early 1900s photograph.

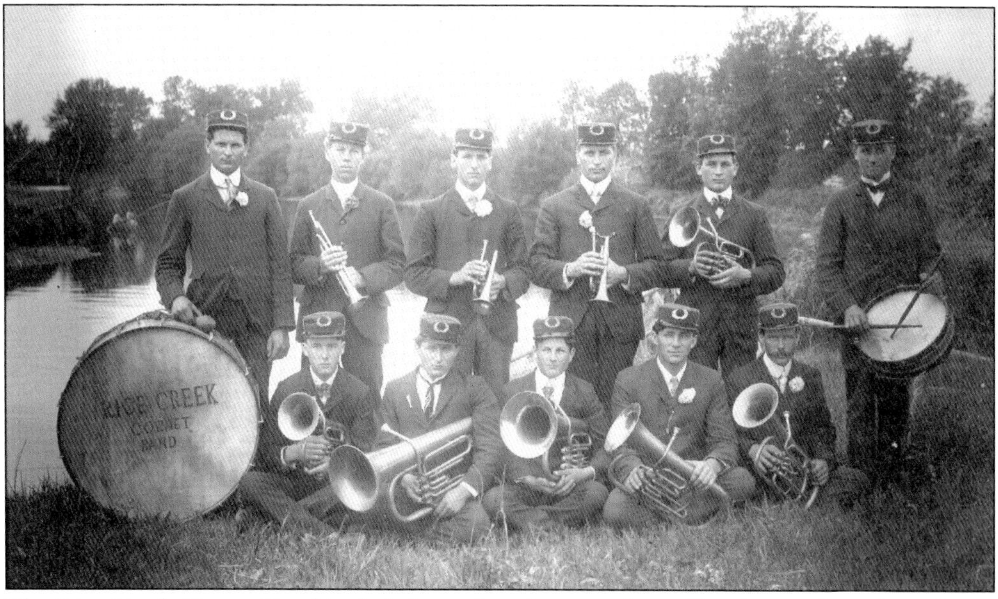

The Rice Creek Cornet Band included members from southern Kanabec and northern Isanti Counties. Along with marches, local bands learned a variety of popular songs so their audiences could sing along. Notice the various sizes of horns, the well-used snare and bass drums, and the festive flowers some band members wore in their buttonholes.

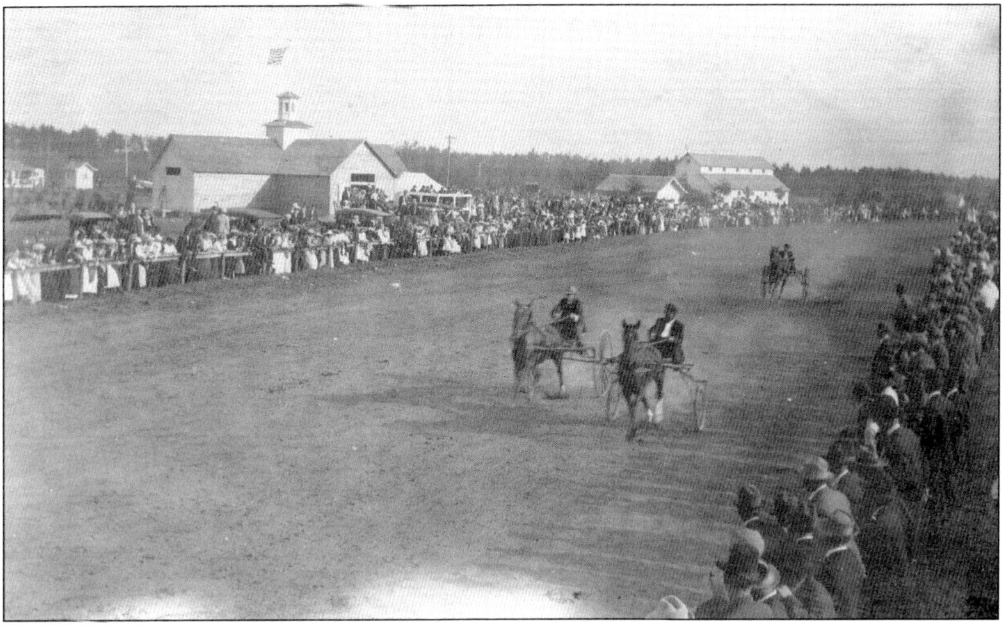

Kanabec County hosted its first county fair on September 29–30, 1896. For a mere 25¢, fairgoers could inspect exhibits created by their fellow citizens, listen to speakers including Gov. David Clough, enjoy a performance by Mora's community band, partake of an elaborate chicken dinner with pumpkin pie for dessert, play games, and watch a variety of races. This harness race took place at the fairgrounds in the early 1900s.

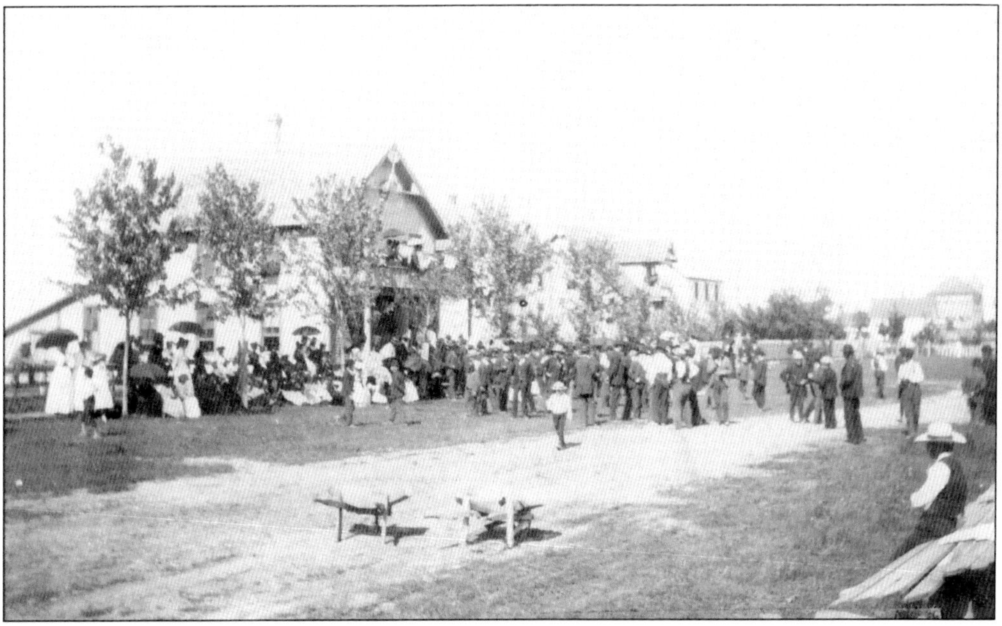

The Fourth of July was a major holiday in early Kanabec County. Residents gathered for parades, programs, dances, races, games, and fireworks. On July 4, 1892, folks turned out in Mora to watch a wheelbarrow race. John Miller captured first place, and Jack Hurd took second. Ole Westling lost control of his wheelbarrow and bolted into the crowd, slightly injuring one unnamed female spectator.

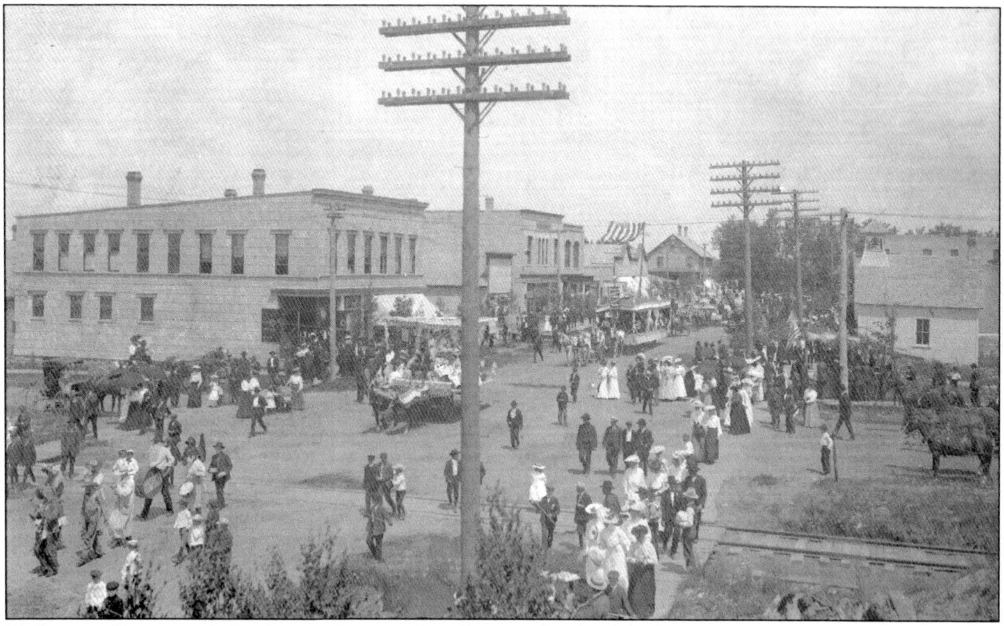

Elaborate floats and the Mora Cornet Band were the highlights of the July 4, 1910, parade in Mora. Hanson & Ziegler won $20 for their first prize float while the Christian Endeavor Society finished second to claim a $10 prize. The parade was followed by a program of singing and speaking at the opera house, a baseball game, and numerous sporting contests including races and a wrestling match.

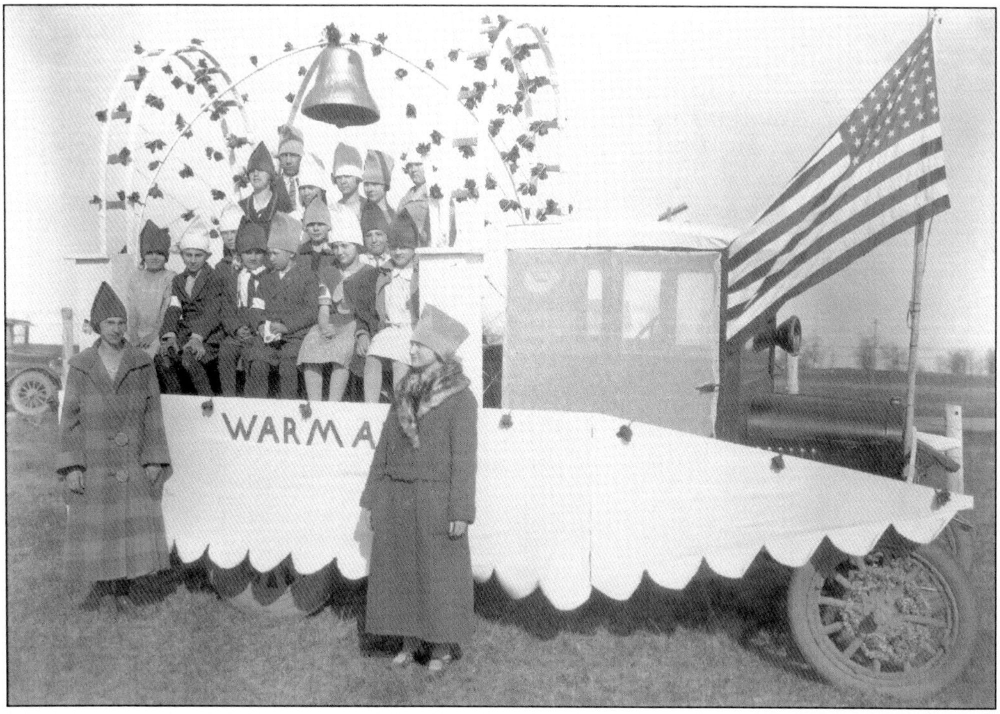

The Warman schoolchildren created this float for a local parade in the 1920s. Notice the patriotic theme, which was very popular at that time.

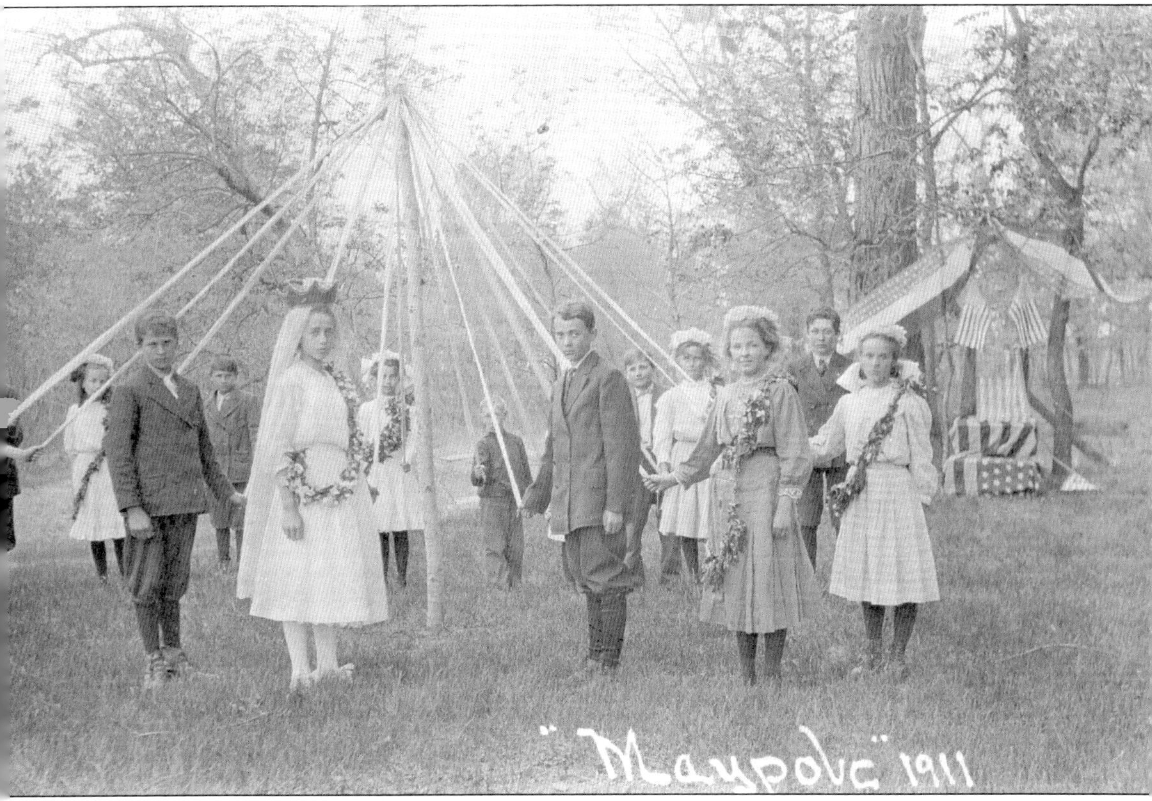

These Ogilvie schoolchildren danced around a maypole to celebrate May Day in 1911. Each child held the end of a brightly colored ribbon, which he or she wound around the pole to create an intricate pattern. As the dance progressed, the children retraced their steps to unwind the ribbons. Hortense Conger (with the crown in front) was selected as Queen of May that year. Her court included Clifford Conger, Gladys Anderson, Myrtle Spindler, William Neiman, Bessie White, Alfred Starry, Rachel Shipton, Mauritz Westlund, Annie Johnson, Harry Toussaint, Ardis Lewis, Bryan Jones, Ella Johnson, Roy Young, Gladys Young, and Wallace Warda. Notice the children's Sunday best clothes, the girls' wreathes of flowers, and the patriotic theme of the booth in the background.

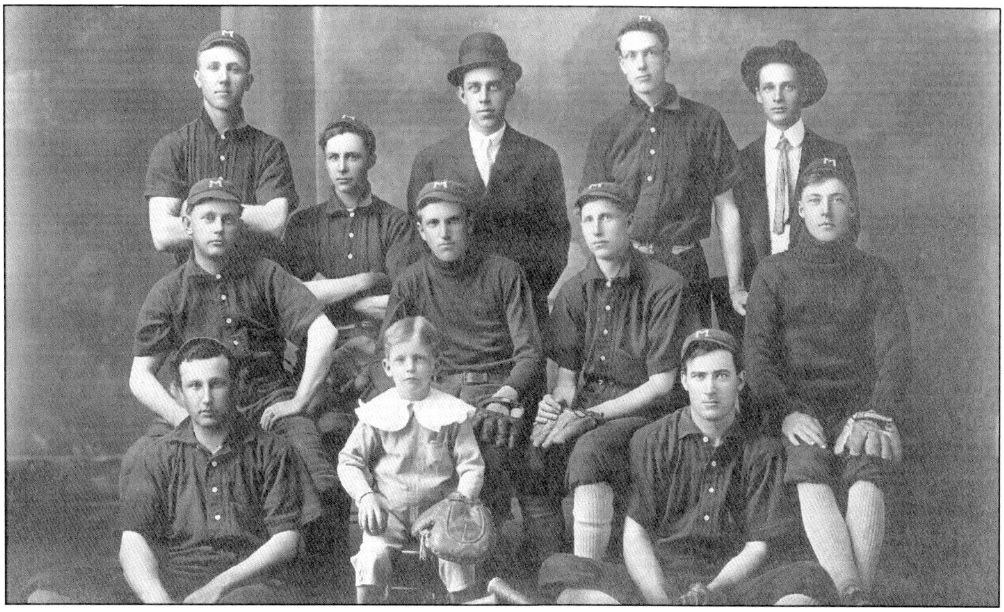

Baseball was the sport of choice in early Kanabec County. The Mora team was organized at a meeting in April 1907. Pat Newport, who was elected chairman, led a committee in drawing up a constitution for the new organization. H.H. Mandefelt was selected as team manager and authorized to secure a pitcher. He also scheduled games, which were played at the diamond on the fairgrounds.

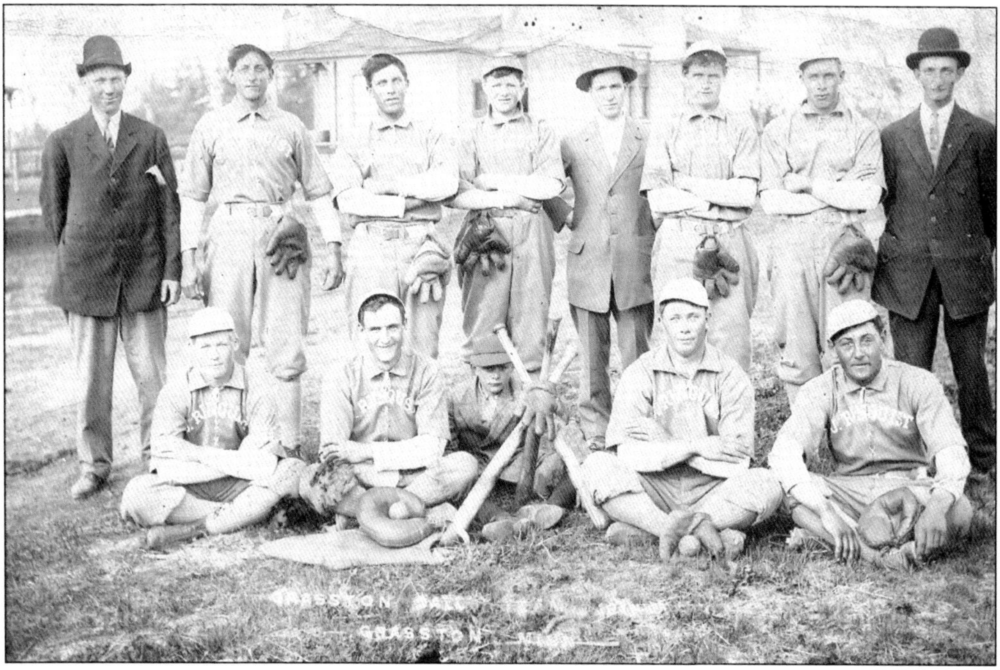

The Grasston baseball team gave the Mora team an "awful scare" on May 28, 1911. Mora had defeated Grasston three weeks earlier, and Grasston was determined to win the rematch, even going so far as to add a university pitcher to improve their lineup. Despite Grasston's best efforts, Mora's team still won 10-9. Baseball game admission cost 25¢ for adults and 10¢ for children.

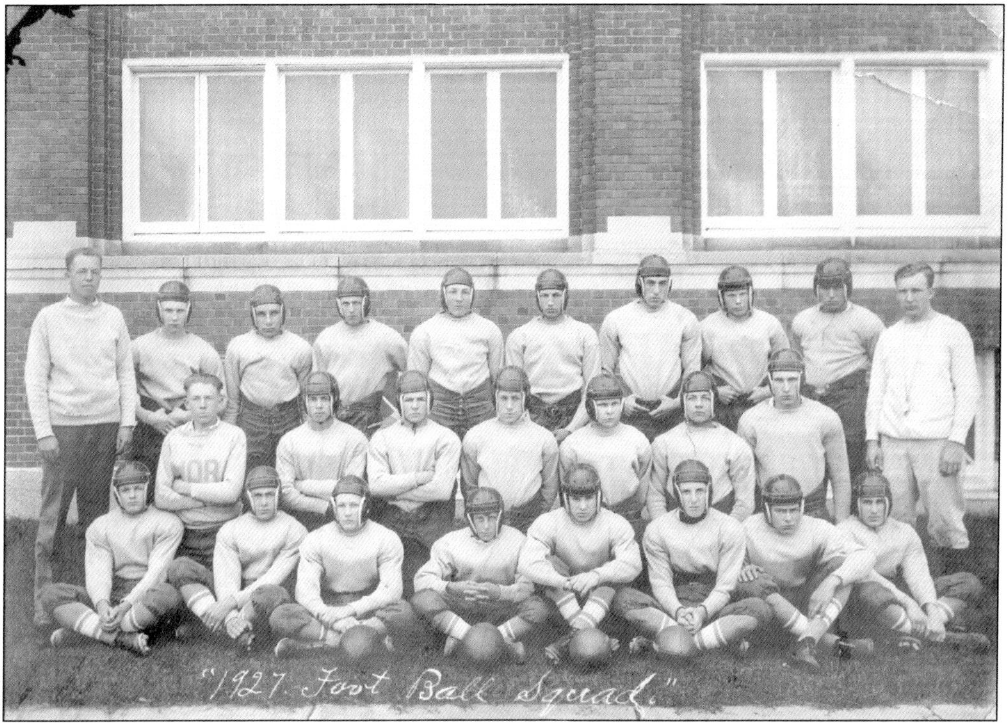

Mora High School's football squad, led by Coach Zemjahn and Captain Dixon, played only three games during the 1927 season. They lost the first one to St. Francis 13-12 on October 14, lost the second one to Pine City 12-6 on October 28, and finally won the last one over St. Francis 13-0 on November 4.

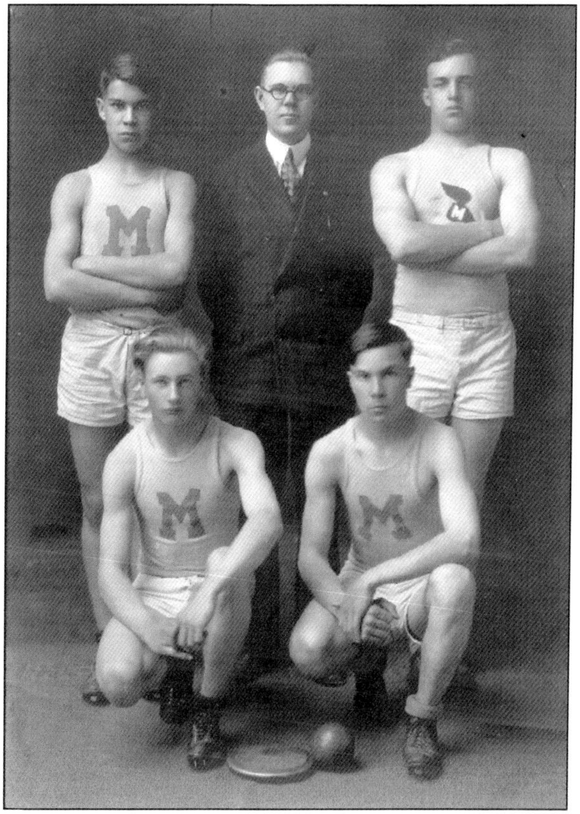

Mora High School boasted a proud track and field team in the 1920s: (kneeling left) Helmer Sundstrom, (kneeling right) James Donavan, (standing left) Rass Boyle, (standing middle) Coach Slettendahl, and (standing right) Raymond Edin.

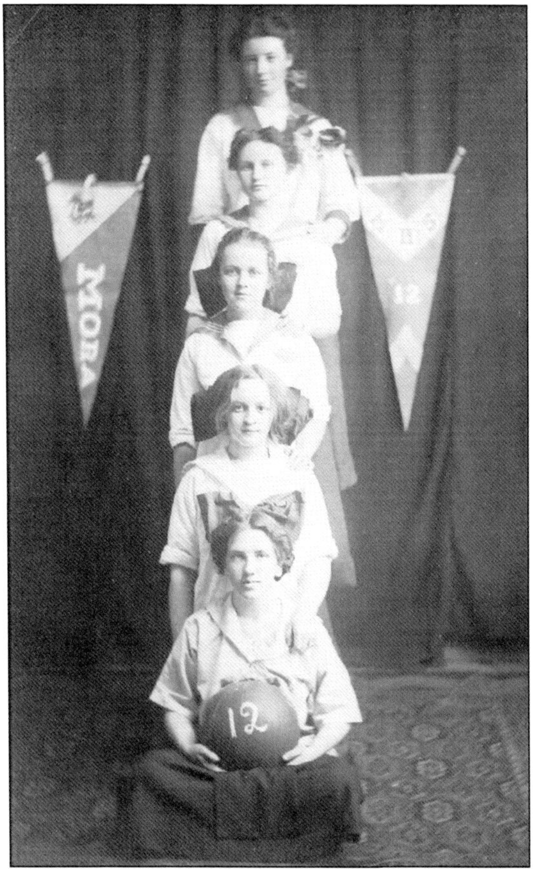

Girls' athletic programs were relatively rare in the early 1900s, but by the 1910s, girls' basketball was beginning to draw fans. Mora High School's team posed for its photograph in 1912: (top to bottom) Mary Powers, Margaret Connors, Grace Peterson, Frances Farrington, and Gretchen Schnittger.

Mora High School's boys' basketball team posed proudly for its photograph in 1916. Basketball games drew scores of fans to the old school gym. Teams competed from late fall through early spring in both regular season games and tournaments. Notice the Mora team's basketball shoes, knee-high socks, and caps.

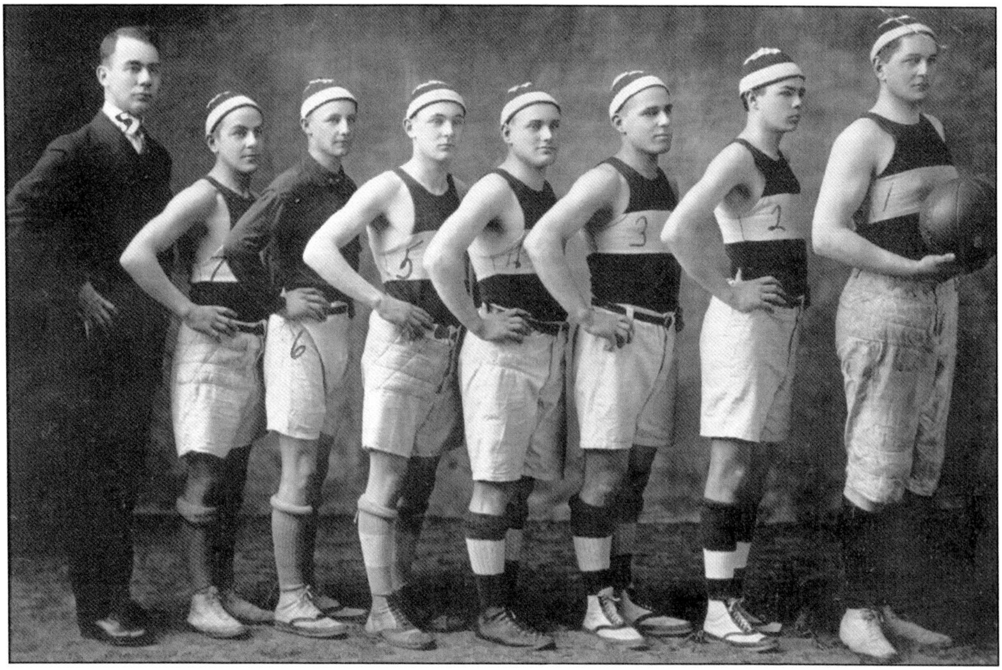

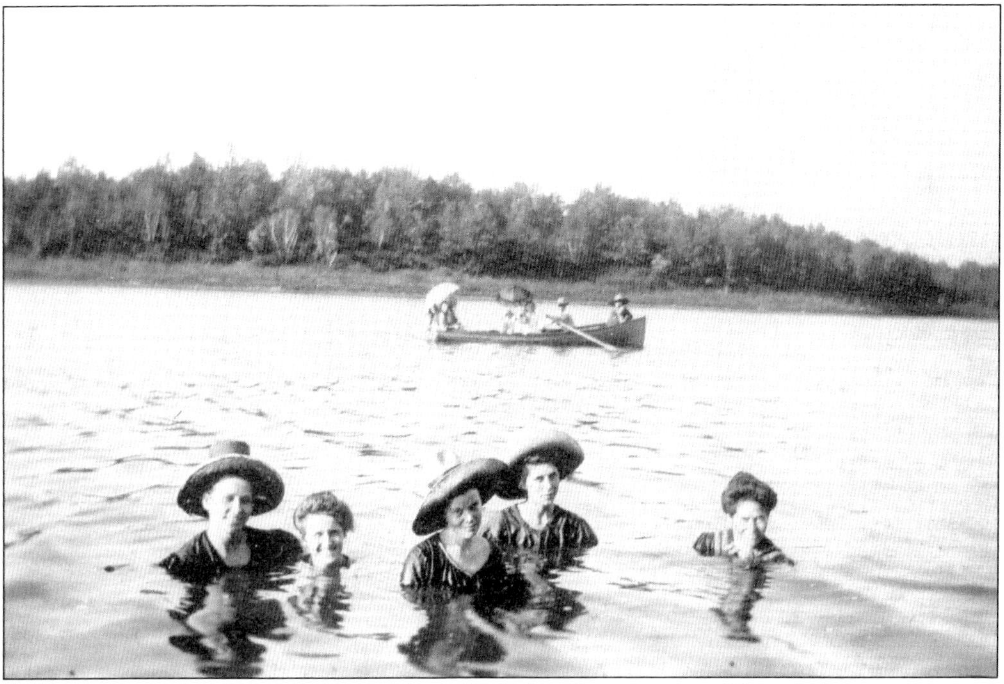

Kanabec County residents have always been fond of outdoor activities. These ladies were enjoying a refreshing dip in Lake Mora in 1907: (from left to right) Mrs. J.O. Werntz, Mrs. R.W. Pope, Mrs. J.C. Cravens, Mrs. John Grahek, and Mrs. C.E. Williams. Notice their bathing costumes and hats. Other ladies preferred to take a ride in a rowboat. They used their parasols to shield them from the summer sun.

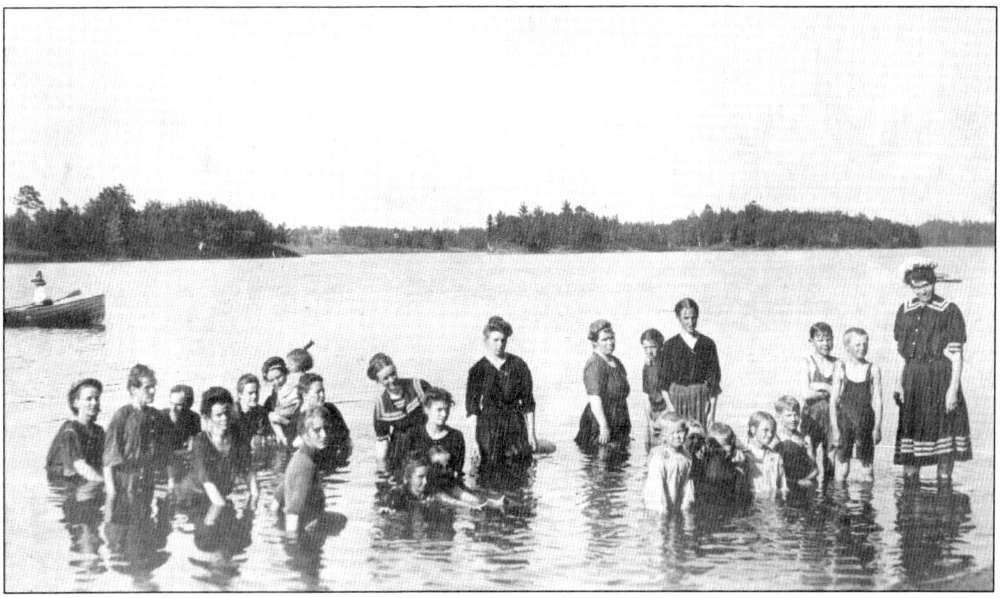

This group of women and children went for a swimming outing at Lake Mora in 1907 to find some relief from the summer heat. This photograph was taken from Maple Avenue looking north.

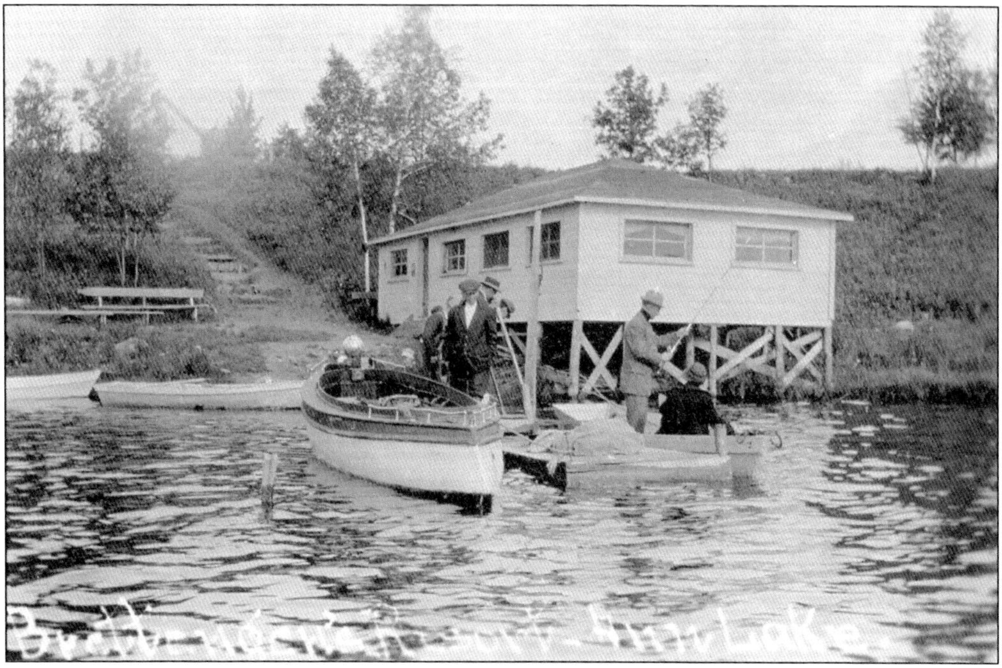

On June 7, 1913, Billy McCall debuted "Billy's Place," a new pavilion on Ann Lake. The grand opening featured a dance for 75¢ and supper for an additional 25¢. McCall also built a launch called The Arrow for fishing trips and pleasure outings on the lake. In 1915, Carl Brettingen bought the pavilion and renamed it Pleasant Hill Resort.

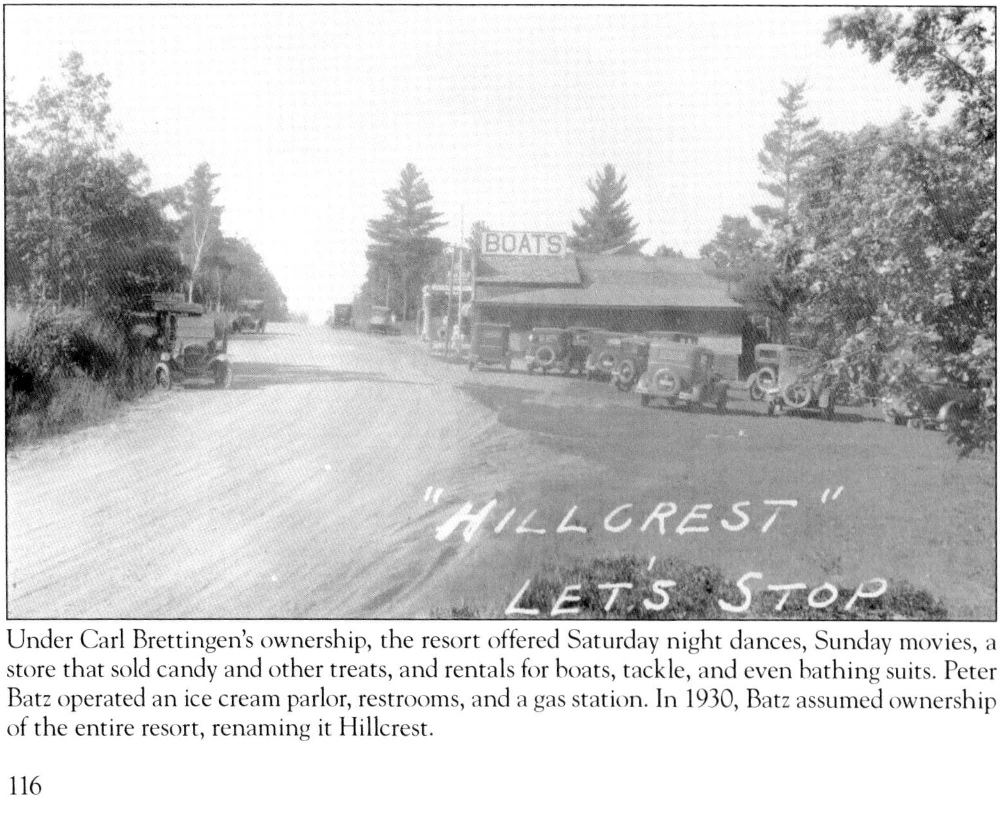

Under Carl Brettingen's ownership, the resort offered Saturday night dances, Sunday movies, a store that sold candy and other treats, and rentals for boats, tackle, and even bathing suits. Peter Batz operated an ice cream parlor, restrooms, and a gas station. In 1930, Batz assumed ownership of the entire resort, renaming it Hillcrest.

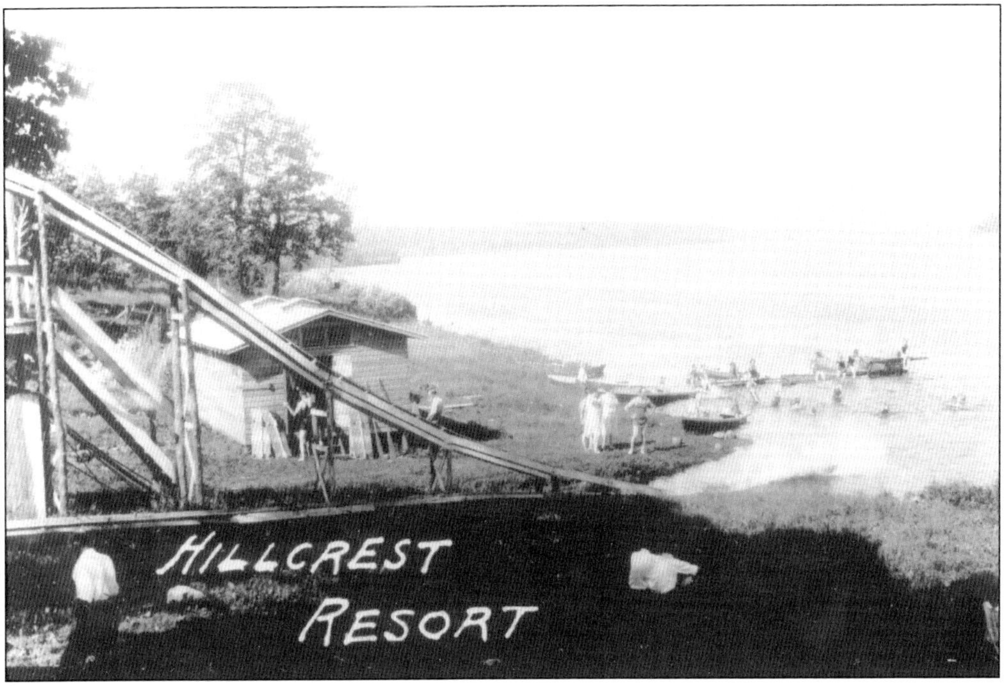

Peter Batz expanded his business to include campgrounds, cabins, a new store, and a new pavilion. A few years later, Joe and Alice Grace bought Hillcrest. The resort burned in 1948 but was soon rebuilt.

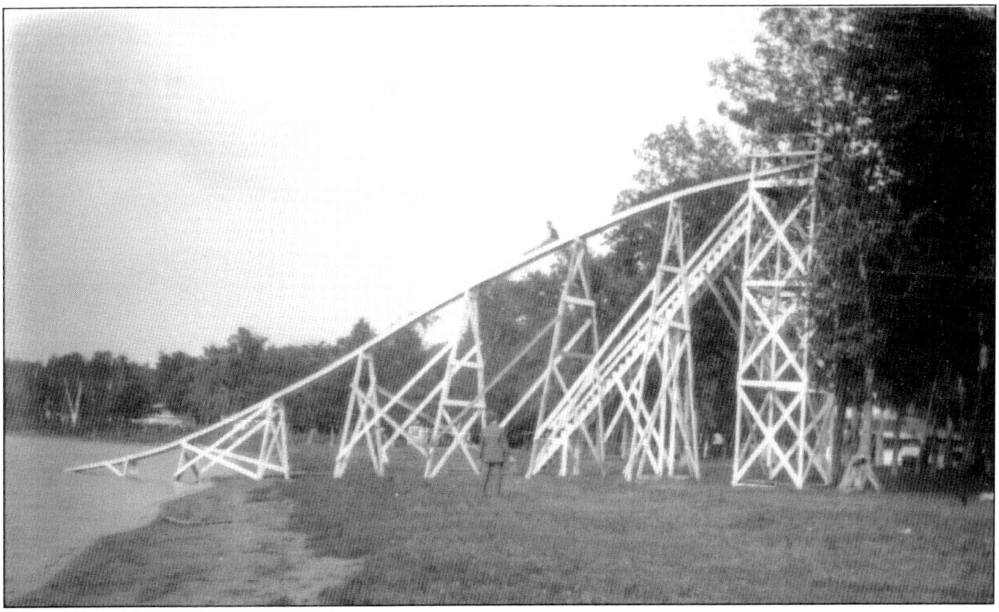
This gigantic slide was a popular feature at Hillcrest Resort for many years. It was used as a water slide in the summer and a snow slide in the winter.

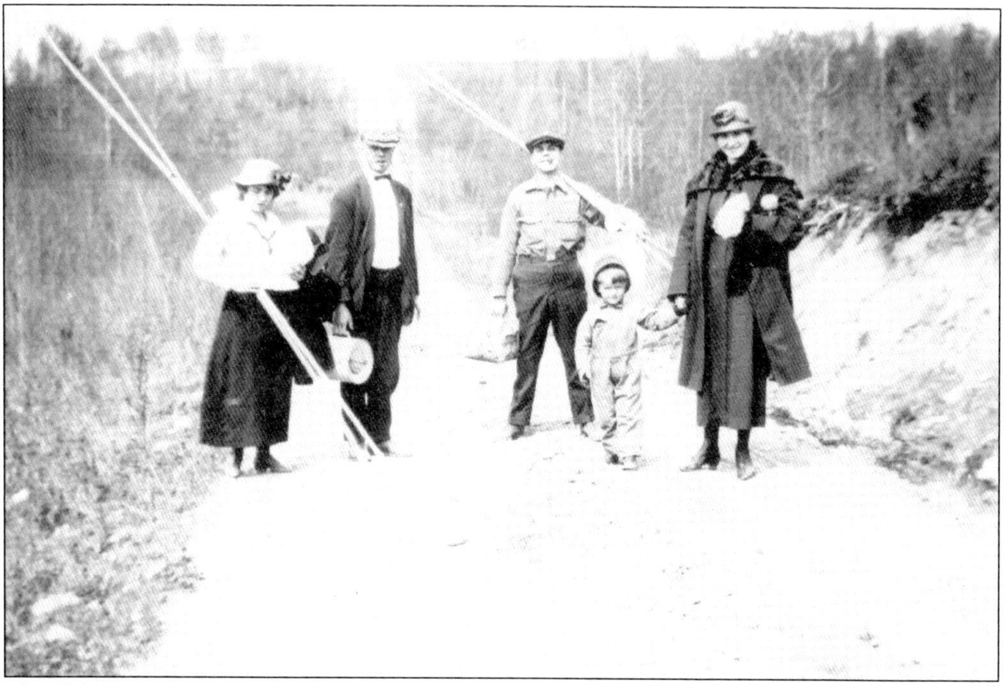

This fishing party was all set for a day at one of Kanabec County's many lakes. Notice their cane fishing poles and picnic supplies.

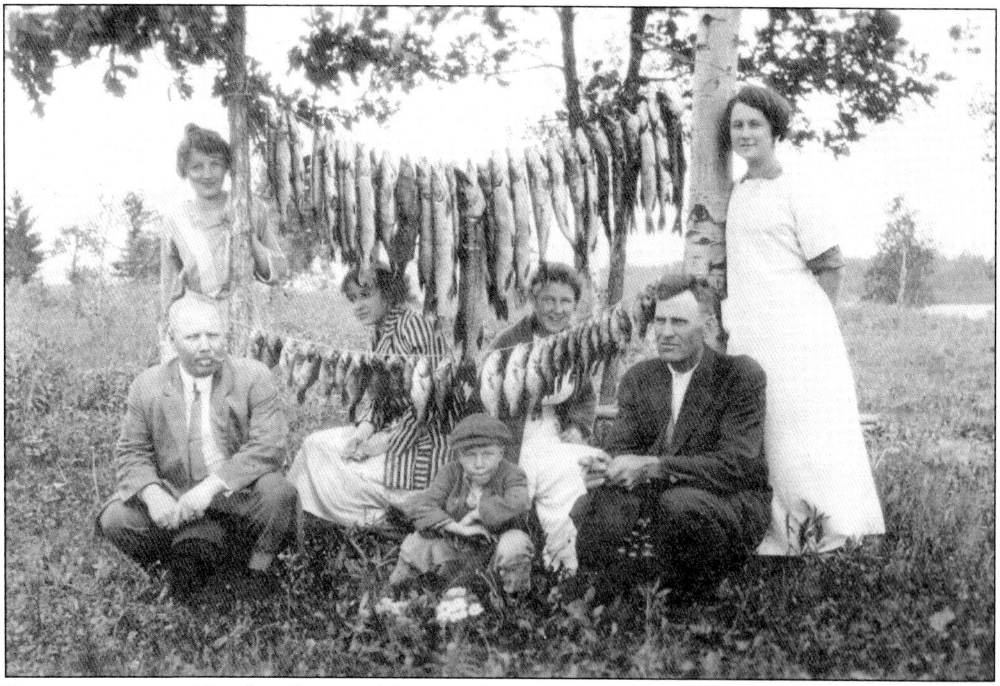

Success met these Kanabec County fishing enthusiasts in the form of over four dozen fish. While some of the fish were probably eaten fresh, others would have been dried, salted, or canned so they could be enjoyed even when summer was over.

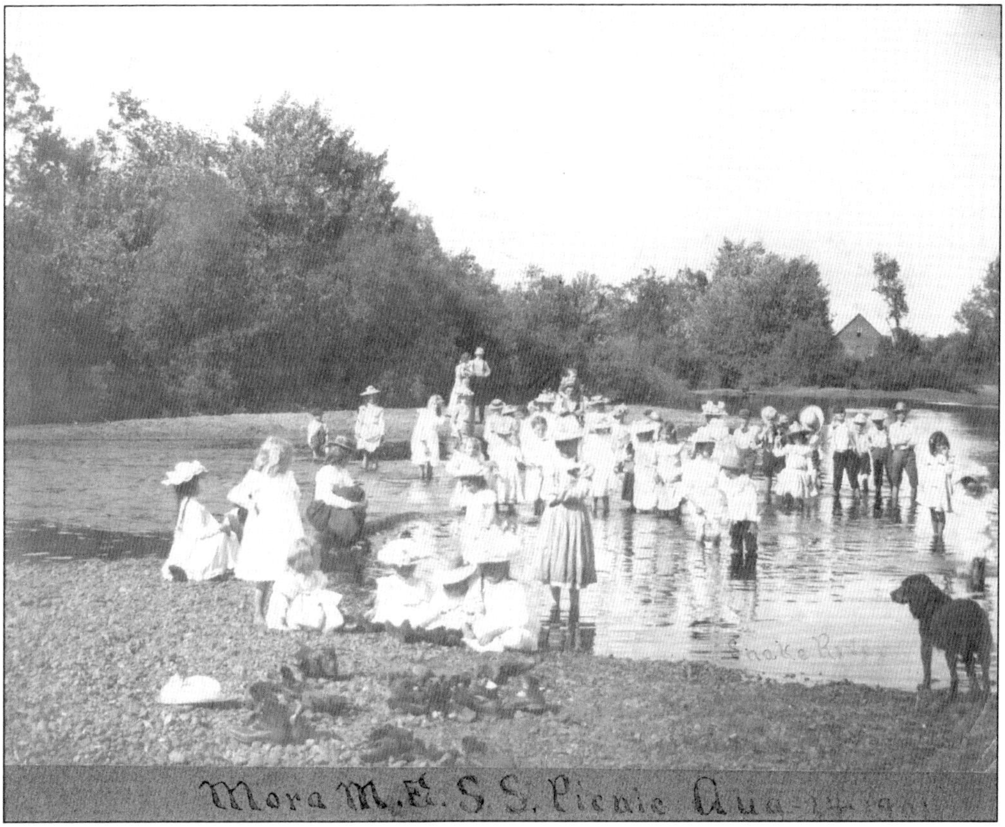

Picnics were a favorite summer activity for Kanabec County residents. The Methodist Episcopal Sunday school pupils and parents gathered near Mora's railroad bridge for their annual picnic on August 14, 1901. Upon arrival at the picnic spot, the picnickers hurried directly into the cool water of the nearby river. Even after consuming a huge meal, nearly everybody had some room left over for a special treat of ice cream.

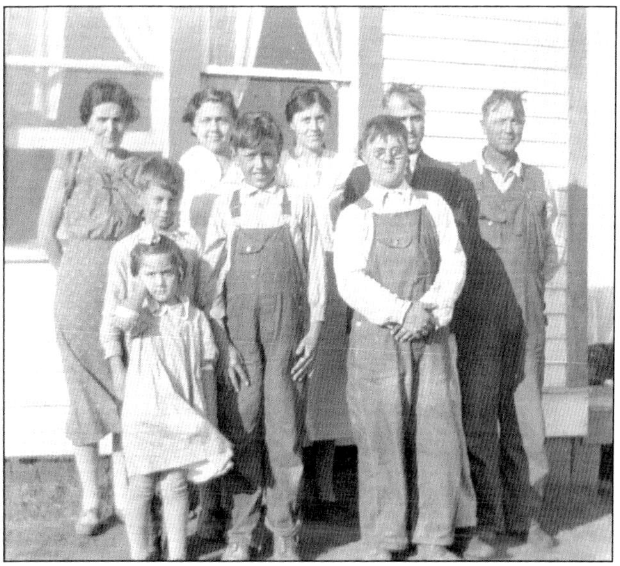

Family gatherings were an important form of recreation in early Kanabec County. Families got together for Sunday dinners, picnics, parties, weddings, and even work days. This photograph of the Points family was taken at Sunny Slope Farm. Curtis Points, his children Kenneth, Elma, Dorotha, John, Ansel, and Helen, and his sister-in-law and brother Belle and Ross Points all smiled for the camera while Curtis's wife, Callie, took the picture.

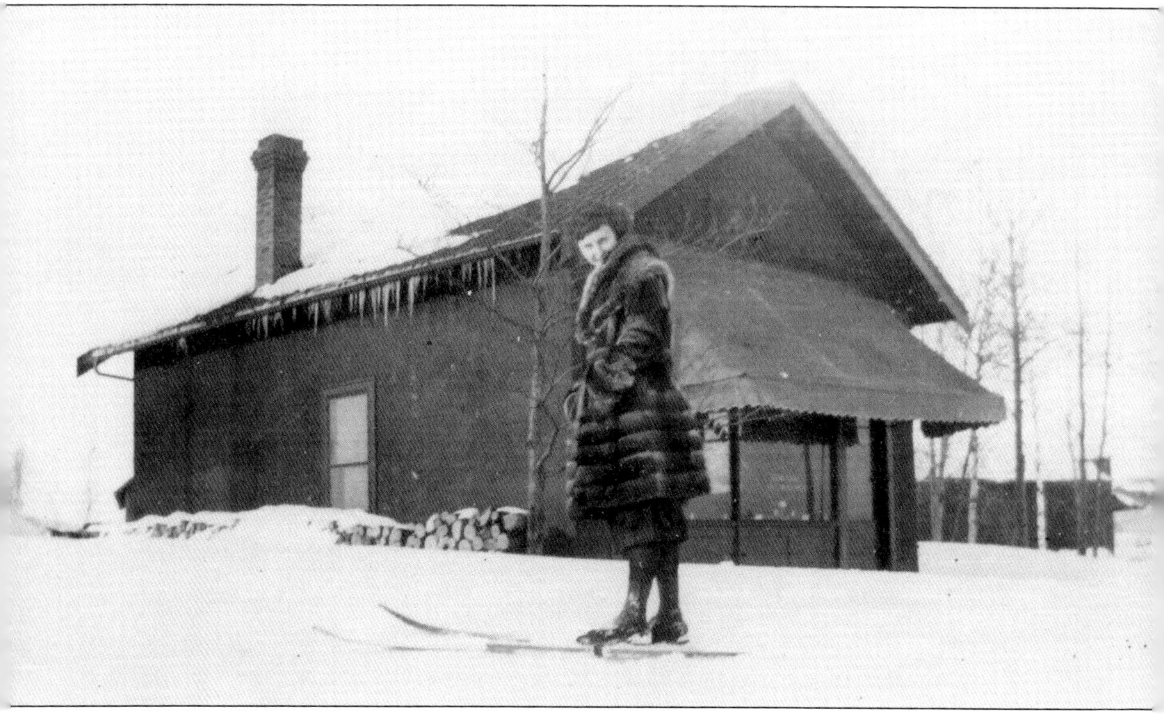

Winter sports like cross-country skiing have always been just as popular as summer sports among Kanabec County residents. Mary Powers Woodbeck, clad in her raccoon coat, skied to her job at Quamba State Bank nearly every morning in the 1920s and 1930s. About 40 years later, in 1973, Mora hosted the first Vasaloppet cross-country ski race. Modeled after a ski race in Mora's sister city, Mora, Sweden, the first Vasaloppet was sponsored by the Mora Jaycees, Mora Commercial Club, and Kanabec Conservation Club, and 96 skiers completed the 30-kilometer course. Over the years, the Vasaloppet has grown into a major annual event with thousands of skiers, a variety of race options, and an international exchange program between the United States, Sweden, Japan, and China. The Vasaloppet is a celebration of cross-country skiing and Kanabec County's Swedish heritage.

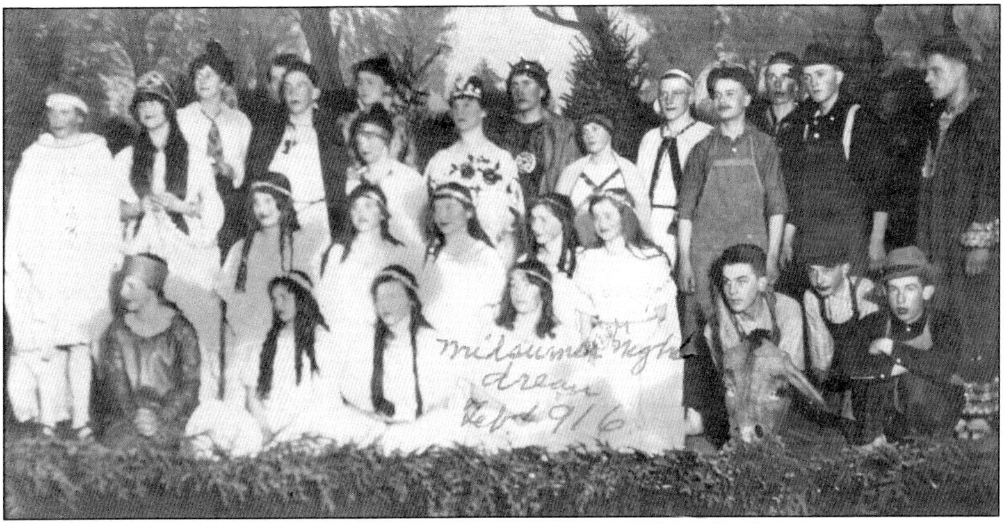

On February 11, 1916, Mora High School students presented William Shakespeare's *A Midsummer Night's Dream* at the opera house. Even though this marked the students' first attempt at such a production, a *Kanabec County Times* reviewer raved about their performance, complimenting the young people on their fine acting and offering special recognition to Ruth Serline for her portrayal of the fairy Puck.

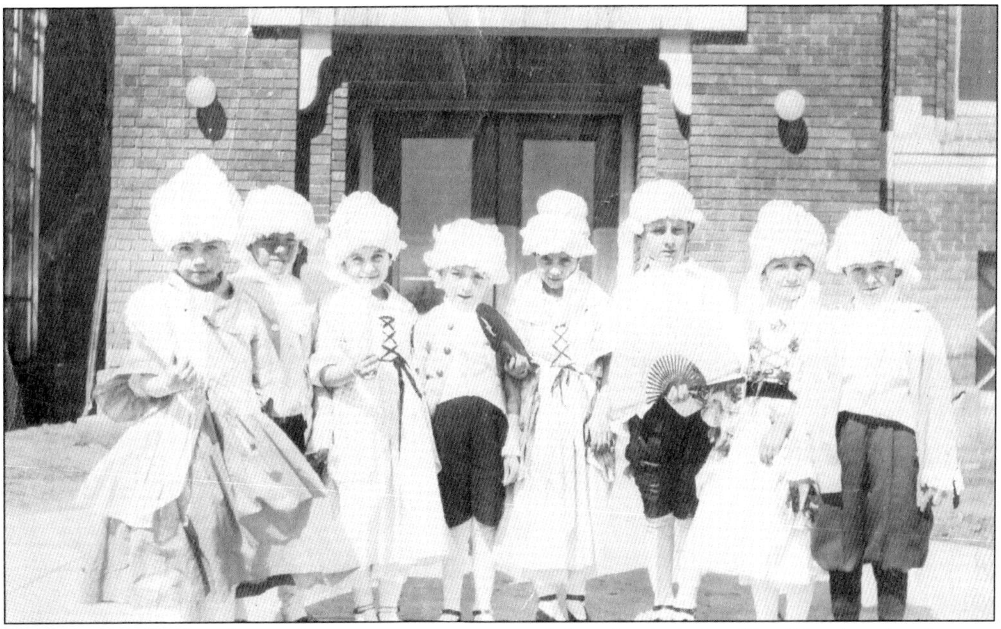

Elementary school students often put on programs and plays for their families, friends, schoolmates, and sometimes even the general public. These Mora children, including Raymond Mattson (second from left), Ruth Crumpacker (third from left), and Ralph Fairbanks (fourth from left), were portraying colonial ladies and gentleman.

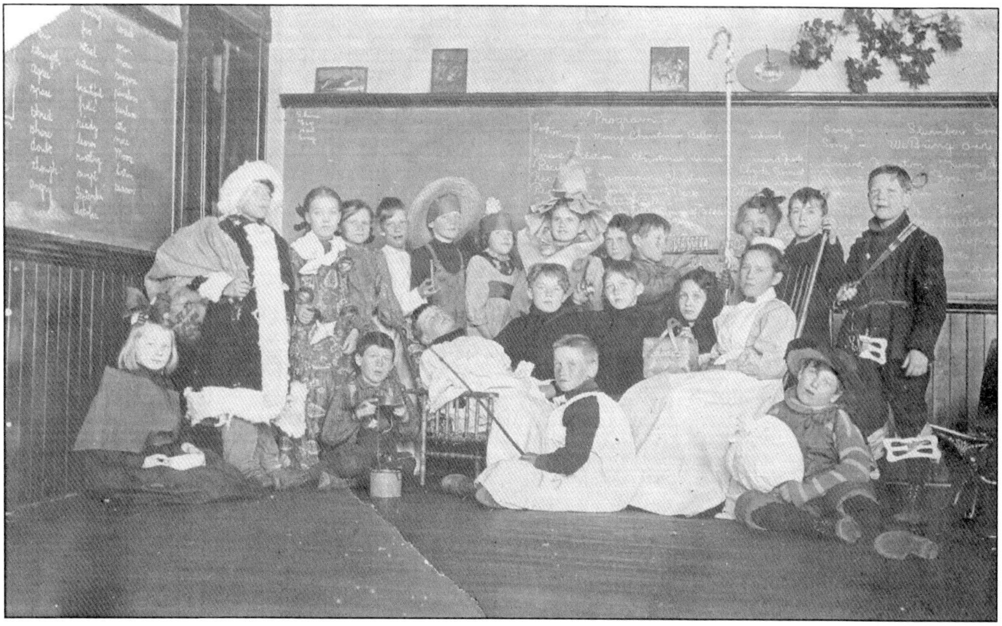

These children were presenting a Christmas program in their classroom. Notice the children's elaborate costumes, the program schedule on the blackboard behind them, and the neatly written spelling words on the blackboard to the left.

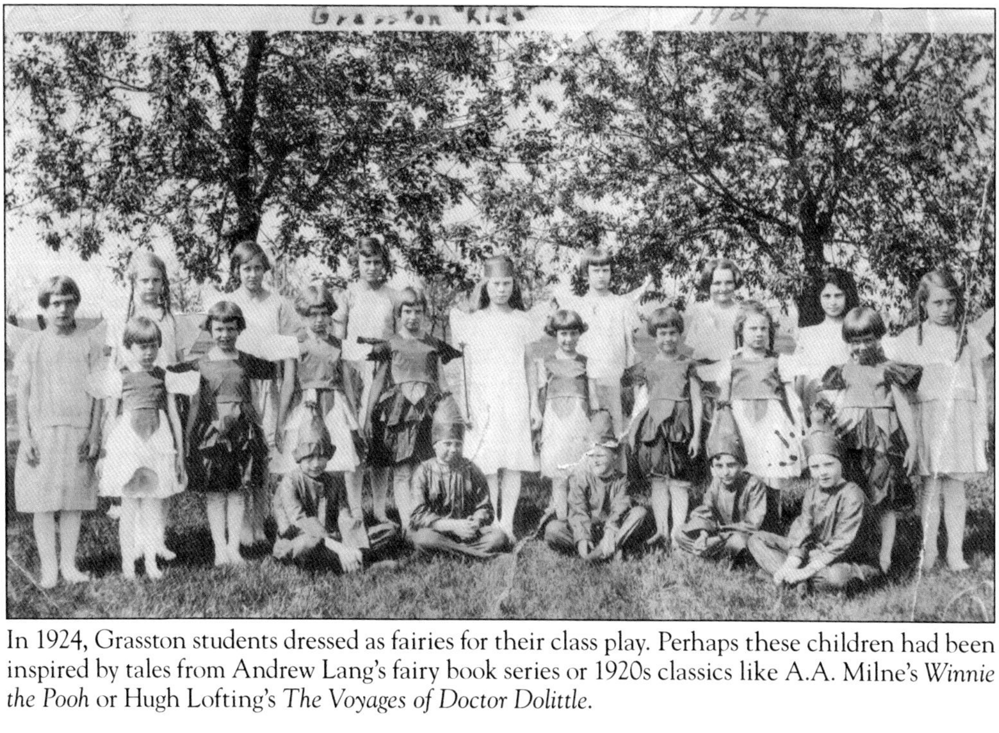

In 1924, Grasston students dressed as fairies for their class play. Perhaps these children had been inspired by tales from Andrew Lang's fairy book series or 1920s classics like A.A. Milne's *Winnie the Pooh* or Hugh Lofting's *The Voyages of Doctor Dolittle*.

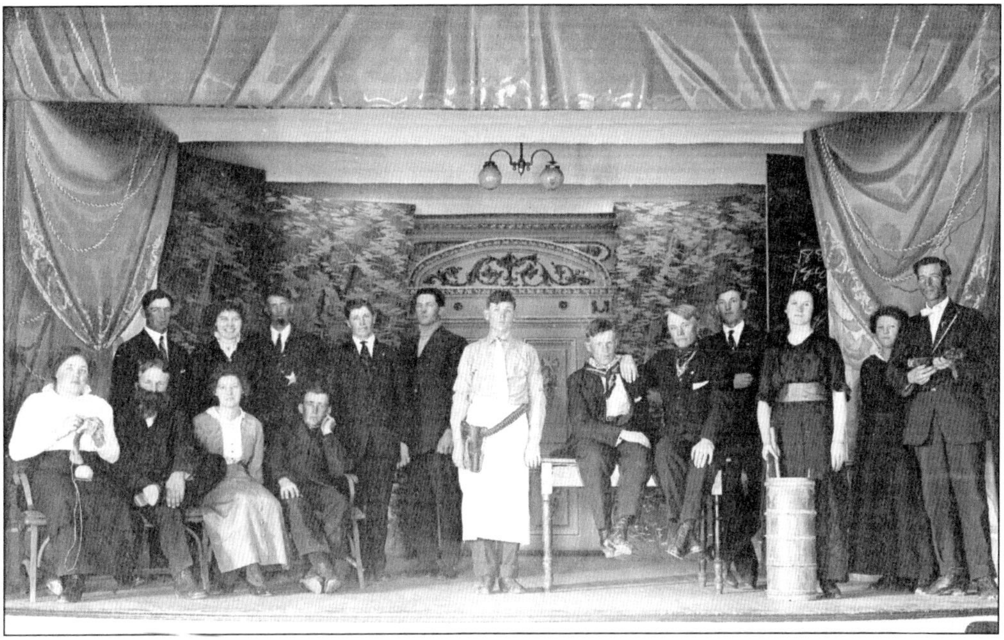

Students were not the only Kanabec County residents to put on plays and programs. Adults organized literary and dramatic societies and performed popular "home talent" plays on the stages of local opera houses. This cast of performers presented its play at Runquist's Opera House in Grasston in the 1910s.

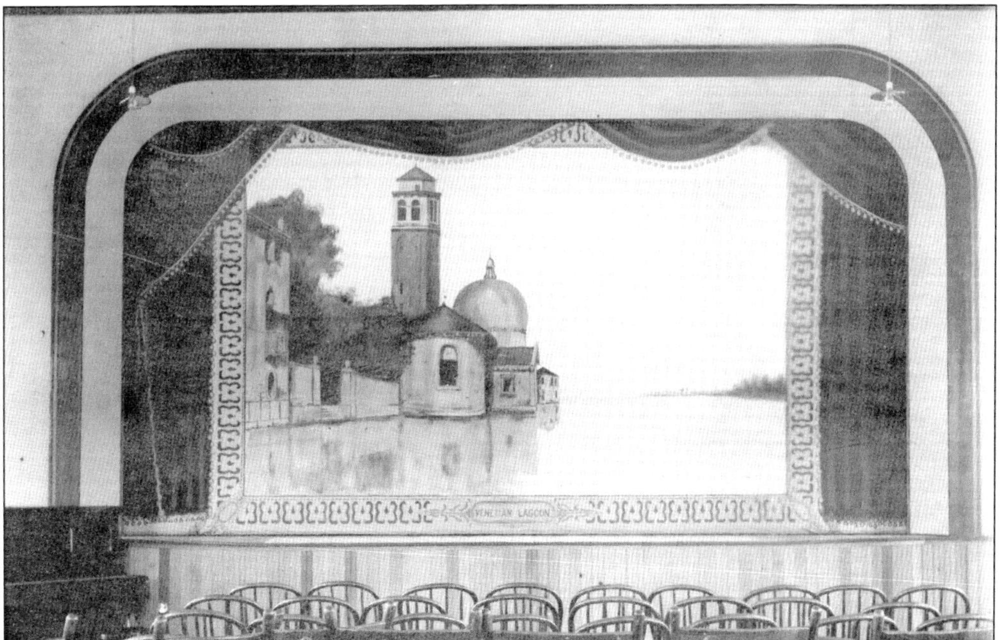

C.E. Williams built Mora's elaborate opera house in 1903 on Railroad Avenue. The opera house hosted Vaudeville acts, home talent plays, minstrel shows, school programs, medicine shows, lectures, masquerade balls, musicals, church festivals, and even roller-skating. In this photograph, the stage was hidden by a luxurious curtain featuring a Venetian scene.

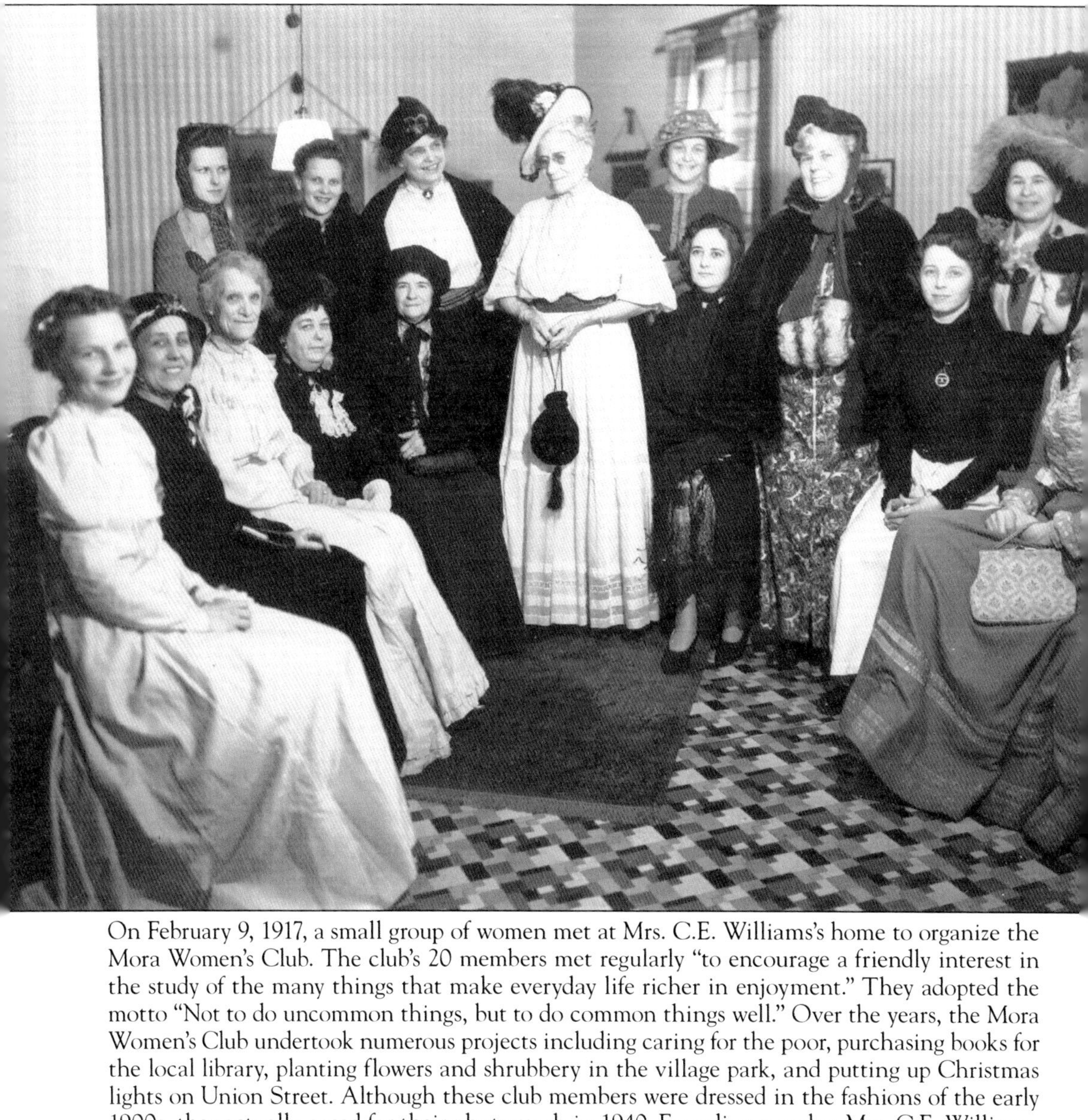

On February 9, 1917, a small group of women met at Mrs. C.E. Williams's home to organize the Mora Women's Club. The club's 20 members met regularly "to encourage a friendly interest in the study of the many things that make everyday life richer in enjoyment." They adopted the motto "Not to do uncommon things, but to do common things well." Over the years, the Mora Women's Club undertook numerous projects including caring for the poor, purchasing books for the local library, planting flowers and shrubbery in the village park, and putting up Christmas lights on Union Street. Although these club members were dressed in the fashions of the early 1900s, they actually posed for their photograph in 1940. Founding member Mrs. C.E. Williams, in the white dress, stood in the center of the group.

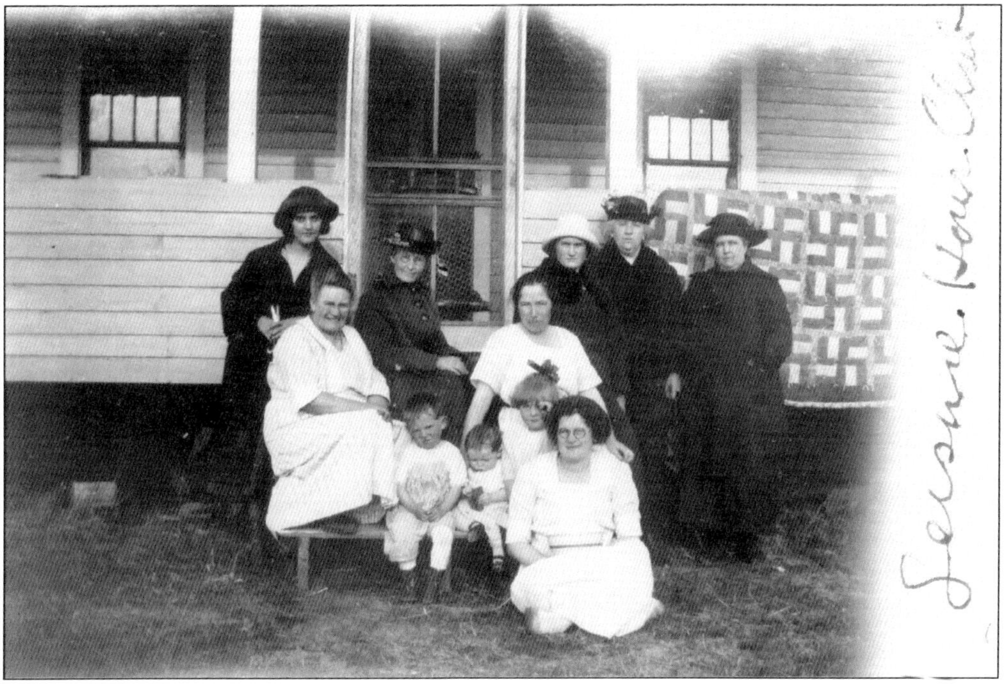

Women often organized small clubs in their neighborhoods. They met frequently to work on their sewing projects and improve their minds by reading, discussing current events, and presenting papers. They also played games, enjoyed meals together, and simply chatted about their lives. The members of the Leisure Hour Club posed for their photograph in 1922.

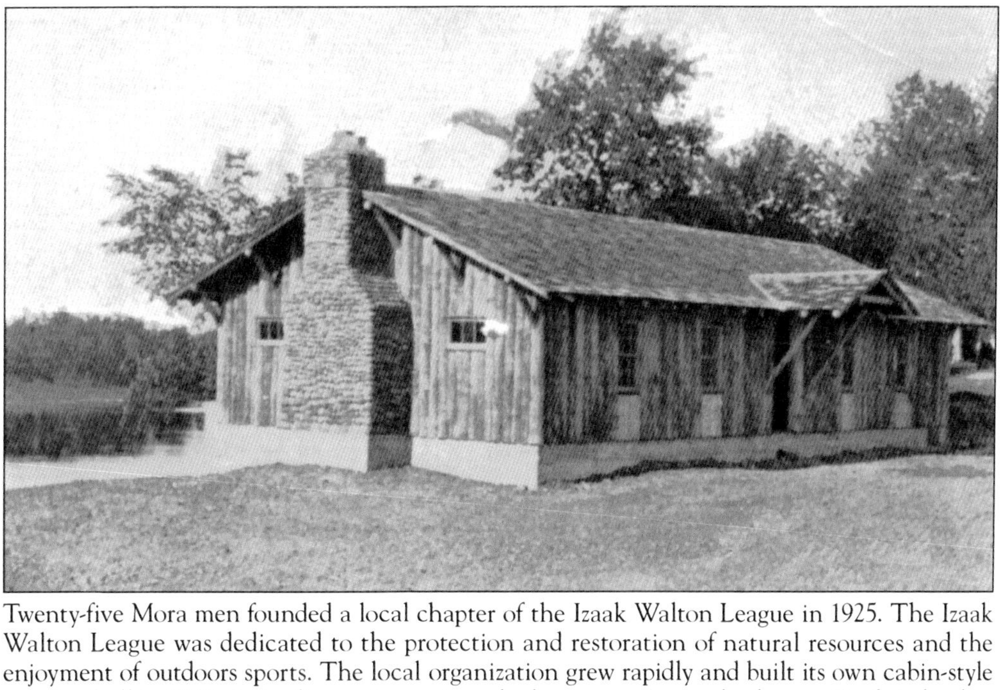

Twenty-five Mora men founded a local chapter of the Izaak Walton League in 1925. The Izaak Walton League was dedicated to the protection and restoration of natural resources and the enjoyment of outdoors sports. The local organization grew rapidly and built its own cabin-style meeting hall in 1930. As its first major project, the league constructed a dam on Knife Lake that raised the water level by six feet.

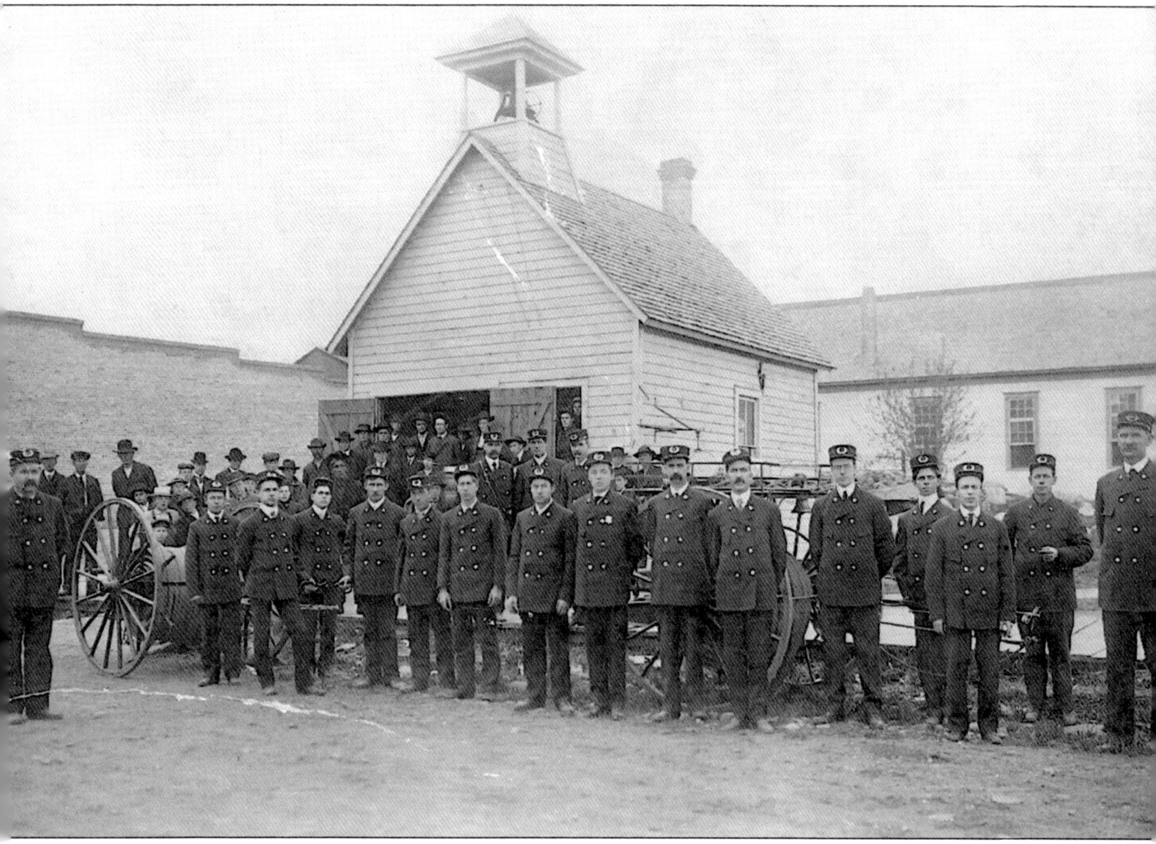

The Mora Fire Department organized in late November 1904. One hundred men attended the department's first meeting and elected C.R. Williams as chief, A.B. Williams as captain, H.H. Mellen as first lieutenant, A.L. Johnstone as second lieutenant, John Berglin as treasurer, and John Lawson as secretary. The village council agreed to provide a fire station at the corner of Railroad Avenue and Union Street. A new hose cart and 600 feet of hose had already arrived. The new fire department answered its first call in February 1905, and in June, a new fire bell was installed in the station, replacing the triangle that had been used as a signal. This photograph was taken in 1907 outside the fire station. The department had already purchased a brand new hose cart built by one of Mora's blacksmiths.

Bibliography

Anderson, Marian. *History of Ann Lake Township and Ann Lake*. Mora, MN: Ann Lake Sportsman's Club, n.d.

Carlson, Karen. *Historic Brunswick Township: The First 150 Years . . . 1858–2008*. Mora, MN: Kanabec Publications, 2008.

Hansen, Shirley, Marge Bjorklund, and Myrtle Telstad. *Grasston 1918*. Grasston, MN: Grasston Community Improvement Committee, 1993.

Hawkins, Dale, Marian Anderson, et al. *Ogilvie Past and Present*. Ogilvie, MN: Back to the Tower Days Committee, 2006.

Kanabec History Center. *2000 Calendar*. Mora, MN: Kanabec History Center, 2000.

Kenney, Dave. *Northern Lights: The Stories of Minnesota's Past*. St. Paul: Minnesota Historical Society Press, 2003.

Kilgore, Paul. "The Timber Industry's Influence on Kanabec County, Minnesota." Paper, Augsburg College, 1978.

White, Bruce. *We are at Home: Pictures of the Ojibwe People*. St. Paul: Minnesota Historical Society Press, 2007.

Zaczkowski, Stephanie, and Jeff Ethan. *A Walk Through 100 Years Under St. Mary's Care*. Elk River, MN: CMC Publishers, 1995.

Ziegler, Frank. *Ken-A-Big: The Story of Kanabec County*. Edited by Robert H. Beck. Mora, MN: B & W Printers, 1981.

Note: The authors used the Kanabec History Center's reference files extensively to glean information from newspaper clippings, unpublished papers, and research notes. Back issues of the *Kanabec County Times* were of invaluable assistance. The authors also consulted a variety of websites for background information and interesting facts.